RECLAIMING THE ROAD

RECLAIMING
Mobility Justice beyond
THE ROAD
Complete Streets

DAVID L. PRYTHERCH

University of Minnesota Press | Minneapolis | London

The University of Minnesota Press gratefully acknowledges the generous assistance provided for the publication of this book by Miami University.

Copyright 2025 by the Regents of the University of Minnesota

All rights reserved. No part of this publication may be reproduced, stored in a retrieval system, utilized for purposes of training artificial intelligence technologies, or transmitted, in any form or by any means, electronic, mechanical, photocopying, recording, or otherwise, without the prior written permission of the publisher.

Published by the University of Minnesota Press
111 Third Avenue South, Suite 290
Minneapolis, MN 55401-2520
http://www.upress.umn.edu

ISBN 978-1-5179-1644-2 (hc)
ISBN 978-1-5179-1645-9 (pb)

A Cataloging-in-Publication record for this book is available from the Library of Congress.

Printed in the United States of America on acid-free paper

The University of Minnesota is an equal-opportunity educator and employer.

UMP BmB 2025

To my fellow traveler Kathleen,
and Eleanor and Vivian for coming along on the ride

CONTENTS

PREFACE   ix

Introduction   1

1. A Short History of the American Street: From Public Place to Pipe for Cars (and Back Again?)   21

2. On the Road to Mobility Justice: Intersecting Approaches to a Just Street   47

3. Multimodalism by Policy and Design   81

4. Slowing the Street   105

5. Opening the Street by Closing It   147

6. Reconstructing the Street as Public Place   193

Conclusion: The Promise and Challenge of Reclaiming Streets Equitably   231

NOTES   241

INDEX   279

PREFACE

Our passions and politics reflect our experiences, which are shaped by places. In my own life, a roadway runs through them all. Like so many Americans, I grew up in car-dependent landscapes. The twisting, sidewalk-free roads of the Delaware River Valley were scenic but didn't offer much mobility to a child. After my parents' divorce, while visiting my father in New York City, I learned the flight-like joy of riding a bike on the carriage paths of Central Park. The ten-speed my mother later gave me enabled teenage freedom to explore the countryside and towns around me. Subsequently, living in a college town and moving to Pittsburgh introduced the joys of walking and transit, as well as the vibrant diversity of a good city sidewalk. As an environmentalist, I'd grown up skeptical of urbanization but came to see walkability and bikeability as linchpins of sustainability. Thus, I consider myself fortunate as an adult to have commuted and lived mostly car-free, thanks to the wonders of well-designed places. Streets have shaped my worldview as a person, geographer, and citizen planner. Many could tell similar stories.

As much as streets can enable mobility, however, they also teach hard lessons about fairness. To share the roadway with cars is to experience stark power asymmetries reinforced by the physical infrastructure of the roadway itself. We learn this as children cautioned against playing in the road, as teens cycling amid busy traffic, and as adults living alongside and navigating the dangers of the typical public street. In fact, this morning I write with my heart still pounding from nearly being struck in a crosswalk on my walk to work. We've all had such experiences, which likely prompt us to ask: Why are streets so inhospitable to non-drivers? Is this situation fair?

Streets are at once so familiar and highly engineered that it's easy not to think much about them at all. It's tempting to think "that's just the way they are." If you step back and look at the big picture, however, something basic yet profound comes into view. Streets are everywhere and take up vast amounts of space. There are more than four million miles of roadways in the United States.[1] If we do some rough math—assuming that each of these has something like two twelve-foot travel lanes plus extra width for gutters or shoulders—the surface area of such roadways totals more than twenty thousand square miles. This area—which doesn't even include sidewalks—is larger than the four smallest states combined. These numbers are even more significant when scaled to the towns and cities where many of us live. Streets often make up more than 25 percent of downtown land area in U.S. cities and 80 percent of urban public space.[2] We spend a lot of our lives on streets, typically an hour a day driving or riding in vehicles, in addition to time walking, biking, rolling, or riding transit.[3] We socialize along streets, whether in passing greetings or long conversations at sidewalk cafés. All of us live adjacent to streets (and unhoused people often live on them). Streets have a vast territory whose geography profoundly structures our lives and how we get around.

Thinking critically about streets invites further insights and questions, both practical and conceptual. For me, this started with crosswalks and what I thought was a simple question: Who has the right-of-way and why? Answering it led me down the branching rabbit holes of traffic law, engineering, and design, which revealed both their intricacies and their powerfully autocentric biases. As a pedestrian and a cyclist, I'd long wondered why streets felt so unfair, but social theory—in geography and across disciplines—gave me intellectual tools to think about mobility as a matter of equity and ask: What would a just street look like, in theory and practice? These questions are both philosophically profound and hugely relevant. I'm sure many would agree that once you start thinking about something as complex as the public street, it's hard to stop.

While such critical inquiry is necessary for reimagining a better city, it's not sufficient. To reclaim streets for more diverse people and purposes takes a planner's talents for articulating policy goals and translating them into design, and ultimately urban space itself, often in close collaboration with transportation advocates and community leaders. For the past twenty years, I've been fortunate to teach urban planning, and for nearly as long I've served my community as a planning commissioner and, more recently, city councillor. Like many readers, I've advocated for Complete Streets policies that affirm the right of all users to safe and convenient accessibility; pushed for multimodal transportation plans and design standards; and fought for crosswalks, bike lanes, multiuse paths, and other ways to make roadways safer for pedestrians and cyclists. Toggling between theory and practice has only sharpened my frustration with autocentrism, my belief that all users deserve their fair shares of the public street, and my commitment to reclaiming the roadway for a just, livable, sustainable city. Reorienting policy from autocentrism to multimodal equity and planning Complete Streets, as many can attest, is a slow, frustrating, yet satisfying process.

Amid such progress, however, a growing number of people began to ask if multimodalism is sufficient to address the street's broader social inequalities and if multimodal improvements might inadvertently accelerate gentrification or even exacerbate racial injustice. To be honest, as a multimodal advocate I struggled with these critiques, and maybe I wasn't alone. Arguments for multimodal equity have long found justification in social inequality, given the strong connection between travel mode and wealth and between traffic violence and social vulnerability (age, race, income). Yet, those approaching equity in terms of identity and social and racial difference could see the street's injustices— and thus solutions—differently. While some might perceive bike lanes as an expression of transportation equity, for example, others might critique them from a social justice perspective concerned with green gentrification and racialized displacement. This kind of cognitive dissonance is not simply intellectual; it affects decision-making: Do we build the bike lane or not? It became more and more evident, at least to me, that we needed to better reconcile distinct and seemingly contradictory approaches to better define mobility justice and effectively plan just streets.

xii   Preface

The watershed moment of 2020, including Covid-19 and racial justice protests, generated unprecedented conversations about streets, social justice, and the connections between them. After decades of grueling work to simply carve out bike lanes from roadway margins, it was thrilling to see cities suddenly close entire roadways for active transport, outdoor recreation, and public gathering. This felt like a tectonic shift in thinking about streets, pushing beyond multimodal infrastructure to their potential as public spaces. Something big was happening. Yet, by remarkable historical coincidence, at that very same moment our country experienced wrenching debates about race and policing, which forced a deeper and more comprehensive reckoning with social justice in America, particularly by those of us who needed to check our privilege. Something profound needed to change to make our cities more just. This accelerated rethinking of both streets and equity challenged me—as a scholar, teacher, and local official—to keep up and make sense of complex political cross-currents. I wondered how planners and community members across the United States were navigating these debates and competing priorities, both in the policy sphere and in the public sphere of the street.

I offer this book as one contribution to the broadening project of understanding the complex, contested, and ultimately shared thing we call the public street. It responds to a pivotal moment in how we think about streets, driven by the growing realization that such public spaces—including the asphalt roadway surface itself—belong to all of us. It draws on a deepening commitment among planners and others to reimagine streets not simply as safer transport infrastructure for all modes but also as livable and vibrant public spaces for people to experience and inhabit. It tries to tackle larger questions about how such public spaces should be shared, connecting vibrant theoretical conversations about equity and mobility justice to the practical work of planners, transportation advocates, and community leaders to reclaim streets for more diverse people and uses.

This book would not have been possible without the contributions of innumerable other people. I am grateful to the community of scholars in transportation geography, planning, and mobility studies for helping to reframe and rethink the street as a space of politics and rights. I am indebted to scholars across disciplines who have explored and expanded our understanding of complicated ideas like equity and justice and applied them to how people get around. I could not have written this book without the scores of planners, advocates, and community members who shared their time and stories with me, providing rich data and—more importantly—inspiration about what's possible when people work together to make their communities better. I hope I've gotten their stories straight and only wish I'd had time to talk with twice as many people and dig deeper into more places and stories.

This book attempts a scholarly, balanced perspective, but inevitably my personal passions, politics, and thus positionality—as a white, male, transportation geographer and planner who walks and bikes everywhere—run through it. I endeavored to learn from and synthesize diverse voices, of both scholars and practitioners, but these efforts are necessarily incomplete. In a way, my own trajectory may reflect the slow bending of our rethinking and planning of streets toward a more just and inclusive city. I am particularly grateful to have been supported and challenged in that journey by careful, constructively critical readers, including two insightful external reviewers who pushed my thinking forward, the University of Minnesota Press faculty board for asking hard questions while getting behind this project, and amazing editorial staff Jason Weidemann, Zenyse Miller, and others for seeing this book through.

Finally, none of this is possible without the support of the people who have traveled with me along this (at times obsessive) journey. My wife, Kathleen, has been with me every step of the way—from hilly Pittsburgh to sunbaked Tucson, and from Valencia, Spain, to small-town Oxford, Ohio—while supporting my civic engagement and even lending her incredible editing talents to this book. My daughters, Eleanor and Vivian, have biked and walked with me since they were little and continue to make me proud in their car-free college lifestyles and deep commitment to social justice. I'm grateful also to work for and serve such institutions as Miami University and the City of Oxford, which haven't always loved my pushy advocacy of pedestrian and bike infrastructure but have proven to be full of wonderfully supportive colleagues.

Ultimately, by sharing and linking insights from dynamic scholarship and planning practice, I hope this book can offer something of a testament to—and perhaps an impetus for—the ways ideally minded people can rethink and remake cities in the image of mobility justice, one block at a time. That's the hope, anyway.

INTRODUCTION

Change, one might say, is afoot. Epochal shifts in urban life can happen both subtly and abruptly, manifesting in distinct times in diverse ways. But few places reveal urban change better than the public street. Streets are central arteries and places where we navigate the city and our dynamic relations to each other. The roadway, being more than simply infrastructure, is a social space—indeed, a public place—where complex forces shaping urban life intersect. Stepping off the sidewalk onto the roadway, we can experience firsthand the diversity, dynamism, dangers, and inequalities of the American city on the move and gain valuable perspective on the road behind and possible futures ahead.

Historically American streets were bustling mixed-use spaces. Though primarily for transportation, they were dominated by pedestrians, who shared them with slow-moving vehicles like horse-drawn carts and later trolley cars, as well as market vendors and playing children. Until the twentieth century, American streets—not just the sidewalk but the entire right-of-way, including the roadway surface—were a public realm, woven intimately with the places around them.

A century ago, however, streets were swept by the epidemic novelties of the automobile and influenza, deadly forces that evolved into endemic features. American cities saw their first cars in the 1890s, but only with mass manufacturing in the 1910s did they begin to flood our streets.[1] The influenza virus likewise emerged and spread quickly on

1

2 Introduction

crowded roadways in 1918—a Liberty Loan parade in Philadelphia is notorious—before emptying them of people and cars: "The life of the city had almost stopped," one medical student recalled.[2] After killing hundreds of thousands across the United States, more than thirty thousand people in New York alone, influenza abated.[3] The epidemic of automobile traffic did not, accelerating to kill two hundred thousand American pedestrians over the 1920s and take over the twentieth-century American roadway, transforming it from public space into vehicular thoroughfare.[4] From this intense and violent historical moment—indeed, a pivot—a new city emerged. Drivers advanced to claim hegemony while pedestrians retreated onto sidewalks (and the influenza pandemic faded into memory). Over the twentieth century, Americans thoroughly remade their streets from public places into pipes for cars.

So autocentric are most streets today—in their social organization, design, and daily use—that we have trouble imagining that they could ever have been or ever could be different. Yet other uses and ideas have stubbornly persisted. The manifold inequities, unsustainability, and human costs of autocentrism have, over recent decades, prompted growing calls for the safe accommodation of pedestrians, wheelchairs, bikes, and transit on accessible Complete Streets designed for all users of all ages and abilities. As part of a so-called Vision Zero movement, policymakers and planners challenged the status quo dangers of our transportation system, which routinely maims and kills people (especially the more vulnerable people among us), to demand safer and more equitable mobility. The push for safe and convenient access for all users—a policy and design movement called "multimodalism"—squarely confronts the urban status quo in the United States by reimagining streets that accommodate all modes, ages, and abilities. This movement has incrementally transformed the planning and engineering of streets, manifested in new or widened sidewalks, bike lanes, improved intersections, traffic calming, and more. Making space on the roadway for nondrivers alone is a monumental, historic project whose impacts we're still just beginning to see. Yet in the process, it also cracked a window for a broader rethinking of streets beyond transportation to their potential as public space and tactical experiments in reclaiming them for social life, like temporarily closing roads for weekend Open Streets events or converting parking spaces into parklets with seating.

Then came Covid-19. This new pandemic again played out on public streets. Roadways suddenly emptied of cars to a degree not seen for a century. In their place, people emerged to seek outdoor, socially distanced recreation and gathering. Cities responded to the health emergency by restricting traffic on Slow Streets to enable open-air, active transportation. Oakland, California, partially closed seventy-four miles of neighborhood streets, limiting vehicular traffic and speeds to prioritize biking, walking, and passing conversation. Others partially or fully closed roadways designated as Open Streets or Shared Streets for slow mobility and outdoor gathering. New York City partially or fully barricaded eighty-three miles of its streets, and suddenly café tables took the place of busy traffic and parked cars. Limited, prepandemic experiments in parklets and street plazas exploded into movement converting parking spaces or entire rights-of-way into public places for dining and social life. San Francisco revamped its public parklet program to quickly issue 1,600 Shared Space permits for outdoor dining and commerce. Over the pandemic and its response, towns and cities across the United States saw activities long confined to sidewalks—walking, playing, gathering, and even sitting down to talk—spill onto the asphalt roadway, inviting people to experience and become acquainted with a long-forgotten and very different kind of street and city.

As if this historical moment wasn't dynamic enough, pandemic streets also witnessed an explosion of street protest and national debate about race and equity following George Floyd's curbside murder by Minneapolis police officers in May 2020. Though immediately focused on race and policing, these protests launched a broader attack on inequality: Black Lives Matter, for example, attacked structural racism and sought to "build local power to intervene" in various forms of structural violence inflicted on Black and other disadvantaged communities.[5] Communities and cities responded in different ways, many seeking to strengthen their commitment to diversity, equity, and inclusion. These efforts connected back to the street. A number of cities converted public roadways into Black Lives Matter plazas. Perhaps more importantly, however, transportation advocates and planners reassessed their approach to equity, moving beyond fair access for all transport modes to encompass social diversity and "needs of those who have experienced systemic underinvestment."[6]

American towns and cities are emerging from a watershed historic moment that forced a reassessment of mobility, equity, and the public street. They have been transformed by the process, much as they were by the violent epidemics of cars and influenza a century ago. Traffic has resumed and many streets returned to their prepandemic norm, but myriad roadways remain partially or fully closed, pedestrians and cyclists continue to share designated roadways with slow-moving traffic (Figure 1), and where parked cars once lined the curb we might find café tables bustling with conversation and dining. These physical changes reflect institutional changes: quickly launched, pandemic programs are being formalized as permanent transportation policies, design standards, and programming. Cities increasingly approach their transportation planning and public investments with an emphasis on equity, defined not simply in terms of transportation access but also in terms of broader social justice. And in many places, people and organizations that had temporarily laid claim to the roadway—from pedestrians to cyclists to playing children to businesses and community organizations—are reluctant to

Figure 1. Simply slowing traffic can encourage people to reclaim the roadway, like on Pittsburgh's Coral-Comrie Neighborway. Photo by author.

relinquish it, even as the uneven distribution of such improvements illustrates the challenges of doing so equitably.

It's too soon to know how lasting these changes will be. Yet even if incremental, they are profound. With every passing month or year that these transformations endure, many of which hearken back to the past, they look more and more like America's urban future. Oakland's pandemic-era street barricades are evolving into a network of permanent Slow Streets; Open Streets are now permanent in New York, including 192 closures spanning all five boroughs; and San Francisco's Shared Spaces parklets are here to stay, in 2024 including more than 1,200 permits for social spaces on sidewalks, curbsides, or the roadway itself (along with thirty full-street closures). If you've dined locally on what was once a parking space, or strolled where cars once sped, you've experienced a trend set by leading cities but widely imitated in towns large and small across the United States. They may be limited in spatial extent, but they suggest a much broader social change.

At this historical juncture, we're invited to step off the curb onto the asphalt roadway to ponder a very different model of the American public street as both transport infrastructure and public place, a model as novel as it is traditional, which challenges the primacy of vehicular traffic. After decades of struggling to retrofit fast and dangerous thoroughfares to accommodate nondrivers, itself an epic task that has only begun, we're witnessing an even more profound rethinking and reclaiming of the American roadway. Looking beyond the basic fairness of multimodal accessibility, cities increasingly prioritize slow access over speedy mobility, neighborhood livability over traffic throughput, and even café tables over traveling or parking. These efforts increasingly cite equity as an explicit goal, whose meaning itself has grown to encompass social inequalities beyond transportation and the roadway. On streets reclaimed for slowness, you can ride or walk or roll with less fear, children can kick a ball, and neighbors can chat. On streets opened for walking and social life, you can wander from curb to curb, shop from a small vendor, or pull chairs around a table with friends (Figure 2). And on curbsides reclaimed by local organizations and businesses, you can sit down and dine in an outdoor space redesigned for social life with a floor, walls, and even a roof overhead. Moreover, these new spaces emerge from unprecedented planning efforts (at least by the standards of roadway design) to address social inequality, promote inclusion, and engage community members. Through and beyond the pandemic, we've had a chance to experience firsthand the potential of streets to be places designed for people and not just cars.

These physical changes, dramatic though they are, manifest something even deeper: a reimagining and reclaiming of the entire roadway, not simply as infrastructure for transport but as a curb-to-curb public sphere serving diverse uses and users. They challenge a dominant—and unabashedly autocentric—social order in place for a century and invite a diversifying set of people to enter and lay claim to the street. We're reminded of something many had forgotten: the street is a shared public space. With that realization, however, we also come face to face with enduring and difficult questions: How did the public street come to be the way it is, and how might it be different? Who and what should public streets be for? How ought mobility and the public street be shared equitably, in theory and in practice? These are ultimately thorny questions

Figure 2. Closing streets to through traffic can open them to slow mobility and public life, such as curbside dining or vending. The Thirty-Fourth Avenue Open Street traverses Jackson Heights, Queens, New York. Photo by author.

of fairness and social justice, which history teaches us that we disregard at our peril.

Reimagining the American Street

This book explores the ongoing reclaiming of American roadways from cars, especially through and beyond the watershed moment of the Covid-19 pandemic, for diverse forms of mobility and broader public life. It ponders what these changes might mean for how we think about mobility and public infrastructure and what might constitute a just street. It is part of a movement to rethink mobility and American streets as significant both in theory and in practice.

Reconceptualizing Mobility and Infrastructure

Mobility and the street are complex and dynamic ideas, as well as physical things. To think about them deeply requires some theory. Twentieth-century transportation geographers, planners, and others predominantly defined, planned, and designed American roadways around physical movement and vehicular circulation, but new mobilities scholarship reinterprets transport not simply as the movement of people or goods but as a social process suffused with what Tim Cresswell and others call the "politics of mobility" in which "mobilities are both productive of . . . social relations and produced by them."[7] To see mobility as political is to raise questions about mobility rights and therefore equity. Environmental justice advocates, led by Robert D. Bullard, have long critiqued inequities in transportation.[8] Transport geographers have worked to define transportation equity.[9] Going even further, sociologist Mimi Sheller argues in *Mobility Justice* for situating mobility in a social context and going beyond the fair distribution of access to encompass "deliberative, procedural, restorative, and epistemic justice."[10]

Rethinking mobility leads to rethinking transport infrastructure. Mobility is shaped by "infrastructural moorings," which (like mobility itself) are what Deborah Cowen calls "socio-technical systems, that are themselves increasingly the object of struggle."[11] And while we have traditionally interpreted infrastructure as a physical system for circulation, a growing number of scholars sees its potential as social infrastructure, or what Alan Latham and Jack Layton call "networks of spaces, facilities, institutions, and groups that create affordances for social connection."[12]

8 Introduction

Streets therefore are simultaneously a transport facility, a contested space of rights, and a possible social infrastructure that can be "more convivial, open and accommodating of difference."[13]

All of which leads to the challenge of defining mobility justice and a just street in both urban theory and planning practice. Planning has what Jason W. Reece calls a "conflicted history" with equity, complicit in urban inequities but capable of enhancing social and racial equity "when this is made a priority in establishing policies and practices."[14] A growing emphasis on equity has brought diversifying approaches, which enrich debate but also present conceptual and practical choices. Geographers and planners have traditionally approached equity from the angle of spatial justice, emphasizing the fair distribution of mobility, access, and street resources across the city. Seen from the perspective of multimodal transport equity, this argues for a fair allocation of the roadway space among modes. Yet, for most people, equity is defined in social terms, focusing our attention on social differences—race, gender, national origin, identity, etc.—and related disadvantages. In his book *Cyclescapes of the Unequal City,* geographer John G. Stehlin powerfully reminds us that "race, class, and gender are durably articulated with mobility practices in urban space."[15] Mobility justice is inconceivable without addressing social difference and inequality. Still others advocate approaching equity as a place-based concern of neighborhood stability or even intergenerational sustainability.[16] In addition to these emphases on substantive equity, we might focus on procedural questions of how to engage people in decisions about their streets.

In this historical moment, we are endowed with a rich and growing diversity of thought about equity and justice, in and beyond transportation. These approaches are distinct and operate on distinct axes, yet they converge on our experience of mobility and the public street. In seeking to define a just city, planning scholar Susan S. Fainstein argues for democracy, diversity, and equity but also to recognize tensions between them.[17] To sort through such ambiguities and tensions is a necessary challenge for operationalizing equity to better plan cities and their streets.

There has not been a more pressing yet opportune moment in a century to fundamentally reframe what we think about transportation, the public street, and mobility justice, while situating these amid broader social and environmental concerns beyond the roadway. Looking beyond a functionalist understanding of roads as physical infrastructure for transport and toward mobility as a social process and streets as public places, we enter into complex political conversations about mobility politics and rights and, thus, knotty questions of justice. We are fortunate to have diverse approaches for thinking about equity, but we are also challenged to somehow reconcile them in a theory of mobility justice that can be both encompassing and nuanced, yet workable for redefining a more just street.

Redesigning the Public Street in Practice

Meanwhile, policymakers and planners are redesigning public streets in practice. The Americans with Disabilities Act applied a civil rights perspective to promote accessibility for people of different abilities. A Complete Streets movement has grown around the principle that "all people ought to have safe, comfortable, and convenient access to community destinations and public places" and envisions "streets for everyone"—that is, designed with safe access for "all people who need to use them, including pedestrians, bicyclists, motorists and transit riders of all ages and abilities."[18] Additionally, a kindred Vision Zero movement contests the dangers of our car-oriented transportation system and calls for "eliminating all traffic fatalities and severe injuries—while increasing safe, healthy, and equitable mobility for all."[19]

To actually transform roadways, however, requires translating multimodal policy principles into the design standards that guide the construction and operation of streets. Streets are engineered according to guidance for highway capacity, roadway geometry, traffic control, and so forth. Their power to collectively shape the city and its public spaces is obscured by their technocratic inscrutability. For nearly a century, transportation policy and traffic design have constructed streets for efficient circulation of vehicular traffic—pipes for cars—but they are now undergoing revision to more fairly accommodate diverse modes. Rejecting the notion that all roads should be highways, a new National Association of City Transportation Officials (NACTO) has emerged with a mission "to build cities as places for people, with safe, sustainable, accessible and equitable transportation choices that support a strong economy and vibrant quality of life."[20]

10   Introduction

Multimodal policies and design guidelines have challenged auto-centrism's inequities, but only very recently have cities begun challenging the core assumption that streets are transport infrastructure in order to reclaim them as public spaces. Prepandemic experiments were quite limited—to only a few cities and often only for temporary periods—but were scaled up over 2020 to facilitate socially distanced mobility and gathering. Cities like Boston expanded their traffic-calming efforts from targeted projects to citywide standards, while Oakland and Pittsburgh drew upon initial efforts to plan bicycle boulevards prioritizing cyclists to designate Slow Streets with signage to reduce traffic volumes and speeds to promote active transportation and neighborhood livability—pandemic programs that are increasingly being made permanent. Elsewhere, cities like New York, Denver, and Los Angeles have closed streets to through traffic or prohibited cars altogether to create Shared or Open Streets that invite both slow mobility and temporary gathering, which are evolving from temporary closures into permanent design standards. And, even more notably and durably, cities across the United States—led by San Francisco, Portland, and Washington, D.C., among others—have converted curbside parking into parklets or "streateries" for dining or public space or the entire right-of-way into public street plazas.

There is no standard nomenclature for these evolving efforts, which go by different names in different cities and exist on a spectrum from merely slowing traffic through partially or fully closing streets for active mobility to more fully remaking the roadway as pedestrianized public spaces. But all have in common the reclaiming of at least a portion of the roadway, some of the time, for a wider range of uses than vehicular travel or parking. And though their spatial extent may be limited, in America's car-centric culture and cities, these changes are a big deal.

Toward an Intersectional Mobility Justice and Street, beyond Multimodalism to Placemaking

As we live through a pivotal moment for reconsidering our ideas about mobility, equity, and the public street, we're simultaneously witnessing a movement to reclaim streets from busy traffic that goes beyond multi-modal access to create public places for social life. These exciting trends raise prospects for a very different kind of street and city, better shared by more diverse people and uses. Yet they also suggest a diversifying set of tensions and choices—between vehicles or active human bodies, transportation or gathering, public or private uses—which prompts the tough question "Streets for whom?"

I suggest that rethinking and reclaiming streets requires both the geographer's broad and integrative perspective on the evolving American roadway and the planner's firm grasp on policy and design tools that can help transform it. This book draws on both to address a set of linked questions: What is mobility justice? What would a just street look like, in theory and in practice? That starts with reconceptualizing mobility as a social process and streets as public spaces of rights, and thus mobility justice. Diversifying claims to streets and approaches to equity, however, demands a way to sort through and reconcile them in practice.

For this we might draw inspiration from and extend the powerful concept of intersectionality, conceived to understand diverse social experiences and structural forces that converge to shape them—toward an intersectional mobility justice. In a foundational 1989 article, Black feminist legal scholar Kimberlé Crenshaw advances the argument that power and marginalization rarely operate on a single axis like race or gender but can intersect to create compounding burdens for people (or, conversely, compound social advantages). Arguing for recognition of "multidimensionality" in the experiences of marginalized people with multiple burdens, Crenshaw uses the public street as a metaphor: "Discrimination, like traffic through an intersection, may flow in one direction, and it may flow in another."[21] More than simply a metaphor, however, intersectionality offers a powerful framework for thinking about how individual experience is shaped by distinct social forces that operate on distinct axes but converge in particular ways. And it prompts us to recognize that, just as forms of advantage/disadvantage operate on different axes, so too can our ideas about equity and the remedies that might follow from them. As intersectionality focused attention on how individuals experience multidimensional social differences and identities, it informed a wider critical race theory that uncovers the ways social power and forms of oppression like racism can become embedded in ostensibly neutral institutional structures like the law, which in turn help reproduce social difference and disadvantage.[22]

These ideas emerged from Black feminist legal scholarship and activism primarily to confront legal bias, but their analytical power is

12 Introduction

not limited to race and gender and can help us see how a wider range of societal forces and structures can converge to create inequality. Intersectionality highlights those axes related to social difference and who we are, but it can also help uncover the material effects of people's "sociopolitical location" in the world.[23] For this reason, intersectionality has been taken up across disciplines.[24] Geographers, among others, have begun to productively engage and extend the concept, bringing to the conversation their own strengths in thinking about broader social and spatial contexts.[25] In the process, these efforts increasingly connect social differences to the situated and embodied experience of unequal mobilities.[26]

I therefore suggest, with the utmost humility and respect for the concept's origins in race and gender studies, that intersectionality offers a powerful framework for thinking about mobility justice and just streets. It invites us to see the experience of being a mobile person as multidimensional, to trace the intersecting structures that create advantages or disadvantages for people depending not only on who they are but also how and where they get around, and to begin to reconcile distinct and sometimes conflicting approaches to equity. As traffic intersections connect streets converging from different directions (what traffic engineers would call "intersection approaches"), intersectionality might be extended to help us think about how different approaches to equity— including and prioritizing social difference, while also encompassing other positional and geographical factors—can be reconciled to think holistically about mobility justice. If intersectionality (like critical race theory) invites us to focus simultaneously on the multidimensional experience of individuals and the different societal structures that make life inequitable for them, the concept might help us see the experience of mobility injustice and confront the ways transportation infrastructure can make it unjust for the mobile. And, finally, just as intersections must reconcile converging traffic, an intersectional theory of mobility justice could help us articulate what a just street might look like and design accordingly as a space not just shared fairly by all but with a more radical belief that the least advantaged people ought to come first—or, to quote Crenshaw, "it can be said: 'When they enter, we all enter.'"[27]

These concepts are powerful, but they are pretty broad and abstract. To operationalize them, I suggest we might benefit from focusing on the street level. The bulk of this book is therefore dedicated to analyzing national policy and design trends and in-depth case studies to explore how the American street is evolving, the ways multimodal and place-making goals are being translated into policy and design, and how planners and key stakeholders are thinking about equity in the process. After setting a foundation of history to understand how American streets became so dangerous and inequitable and articulating a theory of mobility justice and just streets, the book traces how efforts to design multimodal streets for transportation equity have expanded to encompass more diverse ideas of mobility justice and techniques beyond accommodating alternative modes. Just as critical race theory looks beyond identity to structural forces like transportation, mobilities scholarship and planning have increasingly emphasized the importance of individual experience and social equity.

I focus on recent, on-the-ground efforts by planners and stakeholders in some of America's biggest cities—especially during and after the pandemic—to reclaim streets for human-powered mobility and public life, including cities that are slowing their streets (e.g., Boston, Oakland, and Pittsburgh), opening their streets by closing them to through traffic or cars (e.g., New York, Denver, and Los Angeles), or converting roadway space into curbside parklets or public street plazas (e.g., San Francisco, Washington, D.C., and Portland, Oregon). As planners have rethought and redesigned their streets, they have simultaneously shifted their approach to equity, looking beyond fairness among modes to tackle wider forms of social disadvantage. These concurrent and linked trends suggest something important is happening, which bears watching. These cities are not unique in their innovations, and their efforts are uneven, but they represent some of the largest-scale and most creative efforts to rethink and reclaim streets in the United States, while redefining mobility justice in the process.

The research behind this story is woven with diverse sources and methods. To understand historical context, I draw upon both secondary historical sources and primary materials. To build a conceptual framework, I review and synthesize cutting-edge research and theory across urban and transportation studies, in and beyond geography and planning. To establish the foundation for multimodalism, I review the most important policy frameworks and design standards shaping American streets. For case studies, I critically analyze hundreds of policies, plans, design standards, websites, and related media coverage across the nine cities. To understand the thinking and debates behind these changes, I interviewed forty-six transportation planners, multimodal advocates, and neighborhood stakeholders to uncover the history behind evolving policies and programs, the shifting balance among street uses, the relationship between citywide planning and community input, and how decision-makers are approaching the question of mobility justice. These lengthy, semistructured interviews revealed the complex humanity—the dreams and ambitions, the struggles and conflicts—behind planning, policy, and the redesigned street. Though most of this research spanning the continent was remote, I was fortunate to visit some of these cities and observe firsthand their transformed streets.

Admittedly, this story is more about planning and policy than street life itself. An ethnography of any of these streets and their complex social lives would be enormously interesting but beyond the scope of this project. Each transformed block is a rich story unto itself. By exploring so many case studies, I also sacrificed depth for breadth. I try to provide a complete story of evolving policy grounded in the everyday experience of planning and using streets, but each case study of these complex and big cities is necessarily limited. I hope, however, that readers might find value and relevance in my particular weaving of history, theory, policy analysis, and on-the-street storytelling, less as a complete account and more as an interpretive guide for thinking and perhaps reclaiming streets in their own communities.

Mobility, the public street, and equity are big and sensitive topics. The United States is a big country. And these are some big cities. This book and its research are thus necessarily incomplete and partial, conceptually and empirically. Its case studies are representative but cannot encompass diverse planning and experimentation across American towns and cities. Policy analysis and interviews with key informants can only scratch the surface, and they represent official perspectives better than everyday perceptions. But through it all emerges a through line, a compelling story about the rethinking and reclaiming of American streets, one idea, block, and day at a time, through the words of those people who are debating, planning, and experiencing that epochal change.

Overview of the Book

This book unfolds as follows. Chapter 1, "A Short History of the American Street: From Public Place to Pipe for Cars (and Back Again?)," recounts the remaking of American streets from shared public spaces into infrastructure regulated and engineered for vehicular throughput. Building on social histories of the American public street and its contested transformation into thoroughfares, like Peter D. Norton's epic *Fighting Traffic*, I trace how a century of autocentric assumptions became embedded in legal and design standards to thoroughly transform the American street over the twentieth century and in the process prioritized flow over place and speed over safety, and excluded broad classes of users (topics I explore in some depth in my 2018 book *Law, Engineering, and the American Right-of-Way: Imagining a More Just Street*).[28] Amid the motorization of the street, however, we see enduring and growing critiques and movements to question the hegemony of cars and reclaim it for multimodalism, livability, and (increasingly) social life and equity.

To develop a conceptual framework for rethinking the American roadway and equity upon it, chapter 2, "On the Road to Mobility Justice: Intersecting Approaches to a Just Street," starts by reviewing shifting approaches to transportation, from technocratic approaches to newer interpretations of mobility and streets as political, where uneven access and power relations beg issues of fairness. Because *equity* means different things to different people, however, I undertake a broad and comprehensive survey of distinct approaches to mobility justice and just streets, including: a spatial equity focus on the distribution of access across the city, a multimodal equity emphasis on how street spaces are shared among transport users, a social justice approach highlighting human diversity and difference, a place-based focus on stable neighborhoods and a sustainable planet, and a procedural emphasis on fair decision-making. To integrate and reconcile these different and sometimes conflicting approaches, I draw upon and extend the feminist and antiracist concept of intersectionality, whose metaphor of the intersection—as a place where different approaches to advantage and disadvantage, and thus equity, come together—can help us see streets as complex, dynamic, and intersectional spaces where diverse experiences and claims collide and must somehow be reconciled. More than just a metaphor, however, I explore how an intersectional theory of mobility justice might help us critically analyze the multidimensional experience of mobile people and, more importantly for policy and design, define a just street.

Chapter 3, "Multimodalism by Policy and Design," confronts auto-centrism to advocate for the safety and convenience of diverse modes. In the realm of policy, I review the Americans with Disabilities Act prohibiting discrimination against individuals with disabilities, the Complete Streets movement promoting local and state policies to ensure streets accommodate all users of all ages and abilities, and a Vision Zero movement for "safe, healthy, and equitable mobility for all." I then explore how these values have begun to be translated into design standards that shape physical roadways, including highway capacity manuals, American Association of State Highway and Transportation Officials geometric design and bike/pedestrian standards, uniform traffic-control manuals, Americans with Disabilities Act public right-of-way standards, and new NACTO guides for designing complete urban streets. These reveal how discourses of multimodal equity have been increasingly translated into policy and design that reimagine American thoroughfares long defined for "purposes of vehicular travel" toward a vision of multimodal accessibility and equity.

But the heart of the book is dedicated to recent, sudden, and significant street-reclamation efforts that transcend multimodal planning to accommodate alternative modes on otherwise vehicular infrastructure to begin creating shared public spaces for equitable mobility and social life. Chapter 4, "Slowing the Street," traces how many cities are using traffic calming and other techniques to limit through traffic and speeds on Slow Streets to support biking, walking, and neighborhood livability. After briefly reviewing developing traditions of traffic calming and livability in roadway design, I explore recent Slow Streets and traffic-calming efforts in Boston, Oakland, and Pittsburgh. Analyzed through the framework of intersectional mobility justice, we see how efforts to reorient roadways toward low-speed mobility and sensitivity to neighborhood context advance equity on a number of axes, even if they don't really transform streets into truly shared public places.

Chapter 5, "Opening the Street by Closing It," explores more ambitious moves to reorient roadways from (albeit slowed) vehicular travel toward very human-speed public places where nondrivers are considered equal to (or even prioritized over) drivers, while supporting transient forms of social gathering. From diverse American traditions of street closures, I trace the recent emergence of festival-like Ciclovía and Free Streets events, which provided the foundation for Covid-era experiments in Open Streets in New York, Shared Streets in Denver, and Slow Streets in Los Angeles. Many of these pandemic-era closures were temporary but are evolving into permanent programs to calm traffic and pilot full and permanent closure as pedestrian plazas, which reveals the challenges of balancing competing priorities to equitably reclaim streets.

Following these street transformations to their fullest extent, beyond sharing roadways as multimodal facilities to reclaim them for social life, chapter 6, "Reconstructing the Street as Public Place," focuses on durable reconstruction of streets as public realm. Where cars once parked, we increasingly see parklets or sidewalk extensions reclaiming the roadway for sit-down conversation and dining. What were temporary pop-ups during Covid have become established and durable changes, remaking curbsides, entire blocks, or intersections into interim or permanent plazas. This chapter traces the historical precedents for pedestrianizing streets to explore the recent evolution of Shared Streets in San Francisco, streateries in Washington, D.C., and curbside dining and public street plazas in Portland. The ongoing formalization of pandemic pilots into established design guidance and programs illustrates the long-term potential of reclaiming public streets for public life, but it also raises difficult questions of how to do so equitably.

"The Promise and Challenge of Reclaiming Streets Equitably" concludes this book by reflecting on what it means to open our most extensive public spaces to more diverse uses than simply vehicular traffic and parking. There is so much to celebrate in the growing movement to confront the grievous inequities of autocentric streets, which go beyond multimodal accommodation to return the roadway to its historic character as shared public space. It's a momentous change. But these efforts, undertaken amid intense debates about social justice, also raise complicated new questions about how to plan and redesign American streets. The case studies both inspire optimism about the future of American streets and remind us of the challenge to reconcile different approaches to equity toward an intersectional mobility justice that is as conceptually robust as it is workable for decision-makers.

18 Introduction

The Road Ahead

Recent efforts to reclaim streets, mixing cars and bikes and people and café tables and parklets, constitute experiments as exhilarating as they are complex. The parallel movement to redefine mobility, equity, and mobility justice is no less so. These invite us to see and experience the public right-of-way anew and to try to reconcile diverse ways of thinking about, navigating through, experiencing, and ultimately sharing the American roadway as both infrastructure and public space. As people experience evolving streets as places where intersecting social forces come together in new ways, we may gain much by thinking about diverse approaches to equity through an intersectional mobility justice and rebuilding streets accordingly.

These theoretical and policy movements, like the idea for this book itself, predated the pandemic but surged during this unique historic moment. As cities transition to a postpandemic way of life, the fate of these trends remains uncertain. Policies and programs continued to evolve as I researched them. So have streets themselves. Among the millions of miles of roadways and urban streets in the United States, only the smallest fraction were ever slowed, opened, or converted to public spaces. In many cities, these conversions have retreated back from pandemic peaks. The battle for diversity, equity, and inclusion is no less complicated or any better assured. Still, these new ways of thinking about and experiencing mobility and the public street endure not just in these big case-study cities but often in the everyday towns and cities many call home. Whatever they lack in spatial extent they make up for in profound philosophical and policy import. Just as the arrival of the first few cars on American streets heralded a coming revolution, perhaps the novel scene of people walking and dining on the roadway surface suggests a different future ahead. Having survived the pandemic and reclaimed and experienced streets as public spaces, and newly attuned to the complex challenge of equity in its various dimensions, people are not anxious to relinquish these new social spaces or the vision of a better urban future that they offer. As I write, I'm not sure there's any turning around and going back.

Looking ahead, finding our way to a better street and more equitable city requires reflecting on the route that got us here, thinking carefully about the values we want to guide us, getting a firm grasp on the policy frameworks that structure the world, learning from the experience of others, and navigating tough choices that lie ahead. Sometimes historic moments like pandemics push us forward, but approximating justice and making lasting change takes a roadmap and a plan. Hopefully these stories can cultivate both inspiration and care for that journey ahead.

1

A SHORT HISTORY OF THE AMERICAN STREET
FROM PUBLIC PLACE TO PIPE FOR CARS (AND BACK AGAIN?)

To reimagine American streets, we must first understand how they came to be this way and came to be this bad. The geography of today's public roadways reflects societal and historical contexts, whose legacy surrounds us. Reviewing the evolution of the American street, how changing ideas and social forces have shaped its dynamic spatial form is an important step toward rethinking and reclaiming better streets.

This chapter offers a short history of the American public street as an idea, infrastructure, and public space. To set a broad historical context, I trace the shift from slow, multipurpose colonial/frontier streets to the increasing tempo and complexity of industrial streets, to the arrival of automobiles and the reengineering of roads as vehicular conduits. The story of the car's takeover of American streets has been told effectively by others—Peter D. Norton's *Fighting Traffic* is a must read— but recounting it reminds us how changing ideas about mobility have been translated through policy and design into physical infrastructure. A century ago, roadways were remade from public places into pipes for cars. But history also reveals the persistence of nonvehicular uses and countervailing critiques of the costs of automobility for people, cities, and the planet, leading to calls for reimagining streets as multipurpose places for people. Even a brief historical sketch of how streets have been remade in the past helps us understand the present and find inspiration for remaking them in the future.

The Street in History

Origins and European Foundations

Humans are mobile beings who need pathways to move about. We are also social beings, requiring places to gather as a community. Human settlements have always made space for these key functions, from footpaths and clearings to today's boulevards and plazas. What constitutes a street or road, its purpose, and how it ought to be shared differs by society, place, and time. But the need for circulation and public sociality is probably as close as one gets to universal truths in the diversity of human experience.

Streets are intrinsic to cities and emerged with them. Urbanization—starting with Sumerian cities around 7500 BCE—created dense, territorialized landscapes requiring public streets, which pedestrians later came to share with wheeled vehicles introduced around 3500 BCE.[1] But streets were never simply just for circulation. In his monumental *The City in History*, Lewis Mumford argues "the first germ of the city" is not the footpath but the ceremonial meeting place. Streets not only provided local access and circulation, they were also increasingly improved for military command and trade and plazas for public worship, functions that often overlapped within the street itself. Indeed, the Sumerian ideogram for a market as a *Y* could reflect its juncture of traffic routes and trade.[2]

Streets and roads emerged across diverse, ancient world cultures—from China to Mesoamerica, India to Africa—but the most relevant antecedents to American streets are European. The European city can be traced back to the Greek *polis,* which emerged from the transformation of streets and squares into the agora as open space "publicly held and occupiable for public purposes."[3] Hellenistic town plans, the basis for the later American gridiron, embodied the multifaceted role of streets as circulation system, space for trade and ordered military movement, and public places for gathering and civic life, all integral to the overall architectural order. The building of streets and roads was integral to the building of Roman cities and their empire. Within the Forum in Rome, you can still walk the paving stones of the Via Appia, which traversed the city and connected to a network of roads spanning Europe and North Africa from 312 BCE. Romans paved and engineered streets according to their distinct functions. Indeed, the very etymology of the English word *street* comes to us via Old English from the Latin *via strata* (paved road).[4] Roman streets ranged from little-improved rural or village roads to state-maintained *viae publicae* routed for directness and engineered according to anticipated traffic.[5] Most Roman roads were shared but designed with distinct features for different users: smooth paving for wheeled traffic, raised sidewalks and even raised crosswalks for pedestrians. They were also regulated to maintain public order—for example, restricting wheeled vehicles to certain local roadways and noisy carts to daytime use.

Many of these innovations were lost with the fall of Rome, and streets in the medieval city reverted to pathways wending between destinations like home and market and church. Few cities paved their roadways—Paris not until the thirteenth century and London in 1417—so most remained dusty tracks in summer and quagmires in winter.[6] But the Renaissance brought what Mumford calls a "new urban complex" with a new kind of street at its center: straight and often oversized to better serve expanded use of wheeled vehicles and a "hastening of movement and conquest of space, in addition to military displays of power."[7] Not simply designed for efficient vehicular flow, monumental baroque streets served as stages for "the daily parade of the powerful."[8] The military and economic needs of conquest also increasingly found expression in the grid as a key element in planned new towns, like those codified in the Law of the Indies to guide Spanish colonization.[9] With the growing centralization of nation-states, attention returned to road building, particularly to serve the growth in wheeled traffic like passenger coaches.[10] Yet streets remained more gathering place than transportation infrastructure, typically accommodating flow and stasis within the same public space.

The Pre-automobile American Street as Multipurpose Public Space

Frontier Footpaths to Urban Gridiron

Colonists brought European traditions to North America, designing cities based on familiar models adapted to frontier exigencies. The first colonial settlements—whether Saint Augustine (1565), Jamestown (1607), the Plymouth Colony (1620), New Amsterdam (1624), or Boston

24   A Short History of the American Street

(1630)—were little planned. And with the exception of Saint Augustine's grid, America's earliest streets were developed as organically as the towns themselves.

This pattern changed significantly with William Penn's planning of Philadelphia on a rectilinear gridiron in 1680. Envisioning the city as the capital of a great colony, Penn directed planning commissioners to "be sure to settle the figure of the town so as that the streets hereafter may be uniform down to the water from the country bounds."[11] The plan included a hierarchy of streets oriented around north–south and east–west axes, centered on a public-market square and public parks, and introduced the convention of numbering streets and naming them for trees. The gridiron's practicality for circulation and land division set a powerful template and was much imitated in the planning of new towns across North America.

But the political and cultural value of streets—as well as baroque design ideals—crossed the Atlantic too. The planning of a new national capital in Washington, D.C., by Frenchman Pierre Charles L'Enfant integrated a practical gridiron with radial boulevards inspired by Versailles. And these streets were carefully designed for a mix of uses—with carriage traffic down the center and tree-lined pedestrian walks on either side. L'Enfant's baroque approach was little imitated, but elements like ample street widths would become part of the American design vocabulary.

American streets in the settler/preindustrial era, whether developed organically or carefully planned, remained public pedestrian spaces first and foremost. They provided for circulating foot traffic, human and hooved, and limited wheeled, horse-drawn traffic. But such streets—including the roadway surface—were equally meeting places, markets, and open spaces. Few streets were paved, except where heavy wheeled traffic made surfacing with cobble from local rivers worthwhile, and until the mid-nineteenth century, most places tried to limit rather than accommodate vehicular traffic.

Omnibuses, Trolley Cars, and the
Increasingly Bustling Industrial Street

The rapid growth and industrialization of nineteenth-century American cities brought growing volumes and diversity of traffic, starting the road

A Short History of the American Street   25

to vehicularization recounted in Clay McShane's aptly titled *Down the Asphalt Path.*

Unlike colonial cities, whose pattern of streets mostly followed urban development, urbanization in the nineteenth century was planned around a gridiron of streets to structure and accommodate explosive growth with rectilinear patterns that supported orderly property subdivision. Growing carriage and cart traffic prompted cities to require developers to pave new streets and develop their own public paving programs, funded initially by assessing abutting property owners.[12] The expanding size and functional segregation of American districts, spacing emerging suburbs away from factories and slums, also demanded new transportation technologies, including horse-drawn omnibuses and steam railways (which first ran down streets but were later banned and rerouted onto separate rights-of-way). With innovations in horsecar trolleys on fixed rails in the 1850s and the expansion of sidewalks, mixed-use street spaces were increasingly structured around distinct modes of travel.

Increasing conflicts and disorder among pedestrians, horses, wheeled carriages, and later cable and electric trolley cars required new forms of public control. As early as 1866, New York began to control traffic at major intersections, and other cities imposed rules on vehicles mainly to protect street pavements.[13] However, with growing traffic volume and speed, pedestrian use began to rise and cities contemplated regulations to protect public safety and reduce congestion. Local governments devoted increasing resources to improving streets as infrastructure, developing a hierarchy that focused streetcar traffic on improved corridors while orienting local streets around neighborhood life. Heavier traffic volumes and vehicles prompted calls for road widening and improved paving— initially with cobblestone, then with crushed stone macadam suited for carriages, and later asphalt after 1871—while channeling pedestrians onto raised sidewalks.[14]

All this required greater institutionalization of traffic administration and engineering. Instead of decentralized funding and decision-making driven by abutting property owners, which tended toward narrow streets, wide sidewalks, and light paving, cities shifted to centralized municipal street departments and commissions and focused on improving key corridors with taxpayer dollars. A new breed of municipal engineers emerged whose worldview was expressed by prominent engineer Francis Greene in 1890: "The streets of the city are built for the same purpose as railroads between cities—viz. to provide for the transportation of freight and passengers."[15]

Despite these major shifts, the American roadway remained a multipurpose space until the twentieth century, in which travel was "only one form of communication for which urbanites used streets."[16] And, despite increasing improvements, until as late as 1890, half of all American city streets remained unpaved, oriented more to neighborhood conversation than through traffic (Figure 3).

Cars Claim the Street

The Violent Arrival of Autos

Within just a few short decades, this order was swept away by the unprecedented historical force of the motorized automobile. This shift from the pedestrian street to vehicular thoroughfare, and its realignment of the purpose and design of urban public space and infrastructural

Figure 3. Historically, American streets were mixed-use spaces. *Mulberry Street, New York City,* ca. 1900, Detroit Publishing Company photograph collection, Library of Congress, https://lccn.loc.gov/2016794146/.

change, didn't go uncontested. But the hegemony of the car that emerged continues to define the street a century later.

Norton recounts this epic, violent struggle in *Fighting Traffic: The Dawn of the Motor Age in the American City.* "Motorists arrived in American city streets as intruders," Norton reminds us, and "had to fight to win a rightful place there."[17] What began as a trickle of automobiles at the beginning of the century became a torrent as innovations in mass manufacturing brought the car within reach of the middle classes. Car registrations soared from one million in 1913 to ten million in 1923.[18] Not only was the growing volume of cars a public safety problem, but so too was their speed and maneuverability: "Old street uses plus new automobiles equaled disaster," in Norton's words.[19] Under customary assumptions, the city street—like the city park—had been a public space available for use by anyone, as long as they didn't unduly annoy or endanger others.[20] But America's first pedestrian fatality by automobile in 1899 and the many more that followed helped bring about what McShane describes as an "urban traffic revolution."[21]

Interestingly, and perhaps relevant to our recent experience, these social changes coincided with the terrifying 1918–1919 influenza pandemic. The virus emerged in a wartime context of concentrated troops, but it also arrived at a time when mass transportation and urban change had expanded the public places where communicable disease could spread, helping define it for public health officials as a "crowd disease."[22] Though officials were reluctant to close public transit, they promoted social distancing and masking in public spaces and encouraged people to walk instead of ride the streetcar.[23] These measures and public fear helped empty streets.[24] In such a context, however, the automobile offered "solace and refuge from the social and pathogenic threats of public transportation" and became one of the "most desirable tools of pandemic relief."[25] As the war and the influenza pandemic came to a close, people returned to the streets. But the city was never to be quite the same again.

The year 1920 marked something of a watershed moment in the American street. Transit ridership peaked in the United States, only to be followed by a slow and then precipitous decline after 1930.[26] At the same time, car ownership and use soared. With all the new cars on the roadway came unprecedented carnage: two hundred thousand American pedestrians died in traffic accidents over the 1920s.[27] This was a violent struggle between modes of travel, but it had broader social dimensions. Car owners and drivers were more likely to be white, male, middle or upper class, and increasingly suburban. As such people shifted from walking and transit to driving, pedestrians were proportionally more likely to be immigrants and people of color and to have lower incomes. Among pedestrian fatalities, women, children, and urban dwellers were overrepresented.[28] The conflicts had racial dimensions too: by the mid-1920s almost ten adults and children were being struck on the streets of Harlem every day, often by white drivers, making many crashes "interracial affairs."[29]

The public initially blamed reckless motorists and called for stricter traffic control, but as the ranks and political power of drivers grew, public discourse shifted from limiting vehicles to reordering streets around them. Motorists—and a wider lobby Norton calls "Motordom"—weren't content to share the street; they increasingly claimed it for their dominant use.[30] Pedestrians were increasingly marginalized to sidewalks and crosswalks and labeled disorderly jaywalkers when they walked on roadways that had been their domain only a decade before.

Redefining and Redesigning Streets for Cars

This "difficult and sometimes fierce" struggle over the public street was waged among human bodies and vehicles and in the realms of traffic law and design.[31] Prior to the motor age, no city had what can rightly be called a traffic code, but in 1903, New York City—led by pioneering reformer William Phelps Eno—developed "Rules for Driving" that directed drivers to keep vehicles to the right, pass on the left, use hand signals, and travel at a "safe and proper speed."[32] Cities across the United States followed suit, including speed limits that were often stricter than New York's (often 10 mph or less) and adopting traffic codes to clearly define diverse users, delineate street spaces, and assign legal rights to the right-of-way and responsibility in case of conflict.[33] As late as 1926, most national traffic experts still agreed that "streets are primarily provided for general public use," but roadways were increasingly recast from mixed-use public spaces to transportation spaces regulated to promote traffic flow.[34]

Simultaneously, an emerging breed of civil and traffic engineers used design to rationalize competing forms of mobility and street uses.

Cities connected enforceable new rules with new research techniques of systems analysis and controls to design experiments in rotary traffic circles, barriers, signage, and markings. The first traffic signal was installed in 1912 in Cleveland, Ohio. These strategies initially focused on better controlling traffic on existing streets but increasingly sought to reconstruct streets around vehicular speed. To accommodate heavy motorized traffic, engineers looked to smooth rough cobblestone with asphalt paving, and by 1915, Los Angeles claimed it had paved all of its streets.[35] In response to growing congestion, cities across the United States widened streets to add travel lanes, often at the cost of sidewalks and street trees, causing what Jane Holtz Kay describes as "butchery to old buildings and landscapes."[36]

Motorists claimed both ample room to move and plentiful places to park. This too required rethinking and redesigning streets, whose centers had traditionally been kept clear for travel but whose margins were available for a variety of public uses like socializing and mobile commerce. As auto clubs argued for parking as a "fundamental right," customary roadside users and engineers viewed it as a private use infringing on the public domain.[37] Norton cites a Chicago engineer's 1924 complaint: "It seems unreasonable that a comparative few people can utilize the most valuable street space in our cities, practically at will, for their own pleasure and convenience and to the serious inconvenience of thousands of their fellow citizens."[38] Some cities tried banning parking, especially overnight or during rush hours, but with the growing number and political clout of drivers, others began formalizing curb parking with regulations setting time limits and meters (after 1935). Cities increasingly widened streets to incorporate parking while preserving the efficient flow of traffic. In the process, all other uses were displaced.

The epic but little-remembered struggle between drivers and nondrivers between 1915 and 1930 was a "violent revolution," in Norton's words, "less a contest between vehicles . . . than a competition for their urban medium: the street."[39] This transportation and social revolution swept streets only somewhat more slowly than the influenza pandemic it coincided with, but its impact was longer lasting, leaving in its wake roadways reimagined and transformed from public amenities for social life into hard infrastructure, from community spaces into motor thoroughfares.

30   A Short History of the American Street

Planning the City for Automobility

The rethinking of American streets was waged not only at the street level—and in emerging arenas of traffic regulation and engineering—but also at a wider scale by the emerging field of urban planning, which increasingly oriented cities around vehicular flow.

Like the planning discipline itself, this new thinking can be traced to the 1909 *Plan of Chicago,* authored by Daniel H. Burnham and Edward H. Bennett "to bring order out of chaos" by creating a vision for a "well-ordered and convenient city."[40] Lamenting how congestion "paralyze[s] the basic functions of the city," it argued for "removing obstacles that prevent or obstruct circulation" and advocated constructing new thoroughfares that tolerated "no bad turns or kinks" toward a "network of surface thoroughfares equal to the requirements of future generations."[41] The plan conceived of streets as a hierarchical system of general streets, avenues, and wide boulevards to promote urban order and traffic flow. And though it recognized the right of people to assemble, it suggested that gatherings (including parades) be moved off the street.

Such early planning coincided with the first National Conference on City Planning in Washington, D.C., in 1906 and the professionalization of planning as a discipline, which emphasized the importance of streets to orderly development and traffic flow. Perhaps the first general plan adopted by a major city was the 1925 *Official City Plan of Cincinnati, Ohio,* which approached street networks as a "thoroughfare system" to channel vehicular traffic and proposed solving the congestion problem by widening streets. Not only did it assume pedestrians should relinquish the roadway, but Cincinnati's plan also suggested that in widening streets, "the sacrifice of a part of the sidewalk is advantageous."[42]

Codifying and Reengineering the Roadway as Vehicular Infrastructure

Regulating Mobility as Traffic and Streets "for the Purposes of Vehicular Travel"

The battle for the soul and space of the American public street, waged from city to city across the 1920s, led in the 1930s to a new national consensus that streets belonged to cars. Solidifying this new social order required uniform legal and design standards, whose specifics are unfamiliar to most of us but whose impacts are seen across the United States.

Amid local experimentation, reformers and automobile interests increasingly decried "lack of uniformity" in traffic laws, and a National Conference on Street and Highway Safety was convened to address congestion and efficiency. Initially, auto groups opposed traffic regulation on principle, but they came to view uniformity as a way to overturn "prevailing principles of traffic control."[43] A related Committee on Uniformity in Laws and Regulations drafted model traffic legislation called *The Uniform Vehicle Code* codified by twenty-three states by 1930 and a *Model Municipal Traffic Ordinance* adopted by one hundred cities within two years.[44] To update these standards, a National Committee on Uniform Traffic Laws and Ordinances was formed with the motto "Salus, Libertas, Lex" or "Safety with Freedom through Law."[45]

For a century the *Uniform Vehicle Code* (*UVC*) has provided a legal foundation for state statutes governing American streets. At the core of the *UVC* are "Rules of the Road," which define streets as "open to the use of the public for purposes of vehicular travel."[46] In contrast to the unstructured and lightly regulated chaos of the nineteenth-century street, the *UVC*'s "Rules of the Road" impose order by controlling traffic and specifying who can be mobile (and who must yield). Key is the concept of right-of-way, defined as "the right of one vehicle or pedestrian to proceed in a lawful manner in preference to another."[47] Such rights (and inferred duties to yield) are allocated according to different street spaces. On the roadway, cars have the right-of-way, and all others must yield and be limited to the margins. Where pedestrians could once walk across or along the street at will, the *UVC* limited their rights to sidewalks and crosswalks (where present) and imposed the responsibility to not step out onto the roadway suddenly.

Uniform traffic laws transformed the public street, once a mixed-use pedestrian domain, into infrastructure for vehicular traffic (Figure 4). This new order was very explicit in privileging motorists: "Every pedestrian crossing a roadway at any point other than within a marked crosswalk or within an unmarked crosswalk at an intersection shall yield the right-of-way to all vehicles upon the roadway."[48] While other modes had nominal rights to their own portion of the street—pedestrians to sidewalks or crosswalks—such infrastructure was in no way guaranteed. The *UVC* is only a model, but it gained the power of law when adopted by states. By the 1960s, most had adopted such codes, and in 1968 the

Figure 4. By the mid-twentieth century, motorists claimed roadways as their nearly exclusive domain, even in dense cities like New York. Anthony Angel Collection, Library of Congress Prints and Photographs Division, https://lccn.loc.gov/2020636818.

federal government helped finish the process by mandating that states modernize nonconforming laws in line with the *UVC.*

Modeling Street Networks as Pipes for Cars

Translating these social and legal relationships into asphalt, and handling exploding volumes of vehicles and traffic, necessitated new engineering approaches for rightsizing roadways as conduits.

This started with new institutions. A National Advisory Board on Highway Research, founded in 1920, evolved into the Transportation Research Board (TRB) to apply science and engineering principles to model streets to meet vehicular demand.[49] In 1950, the TRB began publishing what remains a marquee publication, the *Highway Capacity Manual,* which reimagined the roadway as a spatial network evaluated in terms of flow: from the uninterrupted flow of freeways to the interrupted flow of surface streets. To measure the performance of streets, the TRB developed a metric known as "Level of Service" (LOS), which graded streets in relation to flow. "Free-flow operation" gets a grade of LOS A and busy streets with traffic, intersections, and pedestrians are given an F. This hydraulic approach to streets—like the field of traffic engineering itself—though initially a response to the challenge of planning new highways, was increasingly applied to urban streets, with outcomes as predictable as they are unfortunate. LOS-focused engineers oversized new streets to meet current and projected future demand and limited complicating factors like pedestrian crosswalks. And since wider streets are more expensive, constrained budgets rendered sidewalks optional.

Such autocentrism was not unique to engineering and became embedded in midcentury urban planning, too. Transportation planners, with their quantitative approach to spatial analysis and modeling of travel demand and supply, found common cause with traffic engineers. Though more careful to put transportation in the context of land use, they still viewed the primary purpose of street networks as transportation, planned mostly for efficient flow. These ideas transcended transportation to influence land-use planning, particularly through the subdivision process that created new streets. Viewing streets as having two functions— mobility across urban space and access to adjoining land uses—planners promoted a street hierarchy: local streets that prioritized access over

34   A Short History of the American Street

mobility poured into collector streets that balanced the two and, ultimately, principal arterials that prioritized mobility and later limited-access highways promoting free flow.

It should be noted that these efforts to plan and engineer new streets and highways, undertaken through the scientific language of flow, reflected a policy bias not only toward automobility but also toward the particular social groups who drove. It is well established that the midcentury boom of road and highway construction, what Kenneth T. Jackson in *Crabgrass Frontier* calls a "concrete colossus," lavished mobility on suburbs occupied primarily by white middle- and upper-class people, with federal funding whose "bias" created "the world's best road system and very nearly its worst public transit offerings."[50] But these biases were more than incidental. The routing and construction of new highways through existing urban areas brought ruinous and disproportionate harm to minority communities. In the recent book *Justice and the Interstates,* editors ask the question "How can a highway be racist?" and answer it by showing how planners and engineers promote a technocratic approach "couched in technical jargon and scientific language that, though undoubtedly precise in its coordinates and angles, obscured the racial implications of its policies."[51] Indeed, not only did Black and Latino communities bear a "greater brunt of the Interstate's destructive force" while receiving fewer benefits, there is clear evidence (particularly from the American South) of "the intentionally vindictive, violent, and racist deployment of transportation infrastructure against the African American community."[52]

By midcentury, transportation and land-use planners were constructing a new suburban America around streets and highways conceived as interconnected conduits, while punching new interstates and widening existing roads through the increasingly diverse urban core. Suburbanites experience this functional hierarchy in the width, volume, and speed of different streets, particularly as we travel from slower and narrower local streets to progressively wider and faster collector and arterial streets. Urbanites experience this as the widening of existing boulevards with new traffic lanes, often at the expense of transit, sidewalks, and even surrounding businesses and homes. In much of this system of auto-dominated throughput, the only vestige of the street's prior public space function may be found occasionally in playing kids and block

A Short History of the American Street   35

parties on local streets (especially cul-de-sacs), but beyond that, we experience streets as they are engineered to be: infrastructure for flow.

Reengineering Streets as Highways
"for the Safety and Convenience of the Motorist"

Having legislated, planned, and modeled streets as a hierarchical network of pipes, the next challenge was to design their physical infrastructure accordingly.

For a century, the most influential voice in the design of American roadways has been the American Association of State Highway and Transportation Officials (AASHTO), whose uniform standards of construction and maintenance evolved by the late 1920s into "standards of practice" embodied in its premier publication *A Policy on Geometric Design of Highways and Streets.*[53] Commonly known as the "Green Book," AASHTO's *Policy on Geometric Design* is known colloquially as the bible of roadway engineering in the United States.

AASHTO is not a governmental agency, but it came to provide the standards by which American public streets are designed and built. The Green Book has made no bones about its autocentrism; its 2011 edition stated, "These geometric design guidelines are intended to provide operational efficiency, comfort, safety, and convenience for the motorist."[54] Envisioning streets as a network of facilities classified based on mobility/movement or access, it then defines users as different kinds of "design vehicles"—including pedestrians, cars, and trucks—with distinct operational characteristics that inform spatial and geometric "criteria to optimize or improve the design" of highways (Figure 5).

Fully transforming public streets into conduits for cars also requires signs and symbols to explicitly communicate a new autocentric order. In 1935, AASHTO (at that time named the American Association of State Highway Officials) joined city and other transportation officials, automobile interests, and the Institute of Traffic Engineers in publishing a comprehensive *Manual on Uniform Traffic Control Devices for Streets and Highways (MUTCD).*[55] The MUTCD was later adopted as a national standard for all federal-aid highways in the 1960s, and by the 1970s, the manual became the required guidance for how streets should be signed, marked, and controlled. What had traditionally been an undifferentiated and uncontrolled public space was increasingly inscribed

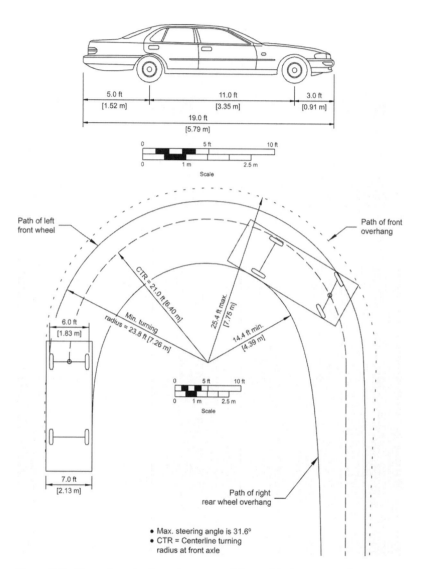

Figure 5. Traffic engineering based on automobiles as "design vehicles" helped remake streets as conduits for vehicular flow. American Association of State Highway and Transportation Officials, *A Policy on Geometric Design of Highways and Streets* (Washington, D.C., 2018). Used with permission.

with signs, symbols, and devices to "promote highway safety and efficiency by providing for the orderly movement of all road users," though defined exclusively as vehicles.[56]

Over the twentieth century, American streets were thoroughly and systematically reengineered and controlled as vehicular conduits. Again, though written in the technocratic language of engineering and design, these standards embodied and reinforced social biases toward people who drove over those who walked, biked, or used transit. And they prioritized speed and throughput over neighborhood quality of life, much less the street's potential as public space. This was an epochal change for both transportation and urban life that we cannot begin to understand without recognizing the powerful role of traffic engineering and control standards, whose uniform institutional frameworks produced uniform street spaces and social consequences.

Questioning the Carnage

Urbanist Critiques

Even as twentieth-century cities and streets were flooded with and redesigned around cars, by 1960 a growing number of urbanists, planners, and others critiqued these trends and their social and environmental costs.

At the broadest level, critics questioned the wisdom of suburbanization and urban disinvestment. Lewis Mumford's monumental *The City in History* reserves special judgment for automobility: "Under the present dispensation, we have sold our urban birthright for a sorry mess of motor cars," he laments.[57] Equally devastating, and even more influential, was Jane Jacobs's *The Death and Life of Great American Cities* (1961), whose defense of big cities started with streets. "Streets and their sidewalks, the main public places of the city, are its most vital organs," she suggests, and she asks rhetorically, "Think of a city and what comes to mind? Its streets."[58] Streets, she continues, "are bound up with circulation but are not identical with it," part of a "marvelous order . . . composed of movement and change, and although it is life, not art, we may fancifully call it the art form of the city and liken it to the dance . . . an intricate ballet."[59] The techniques she advocates to reclaim streets were as heretical then as they are commonsensical today: narrowing roadways to slow cars, widening sidewalks, calming traffic through

38 A Short History of the American Street

shorter blocks and signalization, and tactics like landscaping to "add convenience, intensity, and cheer in cities, while simultaneously limiting automobiles."[60]

At the same time, the struggle for civil rights increasingly intersected with transportation. It's notable that pivotal moments in the civil rights movements took place in transportation spaces, whether Rosa Parks and the Montgomery bus boycott, Bloody Sunday on the Edmund Pettus Bridge, the Stonewall Riots on the streets of Greenwich Village, the National Organization for Women's marches in New York and other cities, or disability activism in Denver and elsewhere that smashed curbs or built ramps for wheelchair access. Streets were settings for many protests, but some activists sought to confront transportation policy and roadway design directly. In Baltimore, Black residents organized in opposition to freeway expansion, arguing in 1968: "We have been asked to make sacrifice after sacrifice in the name of progress, and when that progress has been achieved we find it marked 'White Only.'"[61] In San Francisco, urban redevelopment and highway construction along the city's waterfront brought, according to geographer Damon Scott, "queer San Franciscans into a collective struggle to act as a community, first to defend and then reconstitute their gathering places ahead of the bulldozer."[62] Despite some notable successes, minority communities had difficulty slowing the road-building juggernaut. But even when they lost their neighborhoods to new infrastructure, they didn't easily forget. In Los Angeles, "even though some of the barrios that housed Mexican Americans were bulldozed and gone, the memories of these places persist."[63] These struggles informed and motivated a growing movement to question and resist the building and widening of roadways, particularly at the cost of urban communities.

These critiques of auto-oriented American transportation and roadways—and their consequences for communities—coalesced around the turn of the twentieth century. James Howard Kunstler's 1993 *The Geography of Nowhere* argues bluntly, "Americans have been living car-centered lives for so long that the collective memory of what used to make a landscape or townscape or even a suburb humanly rewarding has nearly been erased."[64] In contrast to designing places for the convenience and speed of vehicles, he suggests streets can "accommodate the automobile and are still charming" by following two rules: respect the presence of humans and pay attention to details.[65] In *Suburban Nation* (2000), architects Andres Duany, Elizabeth Plater-Zyberk, and Jeff Speck call out America's "fundamentally misguided approach to transportation planning" in which what "works best for cars hardly works at all for pedestrians."[66] If you want to make a real town, Duany and his co-authors suggest, trade hierarchical street networks with interconnected street grids and substitute engineering for "automotive sewers" with urban design for "civic thoroughfares."[67] At the same time, Robert D. Bullard and other environmental justice scholars call out transportation racism in *Highway Robbery* (2004), in which transport systems "are planned—and, in many cases, planned poorly when it comes to people of color" with biases that place "an extra 'tax' on poor people and people of color" to reinforce "transportation apartheid."[68]

What's more, these critiques took shape in movements to imagine a better transportation system. In planning and design, a New Urbanism movement emerged whose 1993 *Charter of the New Urbanism* decries urban disinvestment, sprawl, and other forms of social and environmental degradation as "one interrelated community-building challenge" and calls for communities "designed for the pedestrian and transit as well as the car."[69] Published as a book in 1999, the charter places special emphasis on the public street as both problem and solution. In his chapter, architect Douglas Farr argues for streets both "reasonably pleasant and convenient for motoring, but delightful for walking and cycling" through balanced design with sidewalks, bike lanes, and street trees to "reclaim public spaces."[70] Within the environmental justice movement, Bullard argues for a "vision of equitable transportation" in which "safe, clean, efficient, affordable, and equitable transportation should be a right of all Americans."[71]

Accommodating and Designing for Multiple Modes

As urbanists and social commentators confronted car-oriented planning and funding, others focused more squarely on traffic engineering, calling for streets that accommodate all modes of travel. This movement for multimodalism and Complete Streets drew upon ethical arguments about fairness to confront the autocentric status quo.

The Complete Streets movement originated in 2003 when a group of active transportation and other advocacy groups sought greater inclusion of active modes in federal transportation policy. Calling out engineering's lukewarm commitment to "routine accommodation"—which implied nondrivers were guests on the roadway—the group argued that streets that failed to accommodate all modes were "incomplete." In 2005, a Complete Streets Coalition was founded to promote Complete Streets "designed and operated to enable safe access and travel for all users. . . . Pedestrians, bicyclists, motorists, transit users, and travelers of all ages and abilities will be able to move along the street network safely."[72] In *Completing Our Streets,* founding member Barbara McCann describes the movement as beginning with a philosophy as basic as it was radical: "Roads should be safe for everyone traveling along them."[73] In contrast to "mono-modalism," they called on transportation agencies to serve the safety and convenience of people whether they are driving, riding a bus, biking, or walking. The movement demanded streets be safe for a variety of people, including older adults, children on their way to school, and people with disabilities.[74] By reframing the transportation-safety problem to encompass all users, McCann writes, the problem shifted to address the needs of the many Americans who don't drive. The movement advocated for local adoption of Complete Streets policies to articulate a "vision . . . of streets for everyone," defining users to include all modes and ages and abilities, and to apply that vision to "all projects . . . both new and retrofit projects."[75]

The movement for multimodal accommodation required new design standards, which found expression in a variety of policy changes. Passage of both the Americans with Disabilities Act in 1990 and the Transportation Equity Act for the 21st Century in 1998 called upon transportation agencies to accommodate bicycling and walking as a routine part of planning, design, construction, operations, and maintenance.[76] In response, after eighty years of autocentric design, AASHTO began developing engineering manuals focused on so-called alternative modes. And in each new edition AASHTO's Green Book better supported pedestrians and bicycle-focused design, though cars remained the core assumption at the center of both roadway design and the streets they produced, leaving other modes as optional alternatives.

In growing frustration with stubbornly autocentric and highway-oriented traffic engineering, a coalition of large cities, led by New York

Mayor Michael Bloomberg, formed a new nonprofit National Association of City Transportation Officials (NACTO), whose mission is "to build cities as places for people, with safe, sustainable, accessible and equitable transportation choices that support a strong economy and vibrant quality of life."[77] NACTO articulates this vision through a set of alternative design guides rooted in accepted engineering standards to support Complete Streets, including its *Urban Street Design Guide* (2013), *Urban Bikeway Design Guide* (2014), and *Transit Street Design Guide* (2016). I explore these in more depth in later chapters, but in historical terms, NACTO's guidelines offered a major break from AASHTO's car-centric, highly technical, and exorbitantly priced manuals. Conversely, NACTO prioritized the accessibility of streets for multimodal travel and as public places in easy-to-understand text and graphics and provided these resources free on the web for a diverse public. In the process, NACTO articulated a distinct vision of the American street and created guidelines for redesigning it in practice.

As NACTO and others sought to redesign streets for multimodal accessibility, cities began experimenting with ways to reclaim them as public places. Cities have long closed streets for occasional events like parades, but in the twenty-first century cities tried more regular street closures. In the 1970s, Ciclovía events developed in Latin America to close public streets to traffic on certain weekends for active transportation and cultural events, later adopted by a growing number of American cities—including CicLAvia in Los Angeles (2008), Summer Streets in New York (2008), and Philly Free Streets (2016). Around the same time, cities piloted ways to reclaim streets in more enduring ways. In 2005, San Francisco art and design studio Rebar was the first to convert a metered parking space into a temporary public park—installing turf, a potted tree, and a parking bench—for the duration of the meter, which grew into a worldwide Park(ing) Day movement, whose website calls "attention to the need for more urban open space, to generate critical debate around how public space is created and allocated, and to improve the quality of urban human habitat."[78] In 2009, San Francisco began to formalize these pop-up public spaces in a Pavement to Parks program, providing a model for other towns and cities to convert curbside parking into parklets for open space or dining.

42   A Short History of the American Street

These turn-of-the-century movements presented a frontal challenge to the autocentrism of America's public streets. Just as early twentieth-century traffic laws and engineering codified urban experimentation to transform streets into thoroughfares, in the early twenty-first century, novel ideas about multimodal Complete Streets and public space found expression in NACTO standards that sought to "redesign and reinvest in our streets as cherished public spaces for people, as well as critical arteries for traffic."[79]

Reckoning with the Ongoing Dangers and Inequities of America's Public Streets

American Streets, Mostly Still *Dangerous by Design*

Despite the building movement to rethink public streets and accommodate all users, the hegemony of the car built up over the twentieth century remains built into our public streets. Autocentric ideas and systems are as durable—indeed, obdurate—as physical streets themselves. While challenging this status quo was never going to be easy or quick, progress has been discouragingly slow.

A century after the car arrived on the scene, the United States is a thoroughly auto-dependent nation. When the Federal Highway Administration conducted its National Household Travel Survey in 2017, it found that among all trips 83 percent were by automobile and only 11 percent were on foot, 2 percent were by transit, and 4 percent were by another mode.[80] American streets, even in our densest cities, remain car dominated. This system provides ready mobility for many drivers but with high social and environmental costs. For example, transportation is the single largest source of greenhouse gas emissions in the United States, accounting for 29 percent of emissions, the majority from light-duty vehicles and personal travel.[81]

But one of the most direct costs of this system is in human life itself, which continues to climb. Every other year since 2010, the National Complete Streets Coalition has published reports on the state of walking, biking, and rolling titled *Dangerous by Design*. These reports paint a stark portrait of American roads. The 2021 report lists 53,435 pedestrians struck and killed by drivers between 2010 and 2019, more than fourteen people per day on average.[82] Almost two decades into the Complete Streets and Vision Zero movements, these statistics have only gotten worse. Nondrivers struck and killed annually grew 45 percent between 2010 and 2019, with 2018 and 2019 showing the highest deaths since 1990.[83] The report states bluntly, "Our current approach to addressing the rising number of people struck and killed while walking has been a total failure." And while many communities emphasize policing, education, or "blaming the victims," *Dangerous by Design* puts responsibility squarely on "core tenets of acceptable roadway design that actively put people at risk" while those afoot "continue to pay the price."[84]

These human costs are not borne equally. "All people do not experience the benefits and burdens of transportation policy and funding decisions equally," the report argues, noting that vulnerability to traffic fatalities correlates to other forms of disadvantage.[85] Older people between the ages of fifty and sixty-five, and especially those over seventy-five, are particularly at risk. Black and African American people are 67 percent more vulnerable, and American Indian and Alaskan Native people are more vulnerable than non-Hispanic white people. And while data do not exist on the income of victims, pedestrian fatalities occur twice as often in the lowest-income neighborhoods than they do in the highest.

Notwithstanding two decades of Complete Streets advocacy and multimodal design, moving cars at high speeds remains the priority of roadway engineering, operation, maintenance, and performance measurement. Our cities remain car-dependent and streets auto-oriented. These trends, compounded by ever-larger vehicles and more distracted drivers, have made American streets only more dangerous for nondrivers: eighty-four of the one hundred largest U.S. metropolitan areas grew more dangerous since the previous edition of *Dangerous by Design*.[86]

"Whose Streets? Our Streets!" Pandemic, Social Justice, and the Reclaiming of American Roadways

America entered the second decade of the twenty-first century well into an incremental process of redefining and redesigning streets from mere vehicular thoroughfares into multimodal Complete Streets, with incipient experiments in reclaiming them as public places. But few could have anticipated how the coming confluence of Covid-19 and the George Floyd protests would accelerate debates in American cities about the public street, equity, and the connection between the two.

44   A Short History of the American Street

The spread of Covid-19 and widespread stay-at-home orders in the spring of 2020 both emptied streets of automobiles and created new demands for socially distanced mobility and outdoor recreation. Across the United States, personal vehicle trips dropped 45 percent in the early months of the pandemic.[87] Cities like New York experienced a nearly 50 percent decline in bridge and tunnel traffic; the *New York Times* described those empty streets as "post-apocalyptic."[88] This eased travel for drivers but also invited new uses of the street: "With traffic gone," reporter Michael Wilson observes, "so too was basic human awareness of traffic" as people "wandered" onto the street. People continued to need essential services, so even under the height of stay-at-home orders streets continued to serve essential travel. But with the necessity for social distancing and many parks and public places closed, people sought open-air alternatives for active transportation, recreation, and gathering. Conditions that reporters initially described in end-of-days terms presented a novel opportunity for many communities to experience streets in new ways, as these empty spaces invited new uses.

Planners and community members across the United States responded accordingly. They slowed streets by limiting through traffic; closed streets to open the roadway for walking, biking, and temporary gathering; and reclaimed roadways for outdoor dining or plazas. What began as a rapid response to a public health crisis, initially expected to last for several weeks, led to months- and years-long programs. And from experimentation emerged the need for standards. In the summer of 2020, NACTO synthesized many of these in a guide titled *Streets for Pandemic Response & Recovery.*[89] While Covid-19 provided the context, the authors pondered whether "this is a historic moment when cities can change course. . . . These empty lanes provide new possibilities for people to use streets for essential trips and healthy activity right now, and they form the outline of the future cities we need to build."[90]

As cities and their residents reclaimed street spaces amid Covid-19, a growing concern for social justice in the wake of George Floyd's murder and police misconduct also spilled onto the streets. In an immediate and physical sense, the massive protests of summer 2020 focused particularly on public streets, which protesters entered, marched upon, and purposefully claimed. "Whose streets? Our Streets!" was a common

A Short History of the American Street   45

protest call and response. The site of the murder of George Floyd at Thirty-Eighth and Chicago Streets in Minneapolis, center of both protesters and memorialization, is now officially George Floyd Square. This intersection that was formerly curbside parking is now a small public area described as "a gathering place" and "important space for racial healing and justice among many members of the community and visitors."[91]

Calls for social justice helped transform streets in less direct but perhaps even more substantial ways. Public discourse about equity and inclusion, exemplified by the Black Lives Matter movement, transcended protests of police misconduct to confront bias in diverse realms of society.[92] Transportation and streets were no exception. Many have long decried the discrimination and inequities of transportation policy—what environmental justice scholar Robert D. Bullard and others call "transportation racism." Many transportation planners and scholars had been approaching transportation equity primarily as a matter of fairness among transportation users and modes, but sensitivity was now expanding to include the role of social difference in mobility. Advocates like Smart Growth America and the Complete Streets Coalition expanded their definition of Complete Streets beyond safe access for all users to emphasize the needs of "those who have experienced systemic underinvestment, or those whose needs have not been met through a traditional transportation approach, such as older adults, people living with disabilities, people who don't have access to vehicles, and Black, Native, and Hispanic or Latino/a/x communities."[93] Smart Growth America now hosts Equity Summits and the U.S. Department of Transportation's website now advances equity as a strategic goal "with the aim of reducing inequities across our transportation systems and the communities they affect."[94]

The pandemic and the fight for social justice have transformed the American city and our age. In the process, street spaces long dominated by vehicular travel and parking have been reclaimed for more diverse modes and uses and subjected to increasing scrutiny through the lens of equity and sustainability. Both are historical moments that will begin to recede into memory with time but that have altered, in lasting ways, how we think about, design, and use public streets. As a result, the demand for "streets for everyone" has taken on meaning beyond transport.

The Challenge of Sharing Streets

The history of the American street is a history of the American city, changing urban processes, values, and the technologies that facilitate them. Reflecting on that history is essential to seeing the street beyond functional infrastructure to its complexity as a social space and public place.

American streets have taken multiple forms and have been transformed again and again. The nineteenth-century American street was a diverse, mixed-use, often contested mess. In short, it was a public space. The remaking of streets after the 1910s as infrastructure for vehicular flow helped create order, or at least of a certain kind. That autocentric order remains hegemonic today, but growing critiques have begun to affect design standards and physical streets. What began as a struggle for multimodal equity has morphed, particularly since the pandemic, into a wider rethinking of streets as public places central to the broader project of a more socially just city.

What this chapter hopefully reveals more than anything else is that the street is contested: a historical product of intense, even deadly, struggles over who has a right to be and be mobile in its public spaces. Jostling for access and space has always characterized the life of the street, but increasing traffic and the mechanization of transport brought these conflicts to the fore. Over the past century, the result was the institutionalization of legal rules codifying the purpose and allocation of street space and who can proceed (or must yield). Engineering standards have translated these into the physicality of roadway construction, control, and management. Ostensibly technocratic standards have been imbued with ideologies about (auto)mobility that reinforce already-uneven power geometries with the force of policing and asphalt. The uniformity and formality of these infrastructure systems, whose decision-making processes and outcomes are patently unfair to the most vulnerable people among us, mask a raw, bitter struggle with life-and-death consequences. It's hard to think of a better place to witness the stark inequities of urban life than the public roadway or to see a more expansive field for progressive social change.

2

ON THE ROAD TO MOBILITY JUSTICE
INTERSECTING APPROACHES TO A JUST STREET

Reimagining the American roadway and confronting its manifest inequities starts with questioning much of what we take for granted about transportation and infrastructure and thinking carefully about what might constitute an ideally just street. To reclaim streets in practice, we first rethink them in theory.

Scholars, planners, and everyday people alike recognize the importance of streets to urban life, but their very centrality and taken-for-granted banality makes it hard to really see them. And though mobility and streets seem like eminently practical things, they express ideas and ideologies that channel our thinking—like a street channels traffic—in particular ways. We tend to see roadways as infrastructure, for example, a system of asphalt, concrete, signs, and markings logically ordered to facilitate traffic. If streets are highly engineered, however, they're not simply physical infrastructure but also social spaces where we encounter others. And streets are public places—imbued with meaning, uneven power relations, and a sense of place—central to and embedded within surrounding communities. It takes no small amount of critical thinking to deconstruct the everyday street, but it's an essential step toward reimagining something different and hopefully better.

The street therefore has a very complex geography—physical, social, and even ethical—that raises some of the most profound conceptual and policy questions facing cities today. What drives the changing geography

47

of the street? What are mobility and streets for, and who has a right to them and the cities they traverse? How might streets be shared equitably? How can they balance their transportation function with their role as public places, central to livable and just communities?

This chapter seeks to transcend the everyday materiality of the asphalt roadway to broadly rethink mobility and the street. To reimagine mobility itself, we can draw from rapidly evolving debates about transportation in geography, planning, and related disciplines, which have recently shifted from a twentieth-century focus on technocratic approaches and the efficiency of vehicular travel to critical new mobilities writings that look beyond physical movement toward the diverse experiences and contested politics of mobility. Going still further, writings on social infrastructure help us see streets as more than just mobility spaces but as public places with a central role underpinning urban social life. These innovative writings help us see the wider possibilities of transport spaces like streets for both urban circulation and conviviality and remind us that streets are ultimately—and fundamentally—public spaces.

Recognizing mobility as imbued with politics and rights, and the centrality of streets to what social theorist Henri Lefebvre calls "the right to the city," leads to a central and thorny philosophical question: What might constitute mobility justice and a just street?[1] Many people talk about and clamor for equity, increasingly in relation to transportation. However, what they mean by *equity* is not always clear. Ambiguity is a problem enough in theory but even more so when faced with the challenge to translate justice principles into concrete and asphalt. Fortunately, equity and justice (like mobility) are well-established and increasingly vibrant topics among scholars, practitioners, and the public. This chapter can't comprehensively summarize the dizzying breadth and diversity of debates, but I try to outline and differentiate distinct frameworks and approaches before seeking to integrate them.

Among possible roads to mobility justice, we might begin with those that approach transportation systems from a distributional justice perspective focused on how mobility "goods" (e.g., access and rights to infrastructure) and "bads" (e.g., dangers and responsibilities) are spread across society and space. Descending from this map view of citywide distributional fairness, we might take a street-level view of multimodal equity focused on how public rights-of-way are shared among different forms of mobility. Mobility is not just about the mode of travel, however, but also about individual people and groups whose experiences are diverse and shaped by social identity, position, and related advantages/disadvantages—based on their race, gender/sexuality, disability, and other forms of social difference—inviting us to take a more people-centered view of social equity. If all this weren't complicated enough, we must then consider how transportation infrastructures like streets are themselves places and embedded within surrounding communities, prompting us to ask whether streets promote equitable places on a planet shared sustainably (and thus equitably) among present and future generations. Finally, we can approach mobility justice with a procedural equity emphasis on the need for people to have a meaningful say in fair and transparent decision-making processes.

Vibrant debates offer diverse approaches to mobility justice, each with distinct conceptual power and practical implications. But with this diversity come complications and even conundrums. These approaches can operate at different scales and with distinct conceptual vocabularies and emphases, and they can talk past each other in theory. Perhaps more problematic, they can even conflict in practice. For example, a citywide perspective on distributional equity might suggest making transportation improvements where they're not necessarily wanted by neighborhood residents. Advocating bike lanes for multimodal equity can conflict with social concerns about green gentrification. Yet, local resistance to improvements in the present day—for example, by those who fear bike lanes as a harbinger of gentrification—can slow progress to sustainability and thus harm future generations. Top-down planning based on universal values can be in tension with bottom-up procedural equity. Improving mobility for cyclists or transit can literally collide with static use of public space and vice versa. Reconciling these different emphases in theory is hard, but it's even harder for planners who must navigate trade-offs to make decisions on the allocation of public resources and the design of public spaces.

We therefore need a conceptual framework of mobility justice and just streets that is at once open and holistic yet able to reconcile different approaches toward a workable and theoretically informed practice. Here I suggest with humility and respect that we interpret streets—aptly enough—through the idea of intersectionality, a powerful term coined three decades ago by Black feminist legal scholar Kimberlé Crenshaw to highlight how marginalization can operate on distinct but often converging axes, particularly social identities and circumstances like race and gender. She introduced the concept with the metaphor of intersecting streets to emphasize the multidimensionality of individual experience, in which distinct forms of advantage or disadvantage can converge and compound each other.[2] As valuable as the concept is for understanding individual experience, its real power may lie in enabling us to see the structural, political, and representational forces that intersect to shape that experience and produce injustice (or, conversely, equity). Intersectionality has thus become a key concept in feminist and antiracist scholarship and activism, including critical race theory's efforts to understand the legal and other "regimes" that have subordinated people of color and the relationship between such social structures and professed ideals like "equal protection."[3] Yet intersectionality has been taken up across disciplines to think about and confront different forms of inequality. Social geographers employ it to explore intersections of gender and race while "being attentive to matters of inequality and politics."[4] More recently, mobilities scholars have begun applying it to understand the situated and embodied experience of unequal mobilities.[5] In extending the concept, we must take enormous care to respect its social origins and histories in activist Black feminism and not carelessly appropriate it.[6] Yet intersectionality offers an undeniably apt and powerful way to see and reconcile different approaches to mobility and mobility justice, helping us see the connections between individual experience—shaped by differences both social (i.e., who we are) and positional (i.e., how we get around, by choice or necessity)—and societal structures and infrastructures (i.e., street policy and design). Moreover, it offers a way to critically analyze inequitable mobility regimes and to frame a vision of something more just.

Just as intersections connect and manage traffic coming from different directions and streets, our challenge is to trace the distinct roads that might converge in an intersectional theory of mobility justice, which we might use to reimagine and redesign more just streets.

Rethinking Mobility and the Street

Transportation: From Movement to the Politics of Mobility

Geographers and others have long been fascinated by transportation not only as the movement of people and goods but also for its intrinsic role in shaping places. They also increasingly recognize transportation as not just a physical process but one that also involves "meanings, institutions, and social relations."[7] An intellectual movement under the banner of new mobilities has emerged to focus on the "political, cultural and aesthetic implications and resonances of movements . . . the meanings ascribed to these movements, and the embodied experiences of mobility."[8]

Transport geography, which emerged over the twentieth century alongside transport planning and traffic engineering, has traditionally taken a quantitative and materialist approach. New mobilities scholarship contributes critical and qualitative insights from across the social sciences and humanities to highlight how social factors mark mobile bodies and shape their experiences. This shift helps us look beyond the physicality of transportation—and transportation infrastructure like streets—to see the practices and representational schemes that make mobility a highly subjective experience. And instead of modeling the spatiality or efficiency of transport systems, new mobilities research advocates a more "interventionist style" exposing their effects on related concerns like equity, neoliberalization, and sustainability.[9]

Movement can therefore not be understood apart from what cultural geographer Tim Cresswell notably calls the "politics of mobility . . . the ways in which mobilities are both productive of such social relations and produced by them."[10] In launching the instantly successful new journal *Mobilities,* geographer Kevin Hannam and sociologists Mimi Sheller and John Urry called attention to the "relation between human mobilities and immobilities, and the unequal power relations which unevenly distribute motility, the potential for mobility."[11] Interpreting mobility as political implies that it's also ideological. Transportation may often be talked about and planned in technocratic and ostensibly value-neutral ways, but mobility is deeply contested, leading to what geographer Jason Henderson calls "street fights," both figurative and literal.[12] Beyond a clash between cars and pedestrians, it's an ideological struggle among

52   On the Road to Mobility Justice

rationalities, between a transportation engineering approach to streets as conduits for efficient traffic flow and the pedestrian's experience of them as "'place' . . . the intimate context of urban life," in the words of planning scholar and practitioner Jason W. Patton (who we'll hear from in chapter 4).[13]

The politics of mobility take place within a highly structured built environment and its "infrastructural moorings."[14] Infrastructure can mean not only the physical transportation spaces but also the institutions governing them, and it can involve "relations of power and of force rely[ing] on socio-technical systems, that are themselves increasingly the object of struggle."[15] Engineered spaces can seem "decoupled from ideology," but they powerfully reflect and reinforce "assumptions that lead to a particular ideology of mobility."[16] These assumptions, in turn, "are built into the very infrastructure of cities and streetscapes."[17]

All of this leads inevitably to the issue of mobility rights. Mobility, like other forms of contested access to public infrastructure and space, poses complicated questions: Who can claim access and be mobile on the roadway? Who does the infrastructure of the street belong to, and who belongs in its spaces? When claims to mobility collide, who must yield to whom? These are as practically important as they are theoretically complicated. In concrete terms, when we walk or roll onto streets, we all desire safe, convenient, and relatively unimpeded access. Our right to the street is key to a broader "right to the city," what Lefebvre conceives of as the "right to urban life, to renewed centrality, to places of encounter and exchange, to life rhythms and time uses, enabling the full and complete usage of . . . moments and places."[18] Lefebvre's "cry and demand" for rights to the city and its spaces have inspired generations of geographers and other urban scholars, but just as we must share the roadway with others, there is no single right to the city. This makes mobility political and, among competing claims, differences in how we define rights become what geographer Kafui A. Attoh calls "differences that matter."[19]

Streets: From Circulation Systems to Social Infrastructure

Reimagining streets also requires rethinking infrastructure. The *Oxford English Dictionary* defines *infrastructure* broadly as "substructure, foundation" or "permanent installations" for social undertakings.[20] Historians of infrastructure Andreas Marklund and Mogens Rüdiger describe it as "systems or networks that enable exchange and circulation."[21] By taking a broader view of infrastructure's purpose in the "facilitation of activity," social scientists increasingly look beyond technological networks to consider how institutions can also serve as infrastructure and how physical facilities like streets can double as "social infrastructure."[22]

No forms of infrastructure are ever simply physical things; they are what Marklund and Rüdiger call "multi-faceted historical constructs, part technology, part narrative, and part human, but also movement, flow and sets of relations."[23] Geographer Erik Swyngedouw suggests that infrastructure goes beyond mere "circulatory conduits" to help "produce the urban."[24] Indeed, urbanists Stephen Graham and Simon Marvin, in their much-cited *Splintering Urbanism,* define cities in terms of infrastructure as "staging posts in the perpetual flux of infrastructurally mediated flow, movement and exchange."[25] The dual function of transportation infrastructure—as circulation system and public space—makes this point especially salient. While the highly engineered character of transportation infrastructure can obscure its essentially social nature, seeing it as "socio-spatial fabric" reminds us not to leave its design entirely to engineers but instead to seek "active, democratic, and empowering creation of those social-physical environments we wish to inhabit."[26]

We can further reinterpret physical facilities like streets as "social infrastructure," which geographers Alan Latham and Jack Layton define as "networks of spaces, facilities, institutions, and groups that create affordances for social connection."[27] What makes such infrastructure social is its ability to foster social capital by strengthening relationships and interpersonal networks. In *Palaces for the People,* sociologist Eric Klinenberg suggests that we can find such social infrastructure in community organizations (e.g., libraries), commercial "third spaces," and public spaces like sidewalks and parks "that invite people into the public realm."[28] The concept of social infrastructure helps us appreciate those "underappreciated and overlooked spaces not often thought of as public,"[29] and reinterpreting physical facilities like roadways as social infrastructure invites us to imagine them as what Regan Koch and Alan Latham describe as "more convivial" by being open and accommodating of difference, nurturing the ability of people and communities to thrive.[30] Streets are a particular and complicated kind of physical and social infrastructure, engineered for flow but also key to public life. Even if the street's only function were transportation, mobility scholars Marco te Brömmelstroet and colleagues remind us that mobility itself is more than traffic, it is a process that "mediates social and spatial diversity and offers different conditions for exploration, interaction and negotiation of shared (social) space."[31] If streets welcome us to meet friends and neighbors, their concrete and asphalt can transcend physical infrastructure to become social spaces—indeed, public spaces—if designed from a "living room perspective . . . for people and places rather than flow."[32] To the degree the "rhythms of everyday life" are repeated, they can become a form of social infrastructure, which geographer John G. Stehlin suggests can be "relatively long-lasting, even if they do not become objectified in technological systems, or 'hard' infrastructure."[33] Streets, as physical facilities with the potential to shape social relations and the rhythms of everyday life, are thus a particularly important kind of infrastructure, hard and social.

If Streets Are Public Spaces, Who Has a Right to Them?

Streets may be engineered as pipes for cars, but they are social spaces and ultimately public places. Sidewalks, even though intended for pedestrian circulation, afford a place to pause for social life.[34] Even roadways retain social functions that cannot be reduced to traffic or mobility more broadly. By entering the street, we literally and conceptually enter into the complexities of the public realm.

In general terms, *public* is the opposite of *private,* meaning something that belongs to and is "open or available to all members of a community."[35] To geographers and others, however, the meaning of public space goes deeper than simple access. Urban space only becomes fully public—a "meaningful public resource," in geographer Peter G. Goheen's phrase—when the public collectively values it, attributes symbolic significance to it, and asserts claims to it.[36] For urban sociologists like Sharon Zukin, public spaces are particularly important to public culture, as something socially produced "by the many social encounters that make up daily life in . . . the spaces in which we experience public life."[37] Conceptual approaches to public space vary, but most public space scholarship doesn't assume some harmonious copresence. Instead, it focuses on what cultural geographer Junxi Qian calls a contested and ideological process by which "publicness is the outcome of the labours and agencies . . . of diverse people, environments, and meanings."[38] We experience streets as public not just because we can walk or drive on them but also because we help shape them as community facilities, through the ballot box, in planning meetings, at tax time, and in how we share them with others.

This brings us back to the question of rights. Lefebvre's notion of a "right to the city" is fundamentally premised on a right to space, particularly to public spaces like streets, and the ability to participate in its everyday use and decision-making, all contributing ideally to a project of "gathering together instead of a fragmentation."[39] The physical right to access and inhabit space is a critical precondition, yet access alone is not necessarily sufficient.[40] Cultural geographer Don Mitchell reminds us that the right to the city and its spaces are "always a negotiation," which ultimately "give[s] form to social justice (or its absence) in the city."[41] Thus Zukin argues that public culture and spaces are defined in relation to "the right to be in these spaces, to use them in certain ways, to invest them with a sense of ourselves and our communities—to claim them as ours and to be claimed in turn by them."[42]

Scholarly debate about public space has waxed and waned, but surging public and scholarly interest in diversity and equity has emphasized public space as a "central component of our existential conditions and experiences in the city."[43] Because the question of public space is as complex as "Who is the public?," geographers and others have moved past simple definitions to suggest that public space need not be a fixed place at all.[44] Publicness, according to Qian, is "situated, decentred, mobile, emergent, open-ended, embodied, materialised, etc." and perpetually changing.[45] Vigorous debates about urban diversity and inclusion can lead to myriad approaches to public space, but these share a concern for coexistence and "the importance of micro-encounters in everyday life" while maintaining an ideological commitment to presence, inclusion, and accessibility.[46]

Diverse Approaches to Mobility Justice and Just Streets

All these different threads ultimately lead to perhaps the thorniest question of all: What constitutes mobility justice and a just street? Conceptualizing and designing a just street require a way to sort and adjudicate competing claims to share the street fairly. Debates about equity and justice have exploded in recent years and are increasingly applied to transportation and mobility. This proliferation and diversity in approaches leads to a lack of clarity on what justice actually means in terms of transportation.[47] To make sense of all this, it's necessary to trace distinct ways of approaching equity, distinguishing among these different axes and their particular relevance to rethinking streets before reconciling them in an integrative, intersectional, and hopefully clear and workable theory of mobility justice.

Distributive Approaches to Social and Space Justice: How Street Networks Allocate Mobility and Access

Cities are uneven places where societal goods and bads are not distributed equally, often in ways that reflect broad societal structures and systems. So distributional fairness across society and space is a natural starting point for approaching mobility justice. We can analyze this at a variety of scales, but we might start—as most distributional approaches do—with a citywide approach. Any map of mobility and transportation reveals uneven patterns in both the geography of infrastructure networks and the societal structures of advantage and disadvantage. From this broad perspective on social and spatial justice—in other words, sociospatial justice—we can ask: How does the city and its system of streets distribute mobility and access? And is this distribution fair?

Since mobility is political and streets are shaped through political processes, political philosophers offer valuable insights for defining mobility justice in distributional terms. In his 1971 book *A Theory of Justice,* John Rawls defines "justice as fairness." Since societies depend on cooperation, Rawls argues that "truth and justice" are "first virtues in human activities," applying not just to law but to "the basic structure of society . . . the way in which the major social institutions distribute fundamental rights and duties."[48] To know if institutions are fair, Rawls suggests the hypothetical concept of the initial or "original position" of equality. Rational, self-interested people would only consent to a principle of justice—and engage institutions built around it—"as equals when none are known to be advantaged or disadvantaged by social and natural contingencies."[49] By this measure, we should all expect to be treated without bias in how rules systems are administered and how we assign basic rights and obligations. We don't expect the outcomes will be equal, but we at least expect equality of opportunity. These principles can be extended beyond formal, institutional politics to the societal distribution of any good, like mobility and access, to help us imagine a world built for equal opportunity and the just division of social advantages.

This spatial or "map" view of justice appeals to geographers. In his landmark *Social Justice and the City,* David Harvey defined social justice in terms of "territorial distributive justice," whereby competing claims would be adjudicated according to need, contribution to the common good, and merit toward "just distribution, justly arrived at."[50] Achieving social justice in the city therefore requires addressing inequities within the structures of both political power and economic production, distribution, and consumption. In *Seeking Spatial Justice,* Edward W. Soja builds on this idea to argue that geographical unevenness is inevitable but that oppressive and "uneven geographies of power and privilege" need not be. Soja calls for spatial justice as a distinctly geographical approach to confront the "production of injustices and the embeddedness of this production process in the social order."[51] Spatial justice would entail an "equitable distribution in space of socially valued resources and the opportunities to use them." From a spatial justice perspective, the spatiality of street networks can therefore compound or ameliorate other forms of inequality.

Distributive approaches thus lend themselves to transportation scholarship and planning. Seeking to define a "fair transportation system," Karel Martens, Aaron Golub, and Glenn Robinson outline a "justice-theoretic approach" to the distribution of transportation benefits.[52] While traditional transportation and traffic engineering have focused on optimizing the distribution of vehicular mobility, planners Jonathan Levine, Joe Grengs, and Louis A. Merlin advocate a shift from "mobility to accessibility," or from the ability to move to the ease of reaching destinations.[53] Transportation systems may be uneven, but in *Transport Justice* Martens suggests that they should seek the highest possible average access level across neighborhoods and modes while minimizing the gap between areas with the lowest and the highest levels of access.[54] Because accessibility can be measured and mapped, it can inform planning to address "access impoverishment" and make access "more equitable for more of the population."[55]

58   On the Road to Mobility Justice

Transport is part of a social system, and while infrastructure distributes mobility and access as goods, it also delivers rights, opportunities, values, and freedoms. For example, the law helps distribute mobility rights (i.e., the legal right-of-way or the right to proceed uninterruptedly) and responsibility (e.g., the legal duty to avoid harm to others).[56] Mobility can also be interpreted as a kind of capability, leading transport geographers to draw from both economist Amartya Sen and philosopher Martha Nussbaum to call transportation a "catalyser in supporting capabilities by linking them and, thus, enhancing functioning of individuals."[57] Seeking to combine distributive and capability-focused approaches, Pereira, Schwanen, and Banister define transport justice as reducing inequality of opportunity "while aiming to enhance overall levels of accessibility" and prioritizing vulnerable groups.[58] Others suggest that we view mobility justice as both equitable distribution of motility and procedurally "just institutional actions and decision-making processes."[59]

Distributive approaches to socio-spatial justice provide a distinctly broad-scale and systems perspective on fairness in mobility. They attune us to the way transportation systems distribute mobility, access, rights, capabilities, and decision-making across the city. By this measure, transportation systems, like street networks, are equitable if they produce a "just distribution, justly arrived at." Traditional American streets built over the past century distribute excessive mobility to advantaged drivers and suburban spaces, while simultaneously depriving other parts of the city access and burdening them with excessive harms, inequities that often correlate to other social disadvantages related to race or income. By such a measure, they are patently unfair.

Approaching mobility justice from a spatial-distributive equity perspective, one would expect street networks to provide mobility and access, with all of the life capabilities associated with them, fairly to all people. People across the city would share in the system's benefits and harms, rights, duties, and capabilities. Everyone, regardless of their social position or mode of travel, would enter the system from an initial position of equality. The institutions governing streets would ensure equal opportunity for all and freedom from bias, building and administering streets democratically around principles that everyone (including disadvantaged people) would consent to. In practical terms, this requires public planning to map and analyze street networks—their traffic volumes and speeds, bike lanes and sidewalks, and public amenities like street trees—on a comprehensive basis to guide the fair distribution of public funding and improvements to benefit all residents.

This is not to say the system would necessarily distribute mobility benefits and burdens equally to all people in all circumstances. Street networks cannot and should not be extended evenly everywhere. And not all parts of the network will provide the same kind of mobility. Limited-access freeways cannot welcome pedestrians. Conversely, neighborhood streets ought to prioritize nondrivers. Yet, overall, the system should strive to provide something like a just division of mobility advantages and disadvantages across society and space.

The Multimodal Equity Approach: Sharing Street Spaces among Transport Modes

Descending from the citywide map view, we can see how mobility is also uneven at street level, within the public right-of-way where our modes of travel affect how we access and share its resources. Thus, we might approach mobility justice in terms of multimodal equity, asking the question: How do street spaces enable or constrain different modes of travel, and do they do so fairly? This multimodal approach is familiar to planners and transportation advocates, and it is how many popular and policy discourses frame just streets.

Principles of socio-spatial equity and their focus on access as both a mobility good and a human capability can apply to street spaces, but they require scaling down and thinking about how modes relate to each other. Let's start with access, since that's literally the point where one enters the street. If a just transportation system is one that provides sufficient accessibility to all people and modes under most circumstances and is inclusive to ensure the capabilities of vulnerable groups (especially those with "non-chosen disadvantages"), then street spaces should accommodate and include all modes, especially those who—whether by or without choice—travel by nonvehicular means that make them vulnerable.[60] Circumstances dictate some exemptions. Again, interstate highways limit mobility to high-speed vehicles and access to specified exits, and pedestrianized streets do the opposite by limiting vehicular travel. Theoretically, however, streets should provide access to all people

60   On the Road to Mobility Justice

under most circumstances, regardless of their mode, to ensure sufficient access and fair distribution and balanced access. If a particular street doesn't accommodate all users equally, sufficient access ought to be available elsewhere nearby.

Once upon the roadway, mobility becomes the question. As infrastructure designed to facilitate circulation, streets distribute the ability to move across different user groups (cars, bikes, pedestrians, mass transit, etc.), across the public right-of-way, and ultimately through the system and the city. Diverse users must jostle for space along the roadway and their trajectories come together—indeed, can collide—in intersections and crosswalks. For a street to be fair, it should provide sufficient mobility to all users but particularly address the needs of those who choose to or must walk, bike, or rely on transit. A distributional approach emphasizing access and defining transport justice in terms of its sufficiency for everyone can be applied to street spaces just like the wider networks they're part of.[61] To achieve what the Complete Streets movement calls "Streets for Everyone," a just right-of-way would enable people to enter the street from an initial position of equity regardless of mode, distribute benefits and harms fairly to all users, and not disproportionately burden any mode (while compensating for uneven distribution elsewhere).[62] Not all streets can equally accommodate all users, but they should under most circumstances or provide meaningful alternatives nearby.[63] Ideally, street space and infrastructure would enable pedestrians to circulate freely on sidewalks and crosswalks (or down the middle of a shared street) and intersections would distribute movement fairly, safely, and conveniently for all.

Interpreted from the perspective of multimodal equity, public streets legislated and designed almost exclusively for the purposes of vehicular travel are unjust. Streets that provide for one form of vehicular mobility to the exclusion of others fail to distribute benefits like access, mobility, and rights fairly, and they disproportionately burden those traveling by alternative modes with harms like risk, legal duty of care, and pollution. Given the scale of the automobilization of American streets, this constitutes an egregious violation of multimodal equity.

A multimodally just street would thus provide equal opportunities to take advantage of its public spaces and their social goods, including but not limited to mobility and accessibility. Such streets would invite diverse users to enter from an initial position of equality, regardless of their modes of travel. The street and its spaces would equitably distribute benefits and harms, without unfairly privileging one form of travel or social group or burdening others. Streets would be designed for fair and balanced access and mobility for all users and modes but would be particularly attuned to vulnerable modes and people. A Complete Street might be built with sidewalks, bike facilities, transit stops, and travel lanes so everyone can get where they are going, and it should be designed so the visually impaired pedestrian or child walking to school can get across safely. Every single street might not distribute mobility and access evenly—collector streets might need bike lanes but local streets might not—yet the overall roadway network and most streets within it ought to be multimodal, and imbalanced treatments for some users should be compensated for with other benefits, especially targeting the disadvantaged.

Social Justice Approaches: Streets for Diversity, Equity, and Inclusion

Streets may be designed as transport infrastructure to be navigated by different modes, but they are ultimately built for and used by people. Human beings are diverse, not only because of how they get around but also because of who they are. A focus on transport systems and street spaces, interpreted by mode, tells us a lot, but reducing people to their travel mode is, well, reductionist. Increasingly, many approach mobility justice with a social equity and inclusion focus on the scale of the human body, the subjective experience of being human, and the communities that people are part of. This social equity perspective prompts the question: How welcoming are streets to diverse mobile people? Interpreting fairness in terms of social difference and disadvantage is, of course, how public discourse often frames equity. This is no different for scholars.

Social justice approaches focused on social difference and identity have grown in direct contrast to universalist and modernist theories of distributive equity. Indeed, philosopher Iris Marion Young argues in her book *Justice and the Politics of Difference* that ideals of impartiality in distributive systems can create conditions of oppression that can actually reinforce inequity.[64] Social geographers Audrey Kobayashi and Brian Ray likewise emphasize both the "politics of difference" and culturally marginalized groups "for whom difference has been translated into disadvantage" to argue for a less universal and more plural concept of justice that emerges through contested "societal understanding of equitably shared spaces."[65] For many geographers, race and gender provide key lenses for understanding and addressing inequality. Feminist Linda Peake argues for a new kind of urban studies "that takes women's struggles, strategies and everyday desires, but also its own positioning after the modern, seriously."[66] Lynda Johnston emphasizes the "importance and distinctiveness" of people's often nonbinary experiences in confronting hegemonies and "building inclusive spaces and places."[67] Ruth Wilson Gilmore likewise suggests that attention to those most vulnerable to the "fatal couplings of power and difference" is essential to confronting racism and achieving liberation.[68]

Social differences like gender are as critical to understanding mobility as any other geographical phenomenon. Feminist transport geographer Susan Hanson reminds us that gender and mobility are inseparably bound up with each other and that addressing inequities in women's access is critical to achieving social justice and equity.[69] Journalist Caroline Criado Perez powerfully highlights gender bias in data generally and transportation specifically that values male-dominated modes like vehicular commutes over walking or transit trips and cars over pedestrians to argue, "It's time for a change in perspective. It's time for women to be seen."[70] At the street scale, transport researchers show how the frictions of everyday mobility disproportionately affect the experience of women. For example, studies show how gender affects perceptions of walkability in public spaces by adolescent girls and affects participation in bicycle commuting.[71] Such insights led Emilia Smeds, Enora Robin, and Jenny McArthur to argue that "realising epistemic justice requires ensuring that these representations of gendered safety in policy discourses align with the lived realities of people with different gender identities."[72] Streets should be designed for the safety, accessibility, and conviviality of women and girls, and they should be an inclusive place for queer and transgender people to move and gather free from harassment.

Race is also a key critical equity concern in the realms of mobilities and transportation. Bridging mobilities and race/ethnic studies, Genevieve Carpio highlights "the ways actors move through space and how such acts potentially disrupt racial and place-based meanings through their bodies and the technologies that enable those movements," making such systems "key battlegrounds" for contesting power.[73] In *Just Transportation*, sociologist Robert D. Bullard argues that "transportation decision-making . . . often mirrors the power arrangements of a dominant society" to create disproportionate benefits for white suburbanites and "transportation apartheid" for minorities.[74] In his later work, Bullard joins others to advocate for a focus on "people of color because their struggle unites transportation and civil rights in one framework: transportation equity . . . a basic right, a right worth fighting for." Furthermore, dismantling transportation racism requires avoiding disproportionate impacts on vulnerable groups and activism based on "principles of environmental justice and civil rights for all."[75] There is no good reason streets should be less welcoming or accessible to people of color.

A focus on disabilities likewise exemplifies the ways disadvantage can be both a social difference and a function of mobility. In *Disability and Justice*, Christopher A. Riddle applies a capabilities approach to suggest that the experience of disability "can lead our notion of equality to closer approximate justice."[76] Likewise, Aimi Hamraie draws from critical access studies to highlight the importance of knowledge production in shaping "who gets to be in the world and under what condition" and argues for moving beyond disability rights and "nominal formal equity" toward a material "disability justice" built on anticipatory accessibility for the most marginalized.[77] To have a disability often involves nonchosen disadvantages that bear on both identity and mobility, so just streets would be built not simply to accommodate but to enable.

Approaching mobility justice from a social equity perspective emphasizes how social disadvantage—shaped by racism, sexism, homophobia, poverty, ableism, and more—links to transportation planning to reinforce inequity on American streets. It also suggests a pathway toward mobility justice committed to fairness that eschews universalizing principles to focus on the particular experience of people with disadvantages. Mimi Sheller weaves these threads together in *Mobility Justice*, arguing for situating equitable movement within wider social and physical relations to "encompass these many different vectors of class, racial, gender and other injustices across entangled scales."[78] Offering an encompassing set of "Principles of Mobility Justice," Sheller argues for mobility free from constraint by others or threat of violence; protection from exclusion on the basis of gender identity, race, or ethnicity; universal design; protection for the rights of children, older adults, and others needing mobility assistance; public transit that does not arbitrarily deny access and is equitably provided based on minimum access thresholds; Complete Streets that accommodate all modes; multimodal public spaces designed to be shared equally rather than infrastructure that systematically privileges some groups; and public funding for public infrastructure.[79]

By these standards, America's streets are not just inequitable transportation facilities but also unjust social spaces, evident to any nondriver but especially to those with compounding social disadvantages. Roadways are not merely incidentally or mildly unfair; they are what the Complete Streets Coalition bluntly calls "dangerous by design," especially to the least advantaged people among us. It's galling that the benefits of our roadway system accrue so disproportionately to higher-income, able-bodied, nonminority adult drivers, while the risks and harms fall especially on nondriving children, older people, and those with disabilities, particularly those living in low-income communities. Social equity can be framed positively to imagine just streets that would be welcoming, inclusive places for diverse people and put the needs of the least advantaged people first. They would represent and reinforce the diversity and inclusion of a more just society, not simply "accommodating" differences but putting diversity at the center of roadway planning, design, and operation. As both a system and a space, the street would be free from constraint, exclusion, and violence based on who we are and how we get around. At a minimum, streets would be complete, providing multimodal and universal access regardless of mode of travel, age, or ability. Streets should welcome a Black mom walking a second grader to school, not less and perhaps even more than a white commuter. Likewise, a young white or Hispanic man should be able to bike to work free from fear of getting hit by a driver (of whatever race or ethnicity) and in turn ought to yield to an older couple in the crosswalk. Streets are ultimately places for people, so they must be designed as an inclusive social and, indeed, public realm shared equally and with conviviality by diverse people through decision-making that engages diverse voices.

Just Places: Streets That Build Better a Community and Planet

As encompassing as these distinct approaches already are, we must go still further to recognize the power of mobility and streets to shape places, for better or worse. Streets are both places themselves and integral to surrounding neighborhoods. Geographers and planners concerned about livability, affordability, and neighborhood stability increasingly recognize the importance of streets to urban social justice. At the same time, streets are central to sustainability, whether approached as environmental justice today or intergenerational equity in the future. This suggests a distinct question: What role do (or can) streets play in building healthy and diverse places and a more sustainable future?

The complex role of streets as simultaneously transportation infrastructure and public spaces central to their surrounding places defies easy comprehension. A focus on one scale can lead to neglect of others, a point urban scholar Julian Agyeman and sociologist Stephen Zavestoski make in *Incomplete Streets* when they ask whether designing for safe access for transport "users" could sufficiently address the "broader historical, political, social, and economic forces" that shape "the socioeconomic and racial inequalities embedded in streets," which are in turn reproduced by them.[80] They argue that too exclusive a focus on multimodalism and physical design can make certain users and dwellers "invisible" and lead to urban changes that can engender fears of gentrification in low-income neighborhoods of color. Though focused more on critique than theory building, they hint at a vision of just streets and places that can "empower and engage, build civic and social capital, and create opportunities."[81] Melody L. Hoffmann echoes these arguments in *Bike Lanes are White Lanes,* suggesting that cycling advocates "have a tendency to ignore socioeconomic, physical, and material factors that influence people's transportation choices" and that planners can disregard the "racialized and class-based histories" of surrounding neighborhoods.[82] "It is a crucial time," Hoffmann suggests, for bicycle advocates to reflect on their compliance with the status quo and work closer with those transportation activists "who have been fighting for racial equity in their neighborhoods for decades."[83]

Because streets are central to community life and development, transforming them necessarily transforms the places they traverse. Indeed, cities often invest in street design explicitly to enhance mobility, the public realm, and community livability simultaneously. Yet, even improvements with laudable purposes can alter communities already affected by social changes. Scholars of "environmental gentrification" express concern for the ways that public investments to make cities more sustainable can lead to displacement.[84] Those applying principles of environmental justice—what Agyeman calls "just sustainabilities"—increasingly emphasize the important role of local people in defining social justice and environmental goals.[85] Sensitivity to local voices can help ensure that neighborhood improvements are what Winifred Curran and Trina Hamilton call "just-green-enough" to bring improvement but not displacement.[86] These concerns can apply to Complete Streets. Even if bike lanes do not cause gentrification, Stehlin argues, support for them comes from "the same social bloc that gentrification empowers and makes visible."[87] Given the racial significance of infrastructure and urban change, Hoffmann suggests that bike lanes can take meaning as "white lanes."[88] However, purposeful projects with an explicit and overarching goal of social equity can address modal inequities and engage and improve communities.[89]

All of this leads many to advocate for the principle of livability, or what planner Bruce Appleyard—building on the work of his father, Donald Appleyard—calls a "livable street ecology," based on two key ethical principles: one person's pursuit of quality of life shouldn't unduly detract from the livability of others and care should be taken to meet the needs of society's most vulnerable. He calls for a "livability ethics for street/urban empathy, equity, and justice," defined by qualities like easy and equitable access to opportunities, prioritizing the needs of society's less powerful, placing highest value on people's humanity (at rest and in motion), and working to overcome oppression.[90] Livable streets, Appleyard believes, would promote feelings of safety, comfort, and peacefulness; connection, accessibility, and convenience; a positive sense of place; and a sense of ethical empathy, equity, and justice.

Those committed to situating streets in a wider context must acknowledge that justice, while often focused on people living today, also involves people who will live in the future. Equity among different generations is core to the U.N. Brundtland Commission's definition of *sustainable development* as that which "meets the needs of the present without compromising the ability of future generations to meet their own needs."[91] As people confront an uncertain and increasingly dire future, philosopher Joerg Chet Tremmel notes growing demand for a "new ethics of social responsibility" toward intergenerational justice defined so that "the opportunities available to the average person in the next generation are better than those who preceded them."[92] A just street would consider people and communities yet to come. This ethical responsibility should also apply to our nonhuman neighbors, present and future. From this point of view, a bike lane might present green gentrification concerns, or a street closure the risk of hindering low-income workers from driving to work, but reducing vehicular traffic and pollution has benefits for other people (and animals and plants) in the future.

Collectively, these perspectives challenge us to see streets as places within places. From this view, designing our streets and cities as pipes for speeding traffic has been disastrous for the public realm, surrounding neighborhoods (especially those occupied by people of color and people experiencing poverty), and the very future of our planet. A vision of streets as just places, however, suggests that we approach the public right-of-way as equitable transportation infrastructure, vibrant public realm, and a key site for building more livable communities and a sustainable planet. Instead of planning and designing infrastructure out of context, we might approach streets as places that can be a catalyst for positive urban and planetary change. "Just green enough" streets would ensure equitable and sustainable mobility and access while promoting inclusion and neighborhood health within and beyond the public right-of-way, both today and tomorrow.

Procedural Justice: Equity and Inclusion in Street Planning, Design, and Operation

Finally, while most of the above frameworks approach fairness in terms of substantive outcomes, mobility justice cannot be assured without considering the procedural questions of how decisions are made and who can participate. This prompts the question: How can processes behind street planning, design, and operation give all users and neighbors a voice?

Though we might seek spatially just mobility outcomes, Young suggests that distributional equity can obscure the institutional context in which decisions are made, including institutional structures and practices, rules, norms, and "language and symbols that mediate social interactions within them."[93] If these processes aren't fair and inclusive, their outcomes can't be. Bullard suggests that procedural justice in transport-related decisions would follow from uniformity, fairness, and the consistency and involvement of diverse stakeholders, judged in terms of the question, "Do the rules apply equally to everyone?"[94] Sheller's vision of mobility justice emphasizes "meaningful participation of affected populations in the governance of transportation systems."[95]

This is not how transportation planning and design often work in practice, however. For example, technocratic traffic modeling and planning processes—focused on reducing congestion—offer limited discursive room or opportunity for public participation.[96] Performance measures like level of service embed "ideologies of mobility" that prioritize technical knowledge (in theory) and vehicular flow (in practice) that do little to welcome democratic debate about social values or design input.[97] My own research on traffic engineering and roadway standards reveals their permeation with an ideology of vehicular flow, crafted by technical experts in nondemocratic forums, codified in manuals that are prohibitively expensive and written in a technocratic language inaccessible to the general public, and often employed by engineers to make decisions outside public view.[98]

A procedurally just street would thus emerge from democratic, transparent, and inclusive decision-making that engages diverse people, especially underrepresented groups. Decisions about streets as infrastructure, public spaces, and their relationship to surrounding landscapes would include meaningful participation from all affected people, including transportation users, local neighbors, and community members citywide, in language that all participants could understand. Planning and public engagement would take a holistic approach to gain informed consent. Everyday people should be able to have a say in their streets. And given the likelihood of conflicting claims and trade-offs, the process of decision-making must be fair, drawing upon established democratic norms to arrive at majority decisions that respect the rights of minority voices. A just street would afford democratic access along with transportation access. Ongoing operation, maintenance, regulation, and control of streets would embody these same values, providing opportunities for public engagement to ensure streets are designed and managed for all.

An Intersectional Approach to Mobility Justice and Just Streets

Claims to rights and justice—and the different discourses they articulate —can be as diverse as the people using and living along streets. Rethinking and reclaiming our streets not only involve mutual recognition of different claims, but in cities with finite spaces and resources, it can involve trade-offs and tough choices. Diverse people with different perspectives, needs, and wants share the same street spaces. In our roles as pedestrians, cyclists, wheelchair users, transit riders, and drivers we come together to share the street with each other and with the neighbors who live alongside it. Yet our diverse experiences, trajectories, modes of travel, rights-based claims, and relative advantages and disadvantages—intrinsic to who we are and how we travel—can bring us into conflict. These contests can be legal, political, and even cultural. They are also bodily encounters that can have life-and-death consequences. To sort all this out, we need a nuanced and integrative understanding of mobility justice that recognizes and reconciles diverse approaches to a theory of mobility justice, which can be practically adapted to the everyday work of making more just streets. These tensions can be very real and complex for planners. In a world of competing claims and priorities, who do we plan for? How?

The Power of Intersectional Thinking

This brings us back to intersectionality. Kimberlé Crenshaw coined the term to understand the multidimensional experience of marginalized people—her focus is Black women—who experience multiple burdens. Notably, Crenshaw introduces the concept through the metaphor of a public street.

> Discrimination, like traffic through an intersection, may flow in one direction, and it may flow in another. If an accident happens in an intersection, it can be caused by cars traveling from any number of directions and, sometimes, from all of them. . . . But it is not always easy to reconstruct an accident: Sometimes the skid marks and the injuries simply indicate that they occurred simultaneously, frustrating efforts to determine which driver caused the harm.[99]

While mainstream social justice discourses may treat such social inequities as vestiges of bias, Crenshaw argues for intersectionality to highlight the ways "power has clustered around certain categories and is exercised against others."[100] Embracing "the complexities of compoundedness," she suggests, can help rethink discrimination beyond single axes and create a basis for unifying political activity toward greater equity, defined primarily as facilitating the inclusion of marginalized groups.

From the outset, however, Crenshaw's concept of intersectionality looks beyond individual experience and identity to the broader structural, political, and representational forces that converge to create disadvantage. Analyzing violence against women, for example, Crenshaw argues that physical assault is "merely the most immediate manifestation of the subordination they experience," which can include not only race and gender but also job insecurity and poverty. Confronting such violence thus also requires confronting "the other multilayered and routinized forms of dominance that converge" on their lives.[101] Intersectional subordination need not be intentionally produced, she continues, but can be the consequence of "the imposition of one burden that intersects with preexisting vulnerabilities to create yet another dimension of disempowerment."[102] Such structural factors are further compounded by the ways traditional political discourses—often aligned around one axis of difference like gender or race—can fail to address their intersections and whose "mutual elisions" can disempower women of color and the ways marginalized people are culturally constructed through representation.

This structural perspective underpinned the development of the critical legal studies and later critical race theory movements to understand how formal systems like the law are not impartial or apart from society and instead are something that "produces and is the product of social power."[103] Crenshaw and her coauthors advocate critical race theory as a way to uncover "the ongoing dynamics of racialized power, and its embeddedness in practices and values which have been shorn of any explicit, formal manifestations of racism."[104] Even when geared toward liberal ends like affirmative action, they suggest the law is not a "neutral basis for distributing resources and opportunity" but instead can be a "mechanism for perpetuating" the uneven distributions established under hegemonic orders like white supremacy. Critical race theory focuses particularly on social biases built into the law, but it suggests how other ways of thinking and societal structures—even though nominally unbiased on their face—can perpetuate oppression. In their 2019 *Seeing Race Again* Crenshaw, Luke Charles Harris, Daniel Martinez HoSang, and George Lipsitz show how academic traditions of research objectivity, neutrality, and authority across disciplines has led to "colorblindness" as a core orientation and presumption, with consequences for both scholarship and policy development. Challenging postracial and universalized thinking, they encourage diverse fields to "comprehend and critique how contemporary disciplinary practices enable racial structures and inhibit the means to dismantle them."[105]

Intersectionality (like critical race theory) offers a powerful way for scholars, policymakers, and activists to better see how distinct forms and structures of social power or disadvantage converge on individuals. Such work, not surprisingly, has been led by scholars of gender and race to examine how "predominant classification systems such as class, gender, and ethnicity/race co-exist and are simultaneously mutually constitutive."[106] Yet, as Ange-Marie Hancock traces in *Intersectionality: An Intellectual History,* the concept has emerged as a "path-breaking analytical framework for understanding questions of inequality and injustice" that has "traveled far and wide" throughout a variety of disciplines. Such work is diverse and has followed two key trajectories: an analytical approach to relationships between social categories and "a project to render visible and remediable previously invisible, unaddressed material effects of the sociopolitical location" of women of color.[107] Reviewing the breadth of such work is beyond the scope of this chapter, but it's hard not to see the value and appeal of intersectionality—like the metaphorical intersection—for thinking about complex relationships between (and within) individual experience, societal structures, and geographical contexts.

Intersectionality has become an increasingly important concept in geography, particularly by social geographers concerned with social differences like gender, race, and sexual identity.[108] Its broadening application and appeal, Peter Hopkins warns, brings the risk of losing sight of its original emphases and calls for greater care to not "invisibilize" the contributions of Black and antiracist feminist academics and activists.[109] It is essential to avoid superficial appropriation, particularly in traditionally white, male, and colonial disciplines like geography (and planning, for that matter). But intellectual engagement and theoretical extension can bring contributions too. Hopkins, for one, suggests "there are a whole host of knowledges, theories and approaches that geography could bring to bear on the issue of social context and relationality in intersectionality" to advance how "intersectionality is theorized, applied in research and used in practice."[110] As we extend intersectionality, we should continue to foreground social differences but might, with care, broaden our focus to other social and spatial factors, tracing axes that intersect with but are distinct from those related to identity. Indeed, its openness to seeing diverse forms of oppression makes intersectionality too powerful an idea not to extend to the critical analysis of diverse forms of inequity and activism toward a multidimensional justice.

This brings us back to the challenge of mobility justice and just streets. Not surprisingly, intersectionality has proven hard for mobilities scholars to resist as both metaphor and intellectual framework. Just as "intersections are openings where paths cross," Monika Büscher, Mimi Sheller, and David Tyfield suggest that intersectionality can help think about connections between "differential (im)mobilities and uneven mobilities at multiple scales" and categories of social disadvantage by calling attention to "intersectional spatial formations."[111] As critical race theory highlights the power of social structures like the law to construct race, intersectionality can be readily applied to see how transportation infrastructures—as both physical facility and societal system—help construct people as mobile subjects and shape our experience of mobility and mobility justice. Intersectional mobilities research is still new, but it shows diverse possibilities. For example, occupational therapists link disability and mobility justice to understand how people with disabilities—understood as "whole people" and not as functional disability or identity/personhood alone—navigate "systemic, intersectional barriers and enablers to transport access."[112] Others show how gender and disability can combine to shape women's transit experiences, alongside related axes like class, age, and religion.[113] Yet others use the politics of intersectionality to understand the contested space of streets and "reveal gendered and unequal mobilities through situated and embodied experience" to argue for knowledge "situated according to difference and the ways in which intersections of social difference are produced."[114]

Intersectionality is undeniably relevant to thinking about mobility justice, and it exemplifies the way geographers might contribute to both the concept and its practical application. To do so carefully, we should start from a place of sensitivity to individual experience and focus on the compounding social forces/axes that shape the experience of people with social disadvantages. These start with inescapable dimensions like gender or race. Yet intersectionality's power to analyze diverse and overlapping forms of inequality is too great not to encompass other phenomena that are perhaps more situational, like how we get around. Intersectionality can help us see the ways marginalization and privilege can exist on multiple distinct axes and scales, converging on people's bodies and experiences. And as intersectionality takes individual experience as a starting point to understand broader structural forces (like racism or sexism), it can enable us to look beyond the experience of mobility to the infrastructural forces that create mobility justice or its absence. Some of these axes may relate to identity and social difference, requiring analysis from that angle. Others align with more physical dimensions like mode of travel, attuning us to physical infrastructure. Still others might relate to political institutions and processes. By highlighting the ways that different power structures—indeed, infrastructures —combine to shape individual experience and social relations, an intersectional approach to infrastructure suggests the need to trace equity on whatever axes they operate upon. Just as intersections connect approaching streets, and must balance intertwining traffic, intersectionality can help us reconcile diverse theoretical approaches and apply them to imagine and reclaim more just streets.

Toward an Intersectional Mobility Justice

What would such an intersectional approach to mobility, mobility justice, and streets look like, conceptually and practically? Intersectionality starts with human experience, so we might first take an intersectional view of mobile people with diverse needs, wants, and rights. Each of us as individuals arrives at the street with social differences, some chosen and others not. Before we are mobile, we are humans with identities (e.g., race, gender, and sexual identity). These already intersect to make some of us more vulnerable than others: a Black transgender woman walking down the street is at far greater risk than a white, straight cisgender man. We have other dimensions to our being, like chronological age, which also correlate to advantage or disadvantage. In addition to these social markers, however, our experience is shaped by how we need or choose to get around. Are we sitting behind the wheel of a car, walking alongside the road, waiting for a bus, or biking through an intersection? Are we able to walk or do we require an assistive device like a wheelchair to compensate for a disability? These positional factors intersect with but are distinct from our identities. And beyond our individual characteristics, there are geographical factors that can further compound or compensate for disadvantage, like our income, class, place of residence, or the nature of our employment. Are we professionals who can work from home or essential workers who must commute by transit from the inner city to a suburban hospital? Furthermore, each of us has a different position in relation to social power and decision-making structures: an undocumented immigrant cannot experience or participate as fully as a well-established and well-connected voter. We could go on and on. Suffice it to say that myriad factors intersect to shape our experience of mobility, some intrinsic to our being, some positional, and some geographical. These can operate on different axes to compound each other. People of color often have lower incomes and don't own cars, so they walk or bike. This compounding of advantage or disadvantage is usually the case. But they can also, to some degree, offset each other. A white, high-income man doesn't lose his social advantages when riding a bike on the roadway, but busy traffic can pose bodily risks that can make his social position considerably less meaningful or consequential when doing so. In the same sense, a socially disadvantaged person doesn't shed these vulnerabilities when they take the wheel of a car, but driving a large and fast automobile does empower them to a certain degree in relation to nonmotorists (though the risks of driving while Black can negate such mobility advantages). The permutations are endless, reinforcing the idea of mobility as multidimensional, but highlight some key axes like individual identity and difference, social position, mode of travel, and geographic location.

Thus, we might first define mobility justice at the scale of the individual. At a most basic level as human beings, we deserve a right to live and be safe. As transportation users, we deserve a fair share—at least a minimum, but maybe not too much—of the benefits, rights, and harms

On the Road to Mobility Justice   75

distributed by the system. As mobile people we are defined—by choice or circumstance—by different particular modes of travel, which profoundly define our experience of streets. Each of us deserves a fair "mode share" and safe and convenient access to streets. But we're not just our mode; we have particular identities and subjectivities that shape our experiences. We deserve streets that respect and welcome us and our diversity. Because we're not always in motion and we spend much of our lives dwelling in or along streets, we rightfully expect streets to be livable for us and our communities, as well as for people today and in the future. And, finally, as citizens and members of the urban polity, we demand a voice in public decision-making about mobility and streets. These are distinct axes, with different forms of advantage and disadvantage that intersect in each of us in unique and dynamic ways (even as we shift from mode to mode, place to place). But we all have a right to mobility and fair treatment within transportation infrastructure like streets.

Yet the direct object of planning and design remains the street itself. Here too intersectionality helps us critique streets as systems embedded within and central to wider society, built with social values and ideologies as well as asphalt. Like the law, streets are also very powerful structures—indeed, infrastructures—that help construct us as mobile subjects and shape whether or not we experience mobility as equitable. A critical evaluation of American transportation and streets reveals their structural power to reinforce the hegemony of already-powerful drivers at the expense of nondrivers and neighborhoods. Interpreted through intersectionality, we see how forces compound to disadvantage the already disadvantaged. These are on raw display in any suburban arterial where teens or low-income immigrant workers beat footpaths in the absence of sidewalks or dash across multiple lanes of traffic to reach bus stops, trying to avoid getting struck by speeding commuters or shoppers. Such infrastructure may be designed, like the law, through policy and the design language of value neutrality. But it is, as Smart Growth America notes, dangerous by design, particularly for the least advantaged people among us.[115] That person struck crossing in the absence of a crosswalk is likely to be young, older, and a person of color and to have a disability or a low income. That's unjust enough, but should they survive, the police might likely charge them with jaywalking. As the American legal system was built on supremacy of one race over another, the entire legal

Defining a Just Street

Intersectionality is a powerful analytical lens for critique, but it also suggests a positive vision and intellectual framework for thinking about and constructing justice. Below I outline an intersectional theory of a just street, conceived like an intersection in which diverse approaches to equity, which I've outlined throughout this chapter, might converge.

Approached from a distributional equity perspective, *street networks should be planned to fairly distribute access and mobility across society and space.* Seen from a map view, people across the city would have fair access and rights to the system's many benefits, while also sharing its burdens equitably, whether danger, pollution, or legal duties of care. All people should be able to enter into the network—as a physical and institutional system—from an initial position of equality of opportunity and freedom from bias. From this perspective, we would need to map, plan, and invest in street networks that are geographically even and produce just distributional outcomes across the city or region.

From a street-level, multimodal equity approach, *street spaces should be engineered to provide all users and travel modes with fair access and mobility.* As the wider roadway system should seek fair distribution across urban territory, street spaces should ensure sufficient access and safe and convenient mobility for all modes, particularly those more vulnerable, from one side of the public right-of-way to the other. Beyond accommodating alternative modes at the margins, fully Complete Streets should be designed to be shared equitably from the centerline outward. This balance will of course depend on context, with some streets prioritizing some modes over others, but with few exceptions all streets should provide safe access for all users.

In terms of social equity, *streets should provide a welcoming and inclusive experience for diverse, multifaceted people, especially the most socially vulnerable people among us.* As a public space the street would embody the inclusivity of a plural and equitable society, not merely free from bias and accommodating difference but putting human diversity—and especially a focus on the most socially disadvantaged people—at the center of roadway planning, design, and operation. Planning and designing streets to protect the most socially disadvantaged people, rather than to reinforce the hegemony of the most powerful people, would yield very different—and radically more fair—outcomes.

Situated in urban and environmental contexts, *streets should be shared as public places central to building better communities and a more sustainable city.* The public right-of-way is simultaneously transportation infrastructure, public space, and community center. We must design streets as sustainable infrastructure and livable places, with keen attention to their central role in shaping urban changes both good and ill. The livability of streets—as a community living room—is central to the health and stability of the neighborhoods surrounding them. To avoid unwanted urban changes, streets must prioritize the voices of local residents and hopefully be designed to be "just green enough" to ensure equitable and sustainable mobility while avoiding green gentrification. Yet neighborhood interests must be balanced with those of the wider community, while also recognizing that future generations—human and nonhuman—also have a stake in a livable city and sustainable planet.

Streets should be planned, designed, and operated through decision-making processes accessible to all, particularly those who use them and live alongside them. In contrast to closed, technocratic decision-making, we need transportation planning and street design to be open to meaningful participation through accessible language that enables people to understand choices. Procedures should be participatory, welcoming diverse stakeholder input at different stages and scales in the planning, design, and the ongoing management of public spaces for mobility and community livability.

Both people and streets are multidimensional. Each represents a particular confluence and balance of these distinct registers. Thus, we need a contextual understanding of people and their intersecting forms of advantage and vulnerability, just as streets must be contextualized for their roles in both the transportation system and the city. Streets won't all be the same, but each should take these values into account and seek to balance them fairly. And where a particular street disproportionately benefits one kind of user, it should compensate for relative inequities on one axis with relative advantages on another. Where priorities and forms of mobility are irreconcilable in particular contexts—like cars on pedestrianized street plazas, pedestrians in a bicycle lane, or nondrivers on limited-access freeways—alternative opportunities should be afforded close nearby on the network, with particular care taken on the side of vulnerability and sustainability. How we weigh these criteria will depend on context—historical and geographical—but in trying to strike a balance, we may approximate an intersectional mobility justice and just streets as essential elements of a just city.

This all leads us to one final idea—a radical notion, particularly in the United States—that follows from so many of the approaches discussed above but particularly from the radical arguments of intersectionality (and critical race theory). Mobility justice and just streets must go beyond nominal equity and a view that bias is a historical vestige and inequity is a failure of an otherwise neutral system. Roadway infrastructure in the United States, like our legal system, has been unjust by law, planning, design, and operation. It empowers the already powerful and marginalizes the already marginalized. Therefore, mobility justice demands more than substantive fairness in the allocation of mobility as resource or procedural fairness in the distribution of social power. It requires a radical emphasis on raising up the least advantaged people among us and is, to again quote Crenshaw, a project to look beneath prevailing conceptions and challenge complacency with the goal "to facilitate the inclusion of marginalized groups from whom it can be said: 'When they enter, we all enter.'"[116]

Intersectional Mobility Justice from Theory to Practice?

Rethinking and reclaiming the public street are epic challenges. Streets are too durable, physically and socially, to change easily. For a century, American streets have been built around a cramped set of values. The result has been grossly unjust streets, bad in theory and even worse in practice, with often terrible consequences for people, street spaces, urban places, and the planet. Thinking more creatively about mobility, infrastructure, and public space can help us imagine a better transportation system and future for urban places, large or small.

Applying a rigorous and explicit focus on mobility justice—in all of its different facets—enables clearer critical thinking about the status quo street and the chance to imagine something better and more just. Embracing the diversity of people and their experience of streets through the lens of intersectionality, it's possible to recognize and potentially reconcile different claims to mobility that come together within us and the streets we wish to inhabit. Applying the lens of intersectionality, we can see more clearly how distinct forms of injustice converge on mobile people, but it also suggests some ways different approaches to equity—distributional, multimodal, social, place-based, and procedural—might be reconciled to produce a more just street, which is welcoming to all but is especially accommodating of the least advantaged people among us. The question then becomes this: How can we take these insights and ideals to better and more fairly share streets for all?

3

MULTIMODALISM BY POLICY AND DESIGN

It is impossible to understand the dynamic geography of the public street and its historical evolution and ideal futures apart from the discourses and technicalities of policy and design. Streets may be physically made of asphalt, but they are socially constructed through policy and engineering, which translate theory into everyday material practice.

The policy frameworks shaping streets, which evolved over the past century, are unfamiliar to most of us. Roadway design standards, written in technical language and published in expensive manuals, are even more so. They are not exciting reads for the average person. But gaining literacy in them can shed light on the autocentric street we experience today and on both the barriers and the opportunities to reimagining more equitable mobility and urban life. Reclaiming American streets for greater mobility justice begins with reframing their purpose and proper use in policy and then articulating more equitable values through design. In a transportation space like the street, that starts with multimodalism: making streets safer and more accessible no matter how you choose to travel.

Transportation policy and *transportation design* are broad terms. I've introduced a few of these from a historical perspective in chapter 1 and I analyze them in more depth elsewhere.[1] A full review is beyond my scope here. But suffice it to say that the American street of today is the product of a policy regime of automobility that, for a century, has

81

prioritized vehicular flow and speed to the detriment of other modes, vulnerable people, and urban livability.

Fortunately, in recent decades, policymakers have begun to articulate a vision of safe and more accessible streets for diverse transportation users, and they have slowly translated it into design. One of these frameworks is the American with Disabilities Act, which prohibits discrimination against individuals with disabilities in all areas of public life and makes an equity-based argument for redesigning public infrastructure for users of diverse abilities. Another is the Complete Streets movement promoting local and state policies to ensure that streets accommodate all users of all ages and abilities; this push has expanded beyond multimodal equity to encompass broader social justice. And another is the Vision Zero movement decrying the dangers of a roadway system that kills so many users, particularly vulnerable nondrivers, and advocating for "safe, healthy, equitable mobility for all."[2]

Equally important are efforts to weave multimodalism into roadway design and engineering. Among these, this chapter first considers incremental yet significant revision of fundamental national standards like the Transportation Research Board's (TRB) *Highway Capacity Manual,* the American Association of State Highway and Transportation Officials' (AASHTO) *A Policy on Geometric Design of Highways and Streets,* and the U.S. Department of Transportation's *Manual on Uniform Traffic Control Devices.* Beyond the accommodation of alternative modes in such standard manuals, it is helpful to have an overview of emerging, mode-specific guidelines like AASHTO's pedestrian and bicycle manuals, the Americans with Disabilities Act (ADA) *Standards for Accessible Design* and *Public Right-of-Way Accessibility Guidelines,* and emerging federal Department of Transportation multimodal guidance. And perhaps most encouraging of all is the emergence of the new National Association of City Transportation Officials (NACTO) to address the particular needs of urban contexts, including urban street, bicycle, and transit guides, which increasingly look beyond designing for multiple modes toward reimagining streets as places.

The project to reclaim streets may start with retracing history and building theory, but it cannot advance far without first critically confronting and overcoming the autocentrism built into policy and design. At an intellectual level, this helps illuminate how conceptual debates about mobility politics, rights, and, therefore, justice parallel and resonate with growing policy and design movements for safe and accessible "streets for all." But at a more practical level, those who want better and more equitable streets must gain some proficiency in the worldview and language of transportation planning and engineering.

As everyday mobility and public lives unfold through the public right-of-way, policy and design standards are key to understanding and shaping its geography. Though deeply interwoven with the city, the street has geographic boundaries, so there are limits to the power of transportation policy and design to tackle the breadth of urban inequities. After a century of being defined and designed as pipes for cars, however, reframing streets through multimodal policy and design represents a fundamental step toward truly reclaiming them as places for people (and perhaps also for nonhumans and future generations).

Multimodalism by Policy

Policy and design are of course inextricably linked, but they are distinct and worth exploring sequentially. Before streets are engineered, their purpose and the processes for governing them are established through legal and administrative policies. These are too complex to encompass here, especially the maze of federal transportation laws and rules. A few such initiatives for making streets accessible to all modes are worth highlighting, however.

The Americans with Disabilities Act

A fundamental shift in American mobility came with the 1990 passage of the Americans with Disabilities Act. Following decades of activism and organizing, the ADA marked a radical shift in public-policy discourses to connect ethical arguments against discrimination and for social equity to legally mandate fair accommodations in public facilities and infrastructure. In doing so, the ADA challenged ableist assumptions built into public streets and sidewalks, advocated new universal values of mobility justice, and translated them into new accessible design practices.

This movement had origins in both the practical frustrations of life for people with disabilities and the equity values embodied in the wider civil rights movement. Disability rights activists in Berkeley and elsewhere in the late 1960s surreptitiously smashed curbs and poured new curb cuts to enable wheelchair access (a fragment of curb smashed in Denver in 1978 sits in the Smithsonian).[3] Though the major civil rights legislation of the 1960s confronted discrimination on the basis of social markers like race and national origin, the law did not initially afford protection for those with disabilities. The Rehabilitation Act of 1973 banned entities receiving federal funds from discriminating against those with disabilities, but it didn't apply more widely. In 1986, the National Council on Disability published its *Toward Independence* report arguing that while "equality and independence have been fundamental elements of the American form of government since its inception," disabled people faced many complex barriers in "trying to achieve their personal goals and fulfillment." It identified transportation as a "prerequisite" for equal opportunities and decried that "we are far short of a truly accessible system."[4]

The report prompted the introduction of the first draft of the Americans with Disabilities Act in Congress in 1988 by Senator Lowell Weicker, who linked discrimination based on disability to other forms of discrimination prohibited by civil rights law. Weicker argued for the ADA as "a blueprint for the future—a blueprint that says, when a community buys a bus, it buys a bus that everyone can use. A blueprint that says, when new buildings are constructed, they must be usable by persons with disabilities."[5] Representative Major Owens, a veteran of the civil rights movement, argued, "For some of us, the Americans with Disabilities Act of 1988 represents the next giant step in the American civil rights movement."[6] The report and bill focused mainly on transportation services like public transit systems, passenger travel, or vehicles. However, they called out architectural barriers like curbs or stairs in buildings and facilities open to the public and demanded minimum standards of accessible design to ensure public accommodation. The bill languished in Congress until March 1990 when protesters abandoned their wheelchairs to scale the steps of the U.S. Capitol as part of a "Capitol Crawl" to draw attention to the issue.

Passage of the Americans with Disabilities Act in 1990 expressed a powerful, ethics-based argument about mobility, rights, and access to the public sphere. Its findings indict a "serious and pervasive social problem" within American society:

> Physical or mental disabilities in no way diminish a person's right to fully participate in all aspects of society, yet many people with physical or mental disabilities have been precluded from doing so because of discrimination. . . . The Nation's proper goals regarding individuals with disabilities are to assure equality of opportunity, full participation, independent living, and economic self-sufficiency for such individuals; and the continuing existence of unfair and unnecessary discrimination and prejudice denies people with disabilities the opportunity to compete on an equal basis and to pursue those opportunities for which our free society is justifiably famous.[7]

The ADA goes on to state its policy purpose: to provide a clear and comprehensive national mandate for eliminating discrimination against individuals with disabilities; to provide "clear, strong, consistent, enforceable standards" addressing such discrimination; to ensure the federal government plays a central role in enforcing ADA standards; and to invoke the sweep of congressional authority to address major areas of everyday discrimination faced by people with disabilities.[8]

The law confronted a diverse set of disabilities and barriers, but physical mobility and physical infrastructure like streets figured prominently. The ADA specifically targeted the discriminatory effects of architectural, transportation, and communication barriers and established minimum guidelines and requirements for accessible design. It created an Architectural and Transportation Barriers Compliance Board to develop more specific standards. In the process, physical infrastructure like curbs gained symbolic significance, and facilities like curb cuts were central to what disabilities scholar and designer Aimi Hamraie calls a "barrier-free regime" and the "idea that accessibility benefits everyone."[9]

Changing policy discourse and law is hard, but changing the built environment can be even harder. So, soon after the law's passage, the federal government began to develop accessibility guidelines to support a continuous, unobstructed "path of travel" to public accommodations like buildings and services. A Public Rights-of-Way Access Advisory Committee (PROWAAC) was created in 1999 and published a 2001 report, *Building a True Community,* that argues, "For centuries, public rights-of-way ensured the right to passage of all users, humble or grand, on foot or by any other mode," yet only recently has "serious thought been given to the right to access for those who, historically, had never been considered at all in the built environment."[10] In response, it began crafting guidelines guided by the principle "that all users of all abilities have the right to equal access to public rights-of-way" (whose design standards I explore in more depth below).[11]

The ADA, despite halting progress, has utilized civil rights discourses about discrimination to frame a powerful argument about equity. Drawing on American ideals of independence, it defined mobility and access in the public sphere as legal rights and translated these discourses into regulatory expectations for how public facilities (and private ones providing public accommodations) ought to be accessible for all. The ADA confronted the inequity that people with disabilities "occupy an inferior status in our society, and are severely disadvantaged" to offer an equity-based argument and legal mandate for rethinking streets. That's no easy task. In *Building a True Community*, PROWAAC acknowledges that infrastructure is "often created over a period of time by a variety of minds and hands" but argues that streetscapes need to "work at an intimate level" for individuals. Building a more accessible, equitable street calls for "a dramatic change from the way public rights-of-way have been designed in the past."[12]

The ADA highlights the power of policy to reimagine and reconstruct a more accessible street, connecting the language of equity to legal and institutional rules and providing the moral basis for better street design. The ADA, like any policy discourse and framework, is incomplete and should be assessed critically. Hamraie reminds us that struggles for access, belonging, and citizenship are not linear and that universal design is part of contested struggles revealing the "critical work of negotiating, contesting, and remaking access-knowledge."[13] Approached from diverse perspectives, however, the ADA embodies a good approximation of intersectional mobility justice. It advances distributional spatial justice by requiring universal application across urban spaces, promotes barrier-free inclusivity for people with disabilities, which addresses disadvantage that is both mode-specific and key to social identity, improves and boosts the sustainability of public places and neighborhoods (without promoting displacement), and tends toward more transparency in decision-making. While one can critique universalizing discourses of accessibility for all, simple features like curb ramps are symbolically and

Multimodalism by Policy and Design   87

practically important in reclaiming public streets for more diverse people and uses, with a particular emphasis on some of society's most vulnerable members, a key step toward a more just street.

Complete "Streets for All"

Such evolving discourses about accessibility helped inspire a Complete Streets movement advocating for safe and convenient accessibility for all users of all ages and abilities. In 2003, a task force led by America Bikes argued for greater emphasis on alternative modes in transportation policy. Though major federal legislation like the Intermodal Surface Transportation Efficiency Act (1991), the Transportation Equity Act for the 21st Century (1998), and the Safe, Accountable, Flexible, Efficient Transportation Equity Act: A Legacy for Users (2005) increasingly considered the needs of bicyclists and pedestrians, advocates chafed at the technocratic term *routine accommodation* to seek a more compelling way to frame multimodal equity. They proposed the new term *Complete Streets,* whose origin story, recounted by planner Barbara McCann, reveals the power of rhetoric and discourse to policy change:

> I realized that this was more than a new name—it might be a way to reframe the discussion about transportation to include everyone using the roads. . . . The framing of "complete streets" may be most powerful in its implicit definition of its opposite. No one wants to build incomplete streets.[14]

The movement directly confronted the ostensible value-neutrality and technicality of traffic engineering, arguing instead that "they are driven by an underlying political decision" and priorities and values, and so it suggested that an explicit political statement for multimodal streets would offer a clear alternative direction for engineers to follow.[15]

Beyond reframing the conversation, the coalition offered models to guide state and local policy, laid out since 2012 in its *Best Complete Streets Policies* publications. The Complete Streets movement, it suggested, "fundamentally redefines what a street is intended to do" by encouraging and providing safe access for everyone regardless of age, ability, income, ethnicity, or how they travel.[16] In 2013, almost five hundred American communities had already adopted Complete Streets policies; by the time of publication of the most recent *Complete Streets*

Policies of 2023, more than 1,700 states, counties, and localities had done so.[17]

The Complete Streets ethos starts with a focus on fair access among diverse modes of travel and suggests that Complete Streets policies are a "crucial first step to reducing traffic violence, improving health equity, responding to the climate crisis, and rectifying a long history of inequitable transportation practices."[18] The coalition's 2023 report cites the growing rate at which drivers kill people afoot in the United States, with twenty-six thousand people killed while walking between 2018 and 2021. From the beginning, the movement has focused on the mobility disadvantages of older people and those with disabilities, but in recent years it has increasingly addressed disparate impacts on people of color and people with low incomes, suggesting that "Complete Streets can't happen without prioritizing underinvested and underserved communities."[19]

These publications don't exactly offer model legislation, but by highlighting examples of best practices, they seek to guide local policy adoption. These begin with elected officials' explicit commitment to "equitable vision" for how and why the community wants to complete its streets, including "a clear statement of intent to create a complete, connected network and consider the needs of all users."[20] The Complete Streets emphasis on "diverse users" has recently expanded beyond transportation modes to argue that jurisdictions should define their most underinvested and underserved communities.

In the world of traffic engineering, pronouncements by elected officials matter less than institutional and technical design processes, so Complete Streets policies target the organizational behavior of transportation planning and management by suggesting an explicit commitment to Complete Streets principles in all projects and phases. Where multimodal accommodations have often been an optional deviation from the autocentric rule, Complete Streets policies seek to make multimodalism the decision-making norm and any exceptions both specific and subject to high-level approval and public notice. To translate these principles into design practice, these policies guide the use of the "latest and best design criteria and guidelines" and set a timeframe for implementation. Furthermore, these policies look beyond the public right-of-way and the logic of traffic flow to argue for sensitivity to land use and context.[21] In contrast to obscure and technocratic performance metrics (like level of service), the guide argues for measures that are "specific, equitable, and available to the public." The coalition encourages detailed discussion of adapting roads to fit the character of the surrounding neighborhoods and has also come to consider the "unintended consequences such as displacement of residents due to rising costs of living."[22] Finally, it argues for giving meaningful weight to equity criteria in project selection and committing to implementation while involving engagement with underrepresented communities.

The Complete Streets movement and model policies have transformed the conversation about public streets, who they serve, and how they should be designed. According to the Complete Streets Coalition's website, as of 2023 Complete Streets policies have been voluntarily adopted in thirty-seven U.S. states, the Commonwealth of Puerto Rico,

Figure 6. Complete Streets policy and design confront autocentrism and seek to accommodate users of all modes, ages, and abilities. National Association of City Transportation Officials, *Urban Street Design Guide* (Washington, D.C.: Island Press, 2013). Reproduced by permission of Island Press, Washington, D.C.

the District of Columbia, and in more than 1,600 county or municipal governments. This represents remarkable growth, but it is still a small proportion of approximately 3,000 counties, 19,550 municipalities, and 16,000 townships in the nation.[23] Although the adoption of Complete Streets policies is highly uneven across space, it nonetheless reflects a bottom-up commitment to rethinking streets (Figure 6).

Complete Street policies embody key axes of mobility justice, starting with a commitment to multimodal equity for all users across the street network, a universal standard whose implementation should be guided by spatial planning. At the street level, these policies argue for fair access, safety, and convenience for all modes of travel, as well as for people of all ages and abilities. Not simply about nominal fairness, they put special emphasis on those whose forms of mobility are more vulnerable. In their focus on multimodal equity, these policies have been critiqued for neglecting urban and social context. However, the coalition increasingly prioritizes connection between multimodal equity and supporting local land uses, economies, cultures, and natural environments. While it has not been particularly concerned with the role of Complete Streets in gentrification and displacement until recently, the coalition has increasingly argued for an "equity approach" emphasizing affordable housing.[24] Though Complete Street policies have been what Kimberlé Williams Crenshaw might call "colorblind," since 2020 the coalition has sought to address the particular experiences and vulnerabilities of low-income people and communities of color, arguing for social equity interpreted in terms of social justice, reflecting the priority of "advancing racial equity," climate change, resilience, and healthy communities.[25]

The most powerful tool for achieving substantive equity often remains a commitment to procedural equity. In contrast to technocratic and often undemocratic traffic planning and design, the Complete Streets movement advocates greater transparency in debating community goals and accountability in the decision-making processes, opening much more space for people to understand and intervene in transportation policy and roadway design.

Vision Zero

Vision Zero, like Complete Streets, is a movement driven by transportation advocates and planners to redefine what we expect of roadways, specifically by confronting public harms normalized as the inevitable costs of autocentrism, to offer a "Safe System approach" to street redesign.[26] The movement emerged in Europe in the 1990s when the Swedish Transport Administration adopted an "ethical standpoint that no-one should be killed or suffer lifelong injury in road traffic."[27] Rather than treat accidents as inevitable, it argues for a "fundamentally different approach" to traffic safety that takes an integrated approach to complex factors shaping safe mobility—roadway design, speeds, behaviors, technology, policies, etc.—and articulates a clear, shared goal of zero fatalities and severe injuries.[28] The Vision Zero movement applies ethical arguments about transportation benefits and harms through a policy framework to transform them in practice.

What emerged and spread initially across northern Europe has become a worldwide movement. In the United States, New York led in adopting a Vision Zero plan and forging a Vision Zero Network among U.S. cities.

> Each year, more than 42,000 people—the population of a small city—are needlessly killed on American streets and thousands more are injured. . . . For too long, we've considered traffic deaths and severe injuries to be inevitable side effects of modern life. . . . The reality is that we can prevent these tragedies by taking a proactive, preventative approach that prioritizes traffic safety as a public health issue.[29]

Though focused on physical public harms like traffic deaths and injuries, Vision Zero articulates a broadly ethical argument and applies it to roadway design and management.

Vision Zero emphasizes a public commitment to a different vision of streets, articulated through policies and processes. In its publication *Core Elements for Vision Zero Communities,* the Vision Zero Network emphasizes certain fundamental values: traffic deaths are preventable, humans are fallible, the goal should be to prevent fatal and severe crashes, a systems approach is key, and "saving lives is NOT EXPENSIVE."[30] In contrast to popular rhetoric about the freedom of automobility, the Vision Zero Network argues that "because so many fear for their safety on our streets, there is no true freedom of mobility."[31] Like Complete Streets, Vision Zero makes mobility and streets an explicitly political question linked to institutional processes. Their "9 Components of a Strong Vision Zero Commitment" starts with an official commitment by elected officials, followed by creating interdisciplinary teams with high-ranking representation from across city departments and community stakeholders, leading to the development of an action plan with clear strategies and data-driven performance measures. More than just a political expression of values, Vision Zero translates these into the technical language of planning and design, argues for proactive assessment of risk factors and trends, "responsive, hot spot planning," and routine evaluation of safety interventions.[32] The Vision Zero planning process is data driven but, unlike standard roadway performance evaluation prioritizing speed and throughput, puts an emphasis on the human dimension of the roadway experience.

Vision Zero emerged primarily from a public-safety concern with traffic fatalities and injuries to argue for a universal value of zero fatalities or serious injuries. It remains focused mainly on multimodal equity and emphasizes vulnerable users, which in the United States correlates strongly with other forms of social and economic disadvantage, but increasingly emphasizes "inclusive and representative processes, as well as equitable outcomes."[33] Because increased traffic enforcement can lead to inequitable policing, recent policy guidance emphasizes the responsibility of network members "in improving, not exacerbating, these problems."[34] And though it may not emphasize procedural equity, the network seeks to make transportation decision-making better informed by and responsive to public input. Deeply woven with Complete Streets, it seeks to reform both policy and design toward more just streets, though as transportation spaces and not public places.

Multimodalism by Design

These key policy frameworks help to reframe how cities approach streets. However, they do not, with the exception of the ADA, directly reshape streets. That falls more directly to the standard manuals used by engineers to analyze, design, and construct the public right-of-way. What follows is a brief overview of a few of the most important roadway design standards and the ways these have integrated growing concern for multimodal equity, both incrementally and radically.

The Transportation Research Board's *Highway Capacity Manual*

Roadways are engineered as conduits for traffic, which starts with projecting future volumes. This science is guided by the nongovernmental Transportation Research Board, whose mission to promote "innovation and progress in transportation through research" was recently revised to also "foster a high-performing multimodal transportation system that enhances society."[35]

The TRB's marquee publication, the *Highway Capacity Manual* (*HCM*), initially written to quantify demand and thus lane requirements for new highways, has recently been subtitled *A Guide for Multimodal Mobility Analysis.*[36] The *HCM* conceives of roadways as a spatial network and of users in terms of mode, design characteristics, and relations to street space and each other. It interprets capacity as flow and, thus, roadway performance, via the metric of level of service (LOS), which evaluates streets from "free-flow operation" to "extremely low speed." Modeled on a system that values uninterrupted traffic flow, roadways have been designed to prioritize vehicular speed over slower users and volume over livability. The *HCM* now offers analogous LOS measures for bikes, pedestrians, and transit that extend beyond flow to encompass qualitative perceptions like comfort and safety, even as it recognizes that design decisions "can sometimes have an adverse impact on the service provided to another mode."[37]

Though the *HCM* interprets streets as infrastructure for flow and people as users, it has progressed to address multiple modes, even if limited in its ability to balance competing needs. In the manual, vehicular service remains paramount by custom. It's outside the manual's scope to address issues of spatial equity or encompass broader issues of social justice, and its emphasis on flow remains disconnected from streets' myriad qualities as places. However, in terms of engineering streets as infrastructural conduits, the revised *HCM* is slowly advancing greater equity among mobile users.

AASHTO's *A Policy on Geometric Design of Highways and Streets*

Once capacity has been modeled, roadways must be engineered accordingly. The American Association of State Highway and Transportation Officials' *A Policy on Geometric Design of Highways and Streets*—known colloquially as "The Green Book"—is considered "the comprehensive reference manual" for designing or reconstructing roadways.[38] The manual has long been thoroughly and unabashedly car-centric; the 2011 edition's stated purpose was to "provide operational efficiency, comfort, safety, and convenience for the motorist."[39] Since 2016, however, AASHTO has emphasized the needs of all transportation modes and showed greater sensitivity to environmental and community context.

AASHTO's 2018 Green Book has slowly begun to frame streets in more inclusive terms and to design accordingly. This started with how AASHTO defined the purpose and performance of roadways, which now argues for addressing project context and how each transportation mode should be accommodated. Second, it has redefined roadway performance from a level of service away from an exclusive focus on cars toward addressing service provided to each mode.[40] The Green Book incorporates the language of ADA accessibility and Complete Streets to state that each transportation mode "should be considered in the design of every project on the road and street network" under "the guiding design principle" of balancing the needs of diverse modes and community needs. While it is impractical to provide facilities for every mode on every road and street, the policy manual emphasizes that the transportation network should "as a whole" serve all modes effectively and conveniently.[41]

These design principles are applied—and priorities are balanced—differently according to a street's place in the roadway hierarchy. For example, main streets connecting neighborhoods with shopping and the urban core are categorized as "urban collectors" whose purpose is to balance mobility and access for vehicular traffic with alternative modes. To accomplish this, the manual suggests a design that reduces speeds, accepts interrupted flow, limits travel lanes and width, and "should" be provided with sidewalks to serve schools, parks, and shopping (though not requiring accommodations for bikes). Local streets, which prioritize local access over flow, are recommended to have even more limited speeds and widths. The Green Book highlights the particular challenge of intersections and the need for a safe and balanced design that "considers the needs of all user groups" while also meeting other community needs (e.g., environmental, scenic, and cultural) "to the extent practicable."[42] Vehicles remain central, but AASHTO now recognizes that intersections "should" incorporate bike and pedestrian features, though it does not mandate them or address place-based concerns. Such abstract, universalized standards do a poor job of acknowledging social differences or offering a voice for local communities.

AASHTO's Green Book reveals the power of roadway design to translate concepts about proper use of streets into spatial practice. These standards, long premised almost exclusively on the assumption of vehicular mobility, increasingly advocate balance among modes. This alone is progress. Yet vehicles remain the central presumption, with bike and pedestrian accommodations optional, and they don't offer design criteria for car-free or even car-limited streets. Furthermore, they do not address the spatial distribution of nonvehicular improvements or other forms of difference and inequality or meaningfully look beyond the roadway to the urban context. Fundamentally, AASHTO remains focused on designing roadways for traffic flow, but its steps toward multimodalism represent progress.

U.S. Department of Transportation's
Manual on Uniform Traffic Control Devices

Once a roadway capacity has been modeled and its geometry engineered, the last key design step is controlling traffic. The U.S. Department of Transportation's Federal Highway Administration publishes a *Manual on Uniform Traffic Control Devices* (*MUTCD*) whose minimum standards "promote highway safety and efficiency by providing for the orderly movement of all road users." Unlike TRB and AASHTO, the *MUTCD* is published by the government with the force of "law governing all traffic control devices" specifying which elements are mandatory, guidance, or optional.[43] It has sections focused on signs to communicate hazards and the law, traffic markings to guide flow, and controls to "assign the right-of-way." Uniform traffic controls are critical to how people navigate and experience streets, and the *MUTCD* (and versions adopted by states) is a free, downloadable resource for anyone who wishes to understand and perhaps shape street design.

For a century, the manual and its predecessors have conceived of mobility in terms of vehicular flow and signed, marked, and controlled roadways accordingly. The bias favoring cars remains both explicit and implicit: signs are oriented to drivers, markings are made to channel vehicular traffic down the roadway, and traffic signals promote vehicular flow. The bulk of the *MUTCD* is devoted to vehicular traffic and roads, with pedestrian-oriented accommodations secondary, and bicycles last.

Multimodalism has, however, been incrementally woven into the manual. The manual emphasizes the importance of pedestrian-specific markings like crosswalks, though it does not say where and explicitly cautions against installing crosswalks "indiscriminately."[44] Because traffic controls are key to pedestrians' safety and accessibility and in defining their legal rights, it's notable that the *MUTCD* now permits signalization like "leading pedestrian intervals" that enable those on foot to enter the roadway before cars. The revised *MUTCD* explicitly recognizes the legal place of bicycles on the roadway and offers markings to help carve out specific facilities like bike lanes and specific signage to help cyclists assert their rights (e.g., Bicycles May Use Full Lane signage for places lacking bike lanes). These help to promote the safety and mobility of cyclists, but they are unfortunately guidance and not mandated.

The *MUTCD* continues to reflect dominant assumptions about streets as vehicular traffic conduits but increasingly acknowledges the rights of diverse modes and provides strategies to accommodate them, albeit as recommended or optional features. It treats people as transport and does not conceive of other forms of social difference, address issues of spatial and distributional equity, or show sensitivity to neighborhood context. Nor does it consider the role of streets as places or explore streets' relationships with surrounding places. Again, however, better accommodating diverse mobilities on American streets long biased entirely around vehicular flow is a start.

AASHTO Pedestrian, Bicycle, and Transit Guides

For streets to be equitable for all modes, each deserves its own specific design standards and facilities. Thus, in addition to more inclusive design in its Green Book, AASHTO has developed manuals specific for bicycles, pedestrians, and transit.

AASHTO's *Guide for the Planning, Design, and Operation of Pedestrian Facilities* was first published in 2004 and significantly revised in 2021. It opens with the statement that "walking is the oldest and most basic form of travel," yet since pedestrians are also the most vulnerable of users it emphasizes particular attention to their safety.[45] Referencing the ADA and echoing the language of Complete Streets, it emphasizes that planning for pedestrians should serve both alternative transportation and recreational needs, especially where people choose not to or are not able to drive. It laments the disproportionate share of pedestrians among traffic fatalities to argue for more emphasis on designing for safe pedestrian travel. Though pedestrians are not vehicles, AASHTO's pedestrian guide analyzes their specific operational characteristics to inform the design of pedestrian facilities like sidewalks, shared-use paths, and accessible intersections and midblock crossings (Figure 7). In novel innovations, for the first time AASHTO has provided guidance for the pedestrian use of the roadway surface itself on local residential "play streets" that permit children to play, "Woonerf" and "shared streets" with extremely low vehicular speeds to prioritize pedestrians, and "preferential pedestrian facilities" including pedestrian streets, plazas, and transit malls.[46] Incipient AASHTO guidance is quite limited on these facilities, but it represents a major shift in how it defines and envisions the roadway.

AASHTO's *Guide for the Development of Bicycle Facilities,* first published in 1999 with the tepid description of bicycles as a "viable

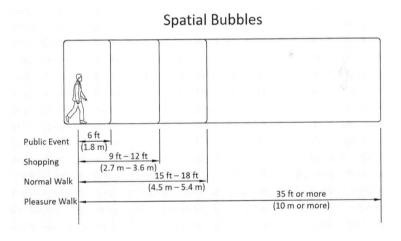

Figure 7. Streets are increasingly engineered for the specific needs of pedestrians. American Association of State Highway and Transportation Officials, *Guide for the Planning, Design, and Operation of Pedestrian Facilities,* 2nd ed. (Washington, D.C., 2021). Used with permission.

transportation mode," was revised in 2012 to call them an "important" transportation mode and "design imperative."[47] It focuses on the unique characteristics of bicycles, which are technically vehicles but have vulnerabilities like pedestrians. AASHTO bike guidelines argue for distinct facilities depending on context. While low-volume, low-speed local streets can be designed implicitly to accommodate cyclists with shared-use markings or "sharrows," the manual calls bike lanes "the appropriate and preferred" bicycle facility on busier streets.[48] Because introducing bike lanes typically requires a reallocation of street space, AASHTO provides various options for doing so, such as "road diets" or separate multiuse pathways or "sidepaths."[49]

Finally, in 2014 AASHTO published its first *Guide for Geometric Design of Transit Facilities on Highways and Streets.* Because public transit is vehicular, past AASHTO guidance simply included buses as design vehicles within the standard Green Book. The new manual recognizes the importance of public transit to serve high passenger capacities in busy corridors, support compact and walkable development, provide mobility for those unable to drive or without access to vehicles, and reduce emissions.[50]

Taken together, AASHTO's pedestrian, bicycle, and transit guides represent a slow shift away from autocentric design to engineering for the particular needs of more diverse transportation users in recent decades. Most of the best practices are recommended guidance and not required, and they do not guarantee equity among modes. Yet, such multimodal guidance—combined with ADA requirements—can help make inclusive design the norm rather than the exception. They make little or no pretense of addressing equity considerations beyond persons as transportation users, and their focus on streets limits their ability to address either the equitable distribution of improvements or the social impacts on communities. Interpreting streets almost exclusively as transportation infrastructure focused on flow, AASHTO is only just beginning to acknowledge the roadway's potential as a public space.

Like the revised Green Book, however, these manuals represent marked progress toward a more balanced and just form of transport infrastructure, even if their engineering perspective shifts their focus away from the public street's greater possibilities.

ADA Standards for Accessible Design and *Public Right-of-Way Accessibility Guidelines*

A key challenge for cities is to translate the legal principles behind the Americans with Disabilities Act into design practice. To do so, the Department of Justice publishes *ADA Standards for Accessible Design* as "minimum requirements" for newly designed and constructed or altered government facilities, public accommodations, and commercial facilities.[51] The Americans with Disabilities Act accessibility standards apply directly to pedestrian routes or vehicular ways that provide access to destinations and very specifically in terms of curb ramps, but making the overall right-of-way accessible presents a daunting task.

PROWAAC has worked for decades under the fundamental principle "that all users of all abilities have the right to equal access to public rights-of-way." To apply ADA standards directly to streets, the committee drafted *Public Right-of-Way Accessibility Guidelines* (*PROWAG*) to "inform federal, state, and local government agencies on how to make their pedestrian facilities, such as sidewalks, crosswalks, shared use paths, and on-street parking, accessible to people with disabilities."[52] After two decades in development and multiple revisions, *PROWAG* was finally approved in 2023 with the argument:

> Despite on-going efforts to improve access, pedestrians with disabilities throughout the United States continue to face major challenges in public rights-of-way because many sidewalks, crosswalks, and other pedestrian facilities are inaccessible. Equal access to pedestrian facilities is of particular importance because pedestrian travel is the principal means of independent transportation for many persons with disabilities.[53]

"To ensure that pedestrian facilities located in the public right-of-way are readily accessible to and usable by pedestrians with disabilities," *PROWAG* standards specify maximum slopes, minimum widths, and ramps and warning surfaces for both on-street pedestrian access routes and intersections, as well as accessibility in signalization controls and timing.[54]

ADA policy and *PROWAG* design guidance require that new and retrofitted streets provide for safe and convenient paths, crossings, and features to accommodate people with disabilities, who are among the most vulnerable mobile people. Try navigating streets as a blind or deaf pedestrian, wheelchair user, or older adult would, and one realizes immediately how frightening and impassable many streets are. Translating the ADA's radical stance for accessibility and inclusivity into design, *PROWAG* improves life for those with disabilities and makes streets safer and easier for others in the process: e.g., parents with strollers, children biking to school, nondisabled joggers. And since accessible design is required by law, such features are built wherever cities improve streets, likely leading to greater spatial equity compared with more discretionary improvements. *PROWAG* does not take into account social differences like race, ethnicity, or gender, but its focus on bodily safety and autonomy can intersect with other forms of being, particularly in diverse urban environments where many people do not drive.

National Association of City Transportation Officials Guides

Perhaps the most interesting and important shift toward fully multimodal design has come with the emergence of the new nonprofit National Association of City Transportation Officials and its growing suite of guides. NACTO was formed in 2004 by major North American cities and transit agencies with the mission to "build cities as places for people, with safe, sustainable, accessible, and equitable transportation choices that support a strong economy and vibrant quality of life." Founded primarily to promote multimodal equity, NACTO increasingly addresses broader inequalities and the street's role in overcoming them. One of its guiding values is "centering justice," which emphasizes that "the ability to move safely, easily, and comfortably through streets and public spaces is a cornerstone of freedom" and that countering diverse forms of discrimination requires policies to "correct structural injustices and advance equitable outcomes."[55] NACTO has built upon the policy arguments of the Complete Streets movement by publishing its own guidelines that are aligned with accepted standards but more sensitive to the needs of diverse users and neighborhood contexts. Where AASHTO manuals are inaccessible to the lay public, being both technically dense and extraordinarily expensive ($342 for a PDF of the Green Book for nonmembers), NACTO guides are published free online in nontechnical language with easy-to-read graphics.

NACTO's premiere publication, *The Urban Street Design Guide,* first published in 2013, argued that beyond being transport infrastructure, streets are also "the lifeblood of our communities and the foundation of our urban economies" and make up more than 80 percent of urban public space.[56] Distinct from traditional transportation design manuals, NACTO's guide explicitly describes streets as places and not simply facilities: at once a "safe place for people to get around" regardless of mode, center of commerce, and front yard for residences. Indeed, its first principle defines streets as public spaces that "should be designed as public spaces as well as channels for movement."[57]

In the guide, these principles are translated into the language of design, suggesting that "street design should both respond to and influence the desired character of the public realm."[58] Instead of a hierarchy of pipes, NACTO conceives of streets via an urban typology ranging from neighborhood streets and alleys to busy boulevards and transit corridors. The guide assumes that streets will be complete, serve all modes, and be designed to "optimize the benefits the community receives from its streets." Instead of engineering for the capacity and flow of vehicular traffic, it argues for rethinking street design elements like lane widths allocated "to serve all needs," pedestrian and bike accommodations, and traffic-calming devices that reinforce "pedestrian-friendly, safe speeds."[59] It focuses particularly on intersections to promote efficient traffic flows for all users and as "street space to bring people together and invigorate a city."[60] Most notably, it begins to reimagine the roadway surface itself as a public space, including "Green Alleys" that retrofit unattractive service lanes into an "inviting public space for people to walk, play, and interact," Shared Streets that prioritize pedestrian traffic, and interim design strategies to extend sidewalks to create parklets or to use "excess asphalt to create public plazas" (Figure 8).[61]

NACTO's *Urban Bikeway Design Guide* further "helps create complete streets that are safe and enjoyable for bicyclists."[62] It recommends treatments such as on-street bike lanes designated for the "preferential or exclusive use of bicyclists," separated cycle tracks, and bike-specific intersection treatments. NACTO bike guidance also outlines strategies for reimagining local streets as "bicycle boulevards" designed for low volume and speeds that give cyclists priority, including techniques for planning "low-stress bikeway networks" that "not only benefit people

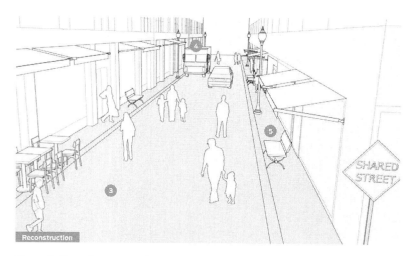

Figure 8. Shared streets go from accommodating to prioritizing pedestrians and cyclists while helping to reclaim the roadway as public space. National Association of City Transportation Officials, *Urban Street Design Guide* (Washington, D.C.: Island Press, 2013). Reproduced by permission of Island Press, Washington, D.C.

on bicycles, but also help create and maintain 'quiet' streets that benefit residents and improve safety for all road users."[63] These standards have been further refined in NACTO's 2017 *Designing for All Ages & Abilities: Contextual Guidance for High-Comfort Bicycle Facilities*, written to "grow bicycling as a safe, equitable mode for the majority of people" and not just experienced cyclists.[64] While some cyclists are young and confident, NACTO argues that existing designs can discourage those who might otherwise ride, including children, older adults, women, bike-share users, people of color, low-income riders, and people with disabilities. It advocates serving a more diverse and often more vulnerable population through more protective facilities like low-speed Shared Streets and bicycle boulevards, buffered bike lanes on streets with lower speeds and volumes, and separate facilities where speed and volume are high.

Finally, NACTO published the *Streets for Pandemic Response & Recovery* guide in 2020 to address the challenges of mitigating the novel risks of Covid-19 by "rethinking streets in a time of physical" distance not only by promoting socially distanced, active circulation and recreation but also by arguing "our streets support more than just movement."[65]

The guide outlines a set of design practices for reallocating street space for critical uses and alternative modes by slowing speeds, extending sidewalks, installing bike and transit facilities, and enhancing crossings. It illustrates how roadways can be converted into places for curbside dining, outdoor learning and recreation, gathering, and even "streets for protest."[66]

Taken together, NACTO guides put multimodal equity front and center and go beyond merely accommodating nonvehicular users to prioritizing pedestrian and bicycle flows. Furthermore, NACTO has increasingly emphasized issues of social difference and equity/justice to prioritize vulnerable populations, though the manuals themselves do not explicitly address social differences like race or gender. Though it emphasizes the importance of planning and participatory decision-making, its design focus on the public right-of-way naturally circumscribes its ability to address spatial-distributional equity or its potential role in urban change such as gentrification. Still, NACTO standards are unprecedented in both their commitment to transportation equity and their more encompassing view of the street's relationship to surrounding places and as a place unto itself. In stark contrast to technically written and expensive AASHTO guides, NACTO's free and easy-to-use manuals significantly advance procedural equity.

The Promise (and Limits) of Rethinking Streets through Policy and Design

The street is a complex, three-dimensional space whose human and physical geography is constructed in the image of societal institutions like policy and design, which must be reformed if we hope to reclaim streets. A single chapter can't summarize their complexities, but a brief review underscores the ways multimodalism and broader equity can be articulated in key public policies and translated through technical standards into a different kind of public right-of-way. Though unfamiliar to many of us, they have enormous power to define what streets are for and who they should serve.

After a century of autocentrism, in which streets have been framed as vehicular transportation space and people as users, these emerging policies and design standards increasingly envision streets for all that fairly accommodate diverse mobilities and people of all ages and abilities.

They increasingly recognize the rights of diverse modes and the need to design for them accordingly, even if multimodal improvements often remain a design option rather than a requirement (with the exception of the ADA). In the United States, this shift to multimodalism is no small feat. Moreover, these new standards link multimodal equity on the roadway to other approaches to mobility justice. From a distributional perspective, they advance spatial equity through their uniformity while addressing the spatial and historic inequities experienced by vulnerable groups. These policies and standards say relatively little about identity or social difference, but in recent years they have started to address the connection between multimodal accessibility and other social vulnerabilities. There is a growing realization that streets are public spaces that ought to be shared and designed with careful sensitivity to urban context. Finally, from a procedural point of view, they challenge the technocratic and often undemocratic nature of decision-making with a greater emphasis on transparency, accountability, and community engagement. These policies and standards continue to assume the centrality of drivers and to accommodate others on the street, but—perhaps inspired by the ADA—they have begun to advance the more radical idea of putting slower and more vulnerable users first on car-limited or car-free streets.

Creating intersectional just streets for everyone will take more than incremental improvements to multimodal policy and design; it will require confronting inequitable legal, political, and institutional systems behind them. That means going beyond multimodal accessibility to encompass diverse approaches to equity toward convivial and inclusive public places. In the incredibly car-centric United States, however, safely accommodating all modes, ages, and abilities is itself a gargantuan challenge. If we hope to advance mobility justice in important and intersectional ways, multimodalism in policy and design is not a bad place to start.

4

SLOWING THE STREET

Multimodal policy and design are critical steps toward equitable streets, but intersectional mobility justice requires moving beyond infrastructure that "accommodates" nondrivers to creating public spaces that welcome diverse mobilities and daily uses. If diverse modes have a legal right to travel American streets, suggesting at least nominal fairness, the reality of auto-dominated roadways and their stark asymmetries in mass, speed, and power reveal deep inequities. While some humans walk, bike, or roll protected by little more than clothing at speeds of 2 to 15 mph, others drive encased in thousands of pounds of steel and plastic at average speeds of almost 50 mph on urban collectors or minor arterials (and almost 57 mph on arterials).[1] These imbalances make mobility a matter of life and death, and they make sharing the roadway surface unimaginable for many nondrivers. A just street would mitigate these inequities, but for a century traffic laws and engineering have only reinforced and amplified them.

The road to a more just street starts with limiting vehicular speeds and traffic. In recent decades, cities have begun to return to slower streets shared more fairly and safely by drivers and nondrivers alike. Pre-automobile traditions of sharing the roadway among relatively slow forms of travel were nearly lost over the twentieth century but persisted on some local neighborhood streets and cul-de-sacs. More recently, advocates of livable streets have looked beyond accommodating alternative modes to more aggressively calm traffic, often inspired by Dutch *woonerf* streets on which slow-moving vehicles must share and even yield to bikes and pedestrians. During the Covid-19 pandemic, some cities radically scaled up these strategies, often under the banner of Slow Streets, using barricades and signage to encourage neighbors to use the roadway for socially distanced mobility, recreation, and gathering.

This chapter explores the emergence, acceleration, and evolution of traffic calming and so-called Slow Streets that reclaim roadways by discouraging through traffic and slowing speeds. While such roadways may not function as the more fully public spaces described in the following chapters, by reducing traffic speed and volume they can become a very different kind of roadway, shared among modes on a more even footing. To understand this shift, the chapter begins by tracing evolving approaches to speed control and traffic calming on American streets, from historical precedents through recent policy debates about livable streets, woonerf streets, and green alleys. These recent models set the stage for the pandemic shift toward Slow Streets, which convert low-volume streets into low-speed shared spaces emphasizing local access. The complexities of these changes can be explored through case studies of Boston's traffic-calming efforts through Neighborhood Slow Streets and speed hump programs, Oakland's expansive Slow Streets, and Pittsburgh's traffic calming, Neighborways, and pandemic Slow Streets. The evolution of these programs—before, during, and beyond the pandemic—reveals both dynamic innovations in American streets and complex equity issues about who has a right to be mobile on local roadways, who streets ought to serve, and the role of community voices in transportation planning and improvements.

Efforts to slow streets can take different names and use different strategies, but they share an overall commitment to making the public right-of-way safer and more livable. Such incremental changes can be a first step away from streets as pipes for cars and toward places for people.

Streets from Slow to Fast to Slow Again?

Slow and Local Streets: From Urban Standard to Suburban Cul-De-Sac

Until the twentieth century, all American streets were, by default, slow streets shared by pedestrians and relatively low-speed vehicles like horse-drawn carriages and surfaced as much for traction as flow. There were certainly asymmetries in velocity and mass among modes that cities, then as now, addressed through speed limits. As early as 1652, officials in New Amsterdam legislated that no wagons or carts be driven at a gallop and required drivers and conductors to lead their horses.[2] In 1757, Boston limited carriages to a "foot pace" to protect churchgoers on Sundays.[3] The late nineteenth-century arrival of omnibuses, horse-drawn rail cars, cable cars, and electric trolleys sped up streets and created new dangers, but they also brought congestion that itself slowed streets. Pedestrians retained the right to walk freely along and across the street, helping to calm traffic with their bodies.

The arrival of rapid, massive, and maneuverable motor vehicles upended the pace and order of historically slow streets. Governments responded first with speed limits. In 1901, Connecticut was the first state to legislate that motor vehicles operating within urban areas not exceed twelve miles per hour.[4] Police viewed speed and safety as mutually exclusive, imposing very low limits: the median state-designated speed limit in American cities in 1906 was 10 mph.[5] Cities continued granting preferential right-of-way to pedestrians.

After the fierce battles in the 1920s between motordom and pedestrians, however, the street was recast as a place for vehicular speed. The first Uniform Vehicle Code adopted in 1926 as a model for state traffic laws granted drivers right-of-way and recommended a standard urban speed limit of 35 mph, 25 mph in residential areas, and 15 mph only under very limited circumstances (school zones, business districts, etc.).[6] Cities increasingly paved roadways to reduce rolling resistance, striped travel lanes to promote traffic flow, and limited pedestrians to sidewalks and crosswalks.

As cities transformed streets into speedy thoroughfares and noisy places, they nonetheless sought to preserve safety and tranquility in residential neighborhoods. Limiting speed to 25 mph helped, but even those speeds aren't very safe for vulnerable pedestrians like children, and they only indirectly control the volume of traffic. In the 1920s, planners subsequently started promoting a hierarchy of roadways to funnel fast and heavy traffic on collectors and arterials while providing slower access on neighborhood streets. At the upstream end of this hierarchy emerged the new innovation of the dead-end cul-de-sac, which eliminated through traffic altogether. Inspired by European garden-city

108   Slowing the Street

planning, the model community of Radburn, New Jersey, was one of the first American suburbs to design housing around cul-de-sacs to keep the annoyances of motorized traffic away and to maintain slow speeds and low volumes to enable people to walk and children to play.[7] In turn, Radburn provided a model for cities beginning to exercise subdivision controls and inspired Federal Housing Administration standards guiding new development.

By midcentury, vestigial traditions of slow sharing had retreated down the street hierarchy to involve only the lowest volume local streets, cul-de-sacs, and alleys. Everywhere else the roadway surface was regulated, designed, and experienced as the exclusive domain of vehicular volume and speed.

Traffic Calming for Livable Streets

Late twentieth-century urban critics and planners came to decry this regime and argued for greater livability on urban streets. While the movement didn't directly challenge the primacy of cars (or even standard speed limits), it sought to mitigate traffic and speed through street design and traffic calming.

Midcentury urbanists like Jane Jacobs and Lewis Mumford lamented the tyranny of the automobile, but only in the 1970s and 1980s did planners apply the science of environmental perception to modify driver behavior through design. Donald Appleyard's pioneering study of local streets in San Francisco reveals differences between dangerous and noisy "heavy" streets, from which people withdrew, and "light" streets, where neighbors interacted and children played. Based on these observations, San Francisco developed urban design strategies to protect residential areas through slowing traffic by narrowing or "necking down" street entrances, bending alignments, landscaping, lighting, and sidewalk treatments.[8]

As cities experimented with such techniques, the Federal Highway Administration sought to synthesize these in its 1980 *State of the Art: Residential Traffic Management* report. Authored by Appleyard, the report argues for "changes in philosophy relative to the role of streets" and "significant departures from customary practice" to engineer streets not simply for traffic but to manage them for the overall goal of "improvement of living and environmental conditions on residential streets."[9]

It outlined "traffic management" strategies to reduce speeds through physical improvements.

These were not formalized in standard guidance until the 1999 Institute of Transportation Engineers and Federal Highway Administration report *Traffic Calming: State of the Practice,* authored by planner Reid H. Ewing, which defines *traffic calming* as "the combination of mainly physical measures that reduce the negative effects of motor vehicle use, alter driver behavior and improve conditions for non-motorized street users."[10] In contrast to traffic controls like signals, the report emphasizes the "self-enforcing" nature of traffic calming, using engineering to reduce traffic speed and volume as "means to other ends such as traffic safety and active street life." The manual outlines a toolbox of speed-control techniques, including so-called vertical and horizontal elements that modify the roadway in those respective dimensions. To limit speed, it includes both vertical elements like speed humps and horizontal measures like traffic circles and bulb-outs to narrow the roadway. To reduce or divert traffic volume, it includes techniques like street closures, though it recognizes that this "most commonly used cure for cut-through traffic" was also "the most controversial." It notes that most communities increasingly relied instead on reducing speed rather than diverting traffic (some even prohibiting street closures altogether).

As planners and engineers increasingly sought to both slow traffic and better accommodate diverse transportation modes, the line blurred between neighborhood traffic calming and the wider Complete Streets movement.[11] In the process, traffic calming matured as a science, with the publication of the American Planning Association's *U.S. Traffic Calming Manual* in 2009 and a "Traffic Calming" chapter within the *Traffic Engineering Handbook* in 2016. These documents recognize the possibility of reducing traffic through closure but emphasize speed-control measures and recommend diverting traffic "only when other volume control measures have proven inadequate."[12]

Neighborhood Bike Boulevards and Woonerf/Shared Streets

Planning for Complete Streets and Vision Zero has focused attention on major roadway corridors where safety and livability issues are most acute, often by adding new facilities like bike lanes. Yet cities have increasingly looked to neighborhood streets to improve walkability, bikeability, and general livability. More than just calming traffic, local planners have begun to reimagine local roadways and alleys as shared spaces where cars might actually yield to nondrivers.

To better support cyclists, cities began planning bike boulevards to retrofit already low-volume and low-speed streets to be safely and comfortably shared by cyclists. Also known in the United States as local street bikeways, quiet streets, Neighborways (and in Europe as *fietsstraat* [Netherlands] or *fahrradstrasse* [Germany]), bike boulevards share what a 2009 Portland State University report calls a "common theme of reducing the volume and speed of motor vehicle traffic (particularly non-local, cut-through traffic), and creating a comfortable space where bicyclists, and often pedestrians as well, have priority along the street."[13] Traffic calming and reduction, signage and pavement markings, and intersection improvements help prioritize cyclists while also supporting pedestrians and neighborhood livability. Bikeways are said to create conditions "like living on a cul-de-sac," according to a 2017 Transportation Research Board presentation.[14] Cities like Palo Alto and Berkeley, California; Portland, Oregon; Minneapolis-Saint Paul, Minnesota; and others use bike boulevards to promote cycling and neighborhood livability.

The woonerf, which can be translated from Dutch as "living yard," is an even more aggressive technique for calming traffic to prioritize nondrivers. First introduced in the Netherlands in the 1960s by residents frustrated with through traffic, woonerf streets are transformed from "channels for the movement of cars" into shared spaces by installing design features like street furniture "to turn the street into an obstacle course for motor vehicles, and an extension of home for residents," and thereby slowing vehicles to a "walking speed" of 9 mph.[15] So successful was the technique that the Dutch government sought to scale up this approach. The relative cost effectiveness of traffic calming over street closures inspired similar programs elsewhere in Europe and later Australia, and it provided lessons on the design benefits and challenges of mixing modes on the roadway. While they enhanced traffic safety, livability, and social interaction, woonerf streets raised issues related to parking, access for those with disabilities, emergency access, and costs of implementation and maintenance.[16] In the United States, these models informed early adopters like Cambridge, Massachusetts, and San Francisco and emerging traffic-calming standards emphasizing speed over volume controls, simple over diverse programs, and treatments focused on a single street up to areawide planning.[17] These ideas helped expand planning experiments to transform backyard alleys into "green alleys" not only to manage stormwater and promote regreening but to reimagine them as shared public spaces reoriented around walking, biking, and play.

These ideas are incorporated in the National Association of City Transportation Officials' (NACTO) innovative *Urban Streets Design Guide*, first published in 2013. Arguing that "streets are public spaces for people as well as arteries for traffic and transportation," NACTO goes beyond multimodal accommodation to outline strategies for putting nondrivers first, particularly on neighborhood streets.[18] To prioritize cyclists, it envisions bicycle boulevards created from existing low-volume and low-speed streets through signage, markings, and speed and volume management (i.e., traffic calming or diversion), which might make neighborhoods more livable in the process. To support pedestrians, NACTO suggests reinforcing the existing de facto sharing of some roadways, whether residential streets, downtown commercial alleys, or crowded downtown streets, by making those behaviors implicit through design and traffic calming. Low-volume residential roadways could be remade as "shared streets" to "meet the desires of adjacent residents and function foremost as a public space for recreation, socializing, and leisure."[19] An alley might be reimagined as "an inviting public space for people to walk, play, and interact." NACTO's companion *Urban Bikeway Design Guide* emphasizes the potential to convert low-volume and low-traffic streets into bike boulevards through traffic calming and signage, giving bicycles travel priority while also creating "'quiet' streets that benefit residents and improve safety for all road users" (Figure 9).[20]

Instead of engineering streets to separate modes of travel, these new standards sought to mix them up again, using traffic calming to radically slow speeds and careful design—including the very absence of roadway markings—to welcome bikes and pedestrians to reclaim the roadway.

Pandemic Slow Streets: Emerging NACTO Guidance

These developing strategies gained sudden relevance when Covid-19 hit and social distancing and park closures prompted people and planners to

Figure 9. NACTO bike-boulevard guidance combines traffic calming, signage, and other design cues to slow traffic and promote neighborhood livability. National Association of City Transportation Officials, *Urban Bikeway Design Guide* (Washington, D.C.: Island Press, 2014). Reproduced by permission of Island Press, Washington, D.C.

eye their local streets. Planners experimented with local Slow Street programs in response, which coevolved with and found nationwide expression in the hastily developed NACTO *Streets for Pandemic Response & Recovery* guidance published in June 2020. The guidance outlines ways to "reallocate our streets and sidewalks for public use during this crisis and for the future" toward "achieving a long-term economic recovery that is equitable, sustainable, and enduring."[21] NACTO drew from local experiments (citing Oakland, for example) distilled as best practices.

Traffic calming was key to many of NACTO's pandemic strategies, which emphasized managing vehicle speeds to "to enhance the safety of all street users" by reducing posted speeds through signage and deploying quick-build strategies to redefine the geometry of the roadway through vertical elements (e.g., barriers). It combined concepts from traffic calming and bikeway planning to propose Slow Streets that "reduce traffic volume and speed to a minimum so that people can walk, bike, and run safely" on existing low-volume and low-speed local streets where alternative through-traffic routes exist and whose entrances could be partially closed.[22] In contrast to full street closures, Slow Streets would limit local access at low speeds (5–10 mph) through barriers and Local Traffic Only signage. Such emergency measures could be physically implemented within a week, but NACTO suggested first engaging residents, stakeholders, and advocates.[23]

Intended as an emergency measure and drawing from traditions in tactical urbanism, these pandemic Slow Streets measures used temporary materials rather than permanent redesign. NACTO made little bones, however, about the potential of temporary conversions to advance a longer-term agenda, suggesting that the changes might be applied to already-planned neighborhood greenways, bike boulevards, or routes awaiting implementation.

Case Studies in Calming and Slowing Neighborhood Streets

American cities have long used traffic-calming techniques, but the planning and design of Slow Streets are relatively new, often vastly expanded in response to Covid-19. While the health emergency may be waning, efforts to rethink proper speed and balance among modes on the roadway continue. What began as experiments are evolving into more institutionalized programs and standardized designs. The following case studies show how local streets can be reclaimed for low-velocity and multimodal mobility and neighborhood livability, as well as the challenges of doing so equitably.

Neighborhood Slow Streets in Boston

Boston has been a traffic-calming pioneer well before the pandemic. Described by some as "America's Walking City," its historic and often narrow streets have nonetheless been dominated by vehicular traffic and parking for a century. The city has committed to multimodalism through Complete Streets and Vision Zero programs, which increasingly focused on slowing streets through traffic calming. These have evolved from an intensively planned Neighborhood Slow Streets program launched almost a decade ago to a citywide commitment to the basic speed hump. The growth of slow streets in Boston suggests the opportunities for reclaiming local streets for safety and livability by slowing them.

Boston adopted a Complete Streets policy in 2013 and shortly thereafter published its innovative *Boston Complete Streets Design Guidelines* to "improve the quality of life in Boston by creating streets that are

114 Slowing the Street

both great places to live and sustainable transportation networks."[24] These new standards adopt a design approach that "places pedestrians, bicyclists, and transit users on equal footing with motor vehicle users." They also assert the powerful way streets can shape neighborhood character. "Great streets for walking, bicycling, and activities are great places for everyone," the guidelines argue, and since streets make up 56 percent of city-owned land, "how we use this land reflects how we want to live."[25]

A commitment to slower speeds underpins Boston's Complete Streets efforts, whose guidelines recommend design speeds of 25 mph on most city streets. While they focused first on retrofitting major and commercial streets with bicycle and pedestrian improvements, they also aimed to calm local streets. These included so-called Neighborways (also known as bicycle boulevards) that use traffic calming on low-volume local streets to slow speeds (20 mph or less), discourage motor vehicle through traffic while still enabling local access, and give priority to bicyclists and pedestrians. Traffic-calming strategies for local streets included curb extensions and chicanes (an artificial narrowing of the roadway), speed tables (broader than speed humps), raised crosswalks, traffic circles, and signs or barricades to divert traffic (though only when part of a wider traffic-calming strategy). They also proposed Shared Streets designed without curbs to blend the sidewalk with the roadway surface, ensuring speeds slow enough—no more than 15 mph—for pedestrians to intermingle with bicycles, motor vehicles, and transit.[26]

The public health and safety values of slowness were reiterated in Boston's 2015 *Vision Zero Boston Action Plan,* which sought to eliminate fatal and serious traffic crashes by 2030 through "reducing speeds and building safer streets." The plan proposed a Neighborhood Slow Streets program to enable residents to apply for traffic calming on residential streets to improve safety by slowing drivers with visual and physical cues "and create residential streets that are safe and inviting for walking, bicycling, and playing."[27] The program was formally launched in 2015, and the website describes it as "a new approach to traffic calming requests."[28] Vineet Gupta, director of planning for the Boston Transportation Department, told me:

> For decades . . . residents have been concerned at the mundane
> level about cars speeding on their street, and even in residential

neighborhoods at intersections it's not always safe to cross to the other side. For decades it has been a critical issue but a difficult issue . . . to try and address that in a systematic way.[29]

Historically, the department had received "one-off requests" for traffic calming, but previous administrations had said, "We don't do speed humps, end-of-story." At this point Gupta and his colleagues recognized, "Wait, we're not getting to the bottom of the problem," and responded by developing a program to approach traffic calming systematically: "If you put a speed hump on one street, the traffic goes to another street, so you have to take a district-wide lens." Gupta continued, "You're talking about hyperlocal politics. . . . This is about people who live in the area." For the first time, the program opened the door to speed humps by neighborhood request but planned carefully within the context of the neighborhood.

Instead of just installing speed humps in reaction to complaints, the pilot Neighborhood Slow Streets program used a robust planning and design process informed by public engagement. It did solicit applications: "We need ownership," Gupta suggests, "You have to talk to your neighbors." These applications were filtered through a selection process and scored based on community support, traffic data, and geographic criteria. Applications also needed to define a geographic area for comprehensive analysis. Once selected, members of the city's Vision Zero team and consulting planners visited the site and walked with residents; collected and analyzed data on traffic volumes, speeds, and accident rates; and began multiple rounds of concept development and community engagement toward final design and implementation.

The program first piloted these methods in two neighborhoods: Stonybrook in Jamaica Plain and the Talbot-Norfolk Triangle in Dorchester. "From the outset, the city decided to do a zone-based approach to planning," according to Conor Semler, a consulting planner involved in the process, bounded by major streets and then neighborhood streets.[30] "We didn't just design and install speed humps on certain streets, but also on adjacent streets in anticipation of diversion," he notes. Designers applied a variety of traffic-calming strategies from "a broader and more creative toolkit," Semler continues, but framed as pilots since "the engineering profession as a whole is a bit conservative and wants to see

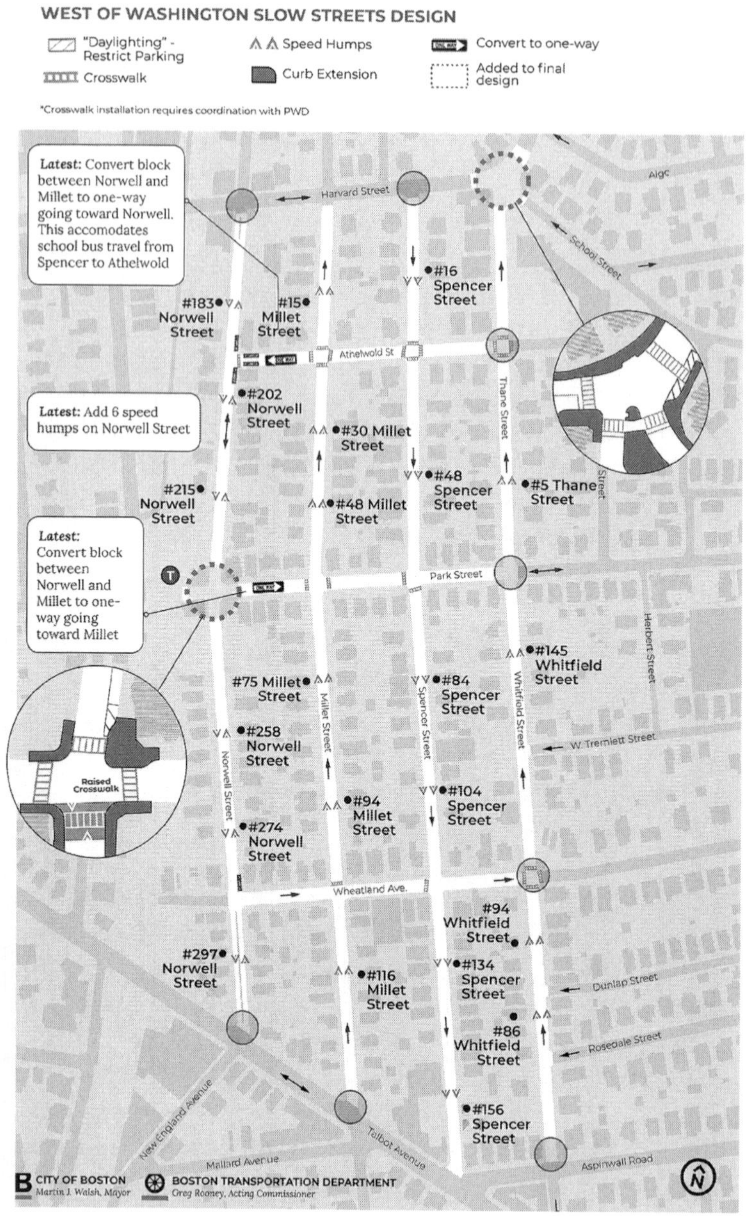

Figure 10. Boston's Neighborhood Slow Street program used intensive, zone-wide planning and community engagement to guide traffic-calming strategies, like in the West of Washington neighborhood in Dorchester. "West of Washington Street," City of Boston, accessed October 28, 2024, https://www.boston.gov/departments/transportation/west-washington-street.

how things work." Yet Boston approached these as high-profile models for citywide application. At a ribbon-cutting for the Stonybrook project, Mayor Martin Walsh called Neighborhood Slow Streets "a concept shaped by our community . . . that we're going to do across the entire city" to enhance safety and "significantly make a difference on quality of life on our different streets." He particularly acknowledged the children in the audience, arguing that "we have to make sure that our streets are safe for them, we have to slow down cars on our streets for their future."[31]

Neighborhood Slow Street pilots engaged residents in neighborhoods more accustomed to enduring safety issues than collaborating with the city. In Dorchester, the Talbot-Norfolk Triangle pilot was spurred when a ten-year-old was struck by a car walking to a park. After the planning process, a local leader told reporters, "I'm a huge fan of Slow Streets. . . . I know what it's done for our neighborhood."[32] In the adjacent West of Washington community, neighborhood association president Laquisa Burke told me, "We had already been working on our plans to get a park in our neighborhood. . . . Throughout the process, Slow Streets came out. . . . We just happened to be the neighborhood adjacent to the neighborhood that was getting it."[33] West of Washington had long suffered from cut-through traffic and speeding; Burke recalls, "People flew right past you, they took the mirrors off your car. . . . People weren't safe, even getting out of your car." As Burke's community group planned the new park, it became even more essential to calm traffic in the area. Through a systematic Slow Streets planning process over 2017 and 2018, planners and community members identified traffic-calming techniques, including establishing new crosswalks (some raised) and speed humps, "daylighting" intersections to improve visibility, and converting some streets to one way. "We wanted to slow people down, direct people to go another way, and really just get people to think," Burke told me; "It's about changing people's ideas." Installed in 2019 and 2020, these features have slowed speeds and reduced traffic, enabled kids to go out and play, allowed day-care providers to bring kids to the park, and helped make the community feel a bit more comfortable. Not only did it help neighborhood safety, she observed, but it also brought a "lot of camaraderie. . . . Everybody wants slower streets." The process even strengthened the neighborhood association and built capacity in a community of color used to being neglected. Burke observed of the city: "Usually for everything they start they start in the white community and it trickles down to us. . . . It was nice for once for something to come to a Black community first."

These Complete Streets, Vision Zero, and Slow Streets strategies converged in the city's long-term mobility plan, *Go Boston 2030,* adopted in 2017, whose overall aim is a region in which "all residents have better and more equitable travel choices" guided not only by a commitment to multimodal access but also to equity defined as "proactively address[ing] transportation infrastructure gaps in chronically under-served neighborhoods."[34] Alongside transportation safety, *Go Boston 2030* emphasizes goals to improve experiential quality so that "every trip will be enjoyable, with continuously inviting, comfortable, and clean public spaces and well maintained facilities." Among diverse strategies, it featured "Vision Zero: Neighborhood Slow Streets" as an opportunity for neighbors to collaborate in improving the safety of their streets.[35] In a related effort, in 2017 the Boston Department of Transportation translated these placemaking aspirations in its new *Tactical Public Realm Guidelines*: "Rather than just serving vehicles as transportation networks, our streets can be spaces in which to convene, create, and experiment" as "living rooms" for public interaction, "canvasses" for creative expression, and "experiments" for testing new technologies.[36]

After the success of these pilots, and bolstered by long-range plans, the Boston Transportation and Public Works Departments rolled out a more permanent Neighborhood Slow Streets program over three to five neighborhood zones each year between 2017 and 2022. Announcing the selection of the first five neighborhoods in the 2017 program, Mayor Walsh suggested, "The Neighborhood Slow Streets program brings us closer to achieving Vision Zero by proactively lowering speeds on streets where Bostonians live, play, and travel."[37] The permanent program involved a rigorous project-selection process that solicited neighborhood applications and scored them based on levels of community support; sociodemographic criteria; geographic criteria, including the presence of public facilities and parks; proximity to rail and bus transit; walking or bicycling routes identified in master plans; crash history; and the geographic diversity of selected neighborhoods. Once neighborhoods were identified, a multistep planning process sought to ensure zone-wide planning and public engagement.[38]

The onset of Covid-19, with its sudden need for socially distanced transportation and gathering, affected Boston as it did every city. Boston suddenly expanded outdoor dining, for example. But unlike other cities, rather than turn to Slow Streets as a pandemic strategy, it instead continued with the trajectory of its already-established program. Planning and construction were delayed and public engagement shifted online, and rather than solicit a new round of applications the city simply rescored previous applications to maintain a pace of three to five neighborhoods per year.

Ultimately, Boston's efforts to slow its streets grew not because of the pandemic but due to the project's infectious success. "Now people from across the city are saying, 'We want what they have,'" said planner Conor Semler.[39] As the program grew in popularity, however, its labor and cost intensiveness posed a problem: Department of Transportation director of planning Vineet Gupta explained simply, "We didn't have the resources."[40] This forced the agency to rethink streets in a more profound way. Where traffic calming had in the past been discouraged and then treated as a special project implemented through careful design, Gupta and agency leaders came to the conclusion that a more universal and efficient approach was needed.

The Boston Transportation Department ended the Neighborhood Slow Streets program after the 2022 funding cycle in favor of standardizing speed humps on local streets. Instead of neighborhood-driven and intensive planning, the new speed humps program rapidly deploys this effective traffic-calming tool based on geographic selection criteria. The new program no longer solicits applications but aims to work "proactively to add speed humps on all eligible streets, in every neighborhood."[41] It set the goal of calming forty to fifty miles of streets across ten neighborhoods per year by adding five hundred speed humps annually, as a "simple tool" to reduce speeds and create a more "comfortable environment for those that live, walk, and bike in our neighborhoods." Reframing speed humps as a "standard tool for safety on our streets," the Transportation Department stated flatly, "We will not be able to host or attend community meetings about their design." In place of in-depth analysis and engagement, the program opted for standardization and breadth of application.

This move away from carefully planned traffic calming to broad application of standardized features gained further prominence in May of 2023 when Mayor Michelle Wu announced a Safety Surge initiative, arguing, "As our City grows, we must act with urgency to make our streets safe for everyone" through a $12 million annual commitment to installing speed humps, redesigning dangerous intersections, and adjusting signals to prioritize pedestrian safety.[42] This shift was pragmatic, emerging from years of design experimentation and experience. While the traffic-calming toolkit of the Neighborhood Slow Streets program had been more creative, planners and designers like Conor Semler learned firsthand the complications of horizontal deflections like curb extensions, which often required the removal of parking and affected drainage, whose associated costs are "orders of magnitude more expensive." Horizontal elements like speed humps proved extremely effective in slowing traffic and didn't affect stormwater flows.[43] Though Semler regrets the narrow focus on speed humps to the exclusion of other techniques, he acknowledges their efficiency. For Gupta, the simplicity of the speed hump is also its power: in contrast to time- and labor-intensive planning, speed humps can be administered and installed more efficiently, and they are less controversial than other improvements like bike lanes. "It should be seen as the same level as a crosswalk or replacing a tree," Gupta continues; just as people in a neighborhood expect crosswalks at intersections as a standard design feature, "they should expect a speed hump on their street."[44]

This shift is also deeply philosophical. Traffic calming in the past has been viewed as a one-off, but Gupta says, "We've decided every street in Boston has a right, it's your right to not have cars drive fast on your street. . . . We're going to act on your right."[45] While the intent of Safety Surge and the speed hump program remain the same as Neighborhood Slow Streets, the city has shifted from tactical responses to universally applicable techniques. Previous programs had been neighborhood driven, with the inequities that result from that, but now the city will roll out these standardized safety features over the next five years through a comprehensive program. To accelerate implementation, the city adopted a Speed Humps Policy and Design Directive stating unequivocally that speed humps are proven, effective safety measures and should be incorporated into any significant street design project where feasible.[46] What were once exceptional treatments are today considered standard. These institutional shifts may seem arcane, but they are key to implementing Boston's broader Complete Streets and Vision Zero goals.

Boston's efforts to calm streets emerged from a Complete Streets and Vision Zero emphasis on multimodal access, evolving through pilots and neighborhood-driven planning to be broadly implemented as a citywide strategy. To what degree do these really reclaim streets from cars, though? Mandy Wilkens, events and communications manager with the

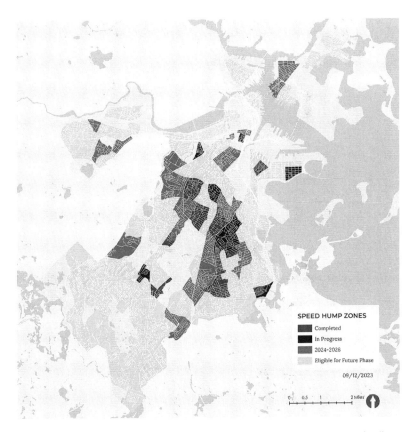

Figure 11. Boston has shifted to a citywide speed hump program that standardizes the installation of this effective traffic-calming technique on all eligible streets. "Making Neighborhood Streets Safer," City of Boston, accessed October 29, 2024, https://www.boston.gov/departments/transportation/making-neighborhood-streets-safer.

Boston Cyclists Union, suggested in our interview that while "speed humps are very good, when they're a piece of the puzzle," there needs to be a more "holistic approach to remaking our streets. . . . Speed humps are only a fraction of the problem in Boston."[47] Traffic humps slow traffic, opening space for alternative modes and improving neighborhood livability, but Wilkens doesn't think they create the kind of pedestrianized, shared public space they could. Vineet Gupta admits that "the slow streets program was less about space. Its driving motivation was safety. . . . It's about space only to the extent that people who live on a street feel safer to be on their street." Yet he sees speed humps as part of an evolution over the long term toward a European woonerf model, using other interventions to make it clear that there are visual signals to both pedestrians and people in vehicles that this is a shared space. He is frank, however: "We can't flip a switch and change things overnight."[48]

From the outset, Boston's program has tried to reconcile different equity approaches. In terms of distributional equity, it began as an application-driven program scored based on geographic criteria. Recognizing that neighborhoods with more capacity know how to claim resources, the agency shifted to a data-driven and citywide approach. The program promotes multimodal equity through aggressive traffic calming, encouraging biking but not fully pedestrianizing the roadway. These improvements do not promote social diversity per se, but they do welcome diverse users while targeting the improvement of places with greater risks of traffic violence and with vulnerable populations (defined primarily in terms of age). Slow Streets are more sustainable than traditional roadways, promoting intergenerational and interspecies equity. Such improvements do affect neighborhood quality of life and desirability, but it seems fewer people are worried about speed humps and green gentrification. Finally, while neighborhood-driven application and high-touch planning advanced procedural equity, Boston has recognized the distributional and social inequities in that approach and now emphasizes a more universal approach. "In every case, you have to find the right balance. . . . That balance is struck with conversations, literally with people on the sidewalk, it's a house-by-house conversation," Gupta admits. Because those conversations are resource and time intensive, there also has to be "some higher-level policy making where we find that balance in the macro-sense."[49]

Slow Streets in Oakland, California

Few cities exemplify pandemic-era experiments in Slow Streets better than Oakland, California. The city built on decades of bicycle planning suddenly expanded a massive Slow Streets and Essential Places program that limited through traffic and speeds on more than twenty miles of local streets "to create neighborhood space for physical and social activity." The program was popular in Oakland, received nationwide attention, and provided a model for other cities. Ultimately the pandemic-era program raised complex equity issues, leading to the end of closures in 2022. Oakland's Slow Streets is now evolving into a permanent program integrated with bike-route planning and paving programs.[50]

Long before the pandemic, Oakland had been slowing streets through multimodal policy and planning. The city adopted a Complete Streets policy in 2013, and in 2016 it created a new Department of Transportation (OakDOT), reorganized to include staff from the Public Works and Police Departments, with the mission to "assure safe, equitable, and sustainable access and mobility," and directed by a planner with experience expanding New York's protected bike lanes. OakDOT's first *Strategic Plan* (2016) pledged to adopt a Vision Zero program, incorporate Complete Streets techniques in standard design, and prioritize ADA compliance in the public right-of-way. "By designing our streets for the most vulnerable Oaklanders," OakDOT's plan argued, "we can place people on equal footing with motor vehicles and protect everyone who uses the street, no matter how they get around."[51] OakDOT's experience in bikeway planning informed the update of its bicycle master plan, *Let's Bike Oakland,* in 2019, which employed an equity framework—highlighting goals related to access, health and safety, affordability, and collaboration—and emphasized Neighborhood Bikeways to provide "continuous, comfortable bicycle routes on the local street network instead of busy arterials" through traffic calming and shared-use markings.[52]

These robust multimodal planning efforts provided a policy context and foundation for Oakland's Covid-19 response in spring 2020. In March, California declared a stay-at-home order and nonessential travel was discouraged. OakDOT planner Jason Patton, Bicycle and Pedestrian Program supervisor in the Safe Streets Division, described how planners' personal experience of working from home helped generate the idea for the Slow Streets program. "We were looking out the window, seeing lots of people on the streets" playing and walking, and with the initially conservative socially distancing guidance, "it doesn't take that much thinking to realize our sidewalks aren't wide enough."[53] Streets were emptied of cars. OakDOT leadership wanted to help address the challenge, Patton admits, and was "seeing it as an opportunity to make a more people-centered use of streets. . . . What's the expression: 'Don't let a good crisis go to waste'?"

In April 2020, Oakland Mayor Libby Schaaf announced a new Slow Streets program to partially close seventy-four miles of neighborhood streets that were already designed as Neighborhood Bikeways to prioritize walking, running, and bicycling. Schaaf announced that "Slow Streets is trying to send a message that we want Oaklanders to recreate in a socially distanced manner" but more broadly suggested that "when we close our streets to cars we open them up to amazing possibilities."[54] Between April and July 2020, the city limited traffic on designated Slow Streets to support physical activity with social distancing while also launching an Essential Places program to temporarily improve pedestrian safety around essential services like grocery stores, food-distribution locations, and Covid-19 testing sites with safety islands, lane closures, signal timing changes, and signage with calming messages such as "Go Slow—It's Essential."

Slow Streets did not prohibit traffic but used so-called soft closures, including traffic safety cones and A-frame barricades with signs depicting a pedestrian and text reading "Road Closed to Thru Traffic," across a travel lane to provide what officials described as a "psychological nudge" to drivers (Figure 12). Warren Logan, the mayor's director of mobility policy and interagency relations, expressed hope: "When they do turn into the street, they do it carefully." As with prior efforts, traffic calming was key. While a department of transportation always wants to design self-enforcing streets, Logan suggested, "we're only going to meet our goals if people respond to design cues with good choices."[55]

The scale and ambitions of Oakland's program generated national attention, positive press, and "made a tremendous splash" in the words of OakDOT's Jason Patton. As the department rolled out closures, trying to balance expedience with care in selection, "that's where it started to get interesting."

Figure 12. Oakland's pandemic-era Slow Streets employed barricades to discourage through traffic, promote outdoor recreation, and support socially distanced gatherings. Photo courtesy of the City of Oakland, California, Department of Transportation.

> Not all neighborhoods had the same experience as the transportation designers and leaders, who live in white-collar neighborhoods. Not all have the same view out their front windows.... The ways we perceive the opportunities and challenges of the world are informed by our own experiences.... With the tremendous social-economic variation, racial variation among Oakland's neighborhoods, what others were seeing was very different from what I was seeing outside my window.[56]

Public feedback on the program thus varied significantly across neighborhoods. The agency was flooded with positive input from affluent flatland neighborhoods but initially heard little from either suburban hillslope neighborhoods or lower-income areas that are traditionally communities of color. In these places, many residents did not have the luxury of working from home and often had to commute to their jobs by car. These same people may have also had different experiences with their local streets in which their social value as gathering places might be diminished by concerns about public safety.

Not only did neighborhoods respond differently to the substance of the program and its closures, but they also reacted differently to the process. Slow Streets were launched as a "transportation thing," according to Justin Hu-Nguyen, co-executive director of mobility justice for the advocacy group Bike East Bay, but communities didn't all see it the same way. Even where "people weren't opposed to it, they were opposed to the process," Hu-Nguyen observed; "The city was rushing it. . . . They didn't do the prework with the communities on how it would impact them."[57] Patton himself felt "dismay" that the city scaled up a new program so quickly rather than building on existing ones. OakDOT began to hear from community partners in lower-income neighborhoods of color, he recalls, that "they didn't think the program was for them or for their neighborhoods . . . which kind of evolved into 'maybe you should just stop doing this.'" Though the agency tried to address concerns through an Essential Places component focused on improving access to social services, OakDOT was "simultaneously trying to address this kind of split in how we were understanding the public response, while trying to manage an internal debate about whether we should be doing it at all." All of this was unfolding in the context of Covid-19 and the murder of George Floyd at the hands of the Minneapolis Police Department, which provoked social unrest and a growing demand for social equity and racial justice. Though "some of us were concerned we weren't really speaking to our equity goals," Patton continues, "there was too much political momentum behind Slow Streets that we couldn't stop."[58]

By midsummer, facing popular support for Slow Streets among some neighborhoods but growing opposition elsewhere, OakDOT paused new installations. In September, it began a process to take "a step back to critically evaluate how the program is and isn't working across the City."[59] Prior to the pause, OakDOT had installed twenty-one Slow Street corridors totaling 21.4 miles, along with fifteen Essential Places, through more than five hundred barricades and more than two thousand posters informing the public of these changes. The agency credited the program with creating space for physical activity and lowering traffic volumes without impeding essential street functions or resulting in fatal or severe crashes involving pedestrians or bicyclists. It found overall support for the program and positive national attention.[60]

Reflecting on the program, OakDOT acknowledged "the realities of Oakland's inequitable distribution of resources and opportunities, and the disproportionate effects of Covid-19 on Oakland's Latinx and

Black communities." Traffic counts and surveys found that usage of and support for Slow Streets varied widely: highest among wealthier and whiter communities and much lower among essential workers and communities of color. Indeed, those identifying as Black and African Americans reported using Slow Streets less than all other groups.[61] Respondents even perceived the design strategies differently, with those in the city's diverse East End believing that the barricades were neither strong enough nor "decipherable from construction materials" to discourage dangerous driving behavior.[62] While many communities were most interested in slowing traffic on neighborhood streets, those in the East End were more interested in safety on major corridors.[63]

These street transformations and tensions played out at the street level in different ways, neighborhood by neighborhood, even block by block. In affluent North Oakland neighborhoods, Slow Streets were welcomed by the community, at least at first. One North Oakland resident who lives on Colby Street told me she and others had argued for traffic calming for decades; OakDOT had installed traffic humps, but "we were advocating taking a more rigorous approach." She explains that they'd had limited success, and then suddenly:

> Fast forward to pandemic. . . . Instantly, with no dialogue, discussion, whatsoever, Slow Streets were implemented. Our neighborhood was over the moon. . . . Our kids got out on the street, talking to neighbors . . . taking over the street, everyone was taking over the street and engaging in ways we hadn't seen.[64]

She even found that her Slow Street became a destination: "People from different parts of Oakland were saying, 'We're going to explore every single slow street.'"

Neighbors on adjacent streets shared this sentiment, among them Andrew Armstrong, a planner and sustainability consultant by professional background. Armstrong supported the idea of Slow Streets at first: "Conceptually, it feels like a wonderful idea, giving people safe recreational space in neighborhoods, and during the pandemic was great." While there was minimal consultation from the city, he and others recognized it was an emergency, and traffic was light all over. Like many, Armstrong embraced the Slow Street on his adjoining street: "Kids could go down and skateboard and scoot. . . . There was a bit of novelty."[65]

As the pandemic waned and traffic volumes increased, the dynamics shifted and people living on streets parallel to the Colby Slow Street started to see spillover traffic. "We went from loving the idea to the unintended consequences on my street," Armstrong observed, which included a "really interesting social dynamic in which residents on the Slow Street loved it and were mobilizing to keep it, but the neighbors on adjacent streets were like, 'Hey, wait.'" Armstrong believes the intent was good and many planners shared his concerns, but without systematic planning, for the broader road network "it felt like there were very few beneficiaries of it and inequities to most everyone else."[66]

Overall, Oakland DOT found Slow Streets and Essential Places programs to be beneficial and recommended continuing them for the length of the stay-at-home order but made significant modifications in the second phase. The agency committed to daily maintenance of barricades and cones, evaluating and modifying Slow Streets according to their context, and placing more emphasis on key corridors. Instead of OakDOT staff selecting locations and design, new or modified Slow Streets would engage community partners and neighbors and seek input through resident surveys. It sought to improve Slow Streets signage, install additional treatments at major intersections, and upgrade barricades to more durable materials, even commissioning a local artist, according to the program's website, "to imagine design solutions that were aesthetic, durable, and culturally relevant to East Oakland neighborhoods."[67] Though still at the start of the pandemic, OakDOT's review of the program in September 2020 looked to the future, hoping to "channel the enthusiasm for Slow Streets into equitable and sustainable programs like pop-up Slow Streets and neighborhood level traffic calming."

As local streets were recast as pandemic places for neighborhood walking and socializing, they also remained a focus of OakDOT bicycle planning. To help advance its 2019 *Let's Bike Oakland* plan, in June of 2021, OakDOT issued a new *Neighborhood Bike Route Implementation Guide.* It defined neighborhood bike routes as comfortable, calmed local streets where bicyclists have priority but share roadway space with automobiles, marked with shared-use arrows and designed for traffic calming. While such guidance did not focus on the place-based function of streets, it emphasized their design for multimodal accessibility and safety through low volume and speeds (20–25 mph). It limited closure to local streets where through traffic was unwarranted, where most residents wanted it, and where there wouldn't be adverse effects on neighboring streets. The guidance focused on traffic-calming techniques and intersection improvements instead. Though the guidance does not cross-reference the Slow Streets program, among ideas for future discussion it contemplated enhanced signage to promote wayfinding and foster placemaking that would "engage communities in a collaborative design process . . . depicting neighborhood identities" while wrestling with proper markings and recognizing that "concerns have been raised that local residents may perceive such markings as a harbinger of unwanted gentrification."[68]

Pandemic Slow Streets and Essential Places came to an official end in January 2022 when OakDOT announced that it was pulling barricades and developing a permanent program embedded within wider planning. In presenting this shift to the public, officials acknowledged the challenges in the first two phases of the program. While intended to be temporary, the program's two-year duration proved too long for temporary materials. With time and reopening, Slow Streets saw declining use as more people returned to driving. Overall, the program saw "waning support" and growing complaints, especially from neighbors concerned about the "privatization" of local streets and the diversion of traffic. The agency admitted that the program drew staff resources that might be better focused elsewhere.[69]

For residents who loved their Slow Street, this reverse was a disappointment. "As fast as it went up is as fast as it went down," an anonymous resident of Colby Street in North Oakland recalled. Neighbors rallied and gathered hundreds of signatures. "We love this and want it to be permanent. . . . We've been trying to put some pressure on," she continued, but "the last response from the department has been, you know, 'We don't have the capacity. This is not a priority.'"[70] Neighborhood resident Andrew Armstrong is more critical: "We've got this situation to where the neighborhood could be slowed, and everyone could benefit," but absent systematic planning of Slow Streets helped to "exacerbate inequities as an unintended consequence."[71]

As it ended the pandemic program, OakDOT acknowledged such "strong and mixed" reactions across the city. According to its website:

130 Slowing the Street

Bicyclist and pedestrian advocates lamented the loss of these streets as active transportation corridors. Residents along the Slow Streets complained about the return of cut-through traffic and higher speeds. People were frustrated by no longer being able to use the streets to socialize with neighbors and let kids play. Other residents welcomed the removal of the barricades that had made it difficult for them to get into and out of their neighborhoods. Residents on nearby parallel streets welcomed the end of traffic being diverted to their streets.[72]

Continuing, OakDOT's website listed some key lessons from the experience:

People want comfortable and safe public places to walk, bike, jog, and socialize. In lower income communities of color, issues like housing, work, childcare, and public safety were more pressing than using street space to recreate. People broadly care about traffic safety. Motor vehicle use on many streets effectively excludes most other uses from those streets. No one likes cut-through traffic or speeding on their street. In the early and dark months of the pandemic, Slow Streets did bring joy to many people, families, and neighborhoods.[73]

Subsequently, drawing on these lessons, OakDOT announced it would develop a permanent Slow Streets program with notable shifts in strategy. First, it proposed continuing and expanding Essential Places' traffic calming with a focus on dangerous corridors and places "serving our most vulnerable residents," using quick-build strategies toward systematic upgrading with permanent improvements. Second, it planned to merge the concept of Slow Streets with neighborhood bike-route planning to better serve pedestrians, bicyclists, and micromobility users and to "advance these streets as community space." New Slow Streets would be selected through long-range planning, designed according to a newly revised *Slow Streets Implementation Guide* (readapting existing bike-route guidance), and implemented through long-range capital and paving plans with proactive community engagement and outreach. Third, it sought to ease permitting for neighborhood-initiated pop-up Slow Streets that close neighborhood streets for block parties, enabling residents "to use their streets as community space." OakDOT was frank in its self-critique of the program to date and the challenges ahead, including ongoing tensions between comprehensive planning and neighborhood initiative, between through movement and neighborhood places, and between local goals and state traffic laws.[74]

In early 2023, OakDOT planners presented the permanent program that maintains the name Slow Streets itself, which it suggested "simply says what it means":

> Slow Streets are for pedestrians, bicyclists, and micro-mobility users with limited local access for motor vehicles. Slow Streets provide public spaces for residents in Oakland's neighborhoods. Slow Streets are slow in practice and in name. Slow Streets form a network for human-powered movement and play.[75]

OakDOT redesignated a Slow Streets network from seventy-five miles of neighborhood bike routes already in its 2019 bicycle plan, systematically evaluating the city's hierarchy of streets to reclassify some collector roadways as local Slow Streets and revising bike-route plans to set target volumes and speeds for vehicles. In presenting these changes to policymakers, OakDOT planners emphasized the goal of balancing multimodal access with the street's potential as open space. The permanent program aims to balance through traffic by walkers and bikers with neighborhood livability through public engagement with standard citywide mechanisms like design guidance, capital improvements, and paving plans.

Designating a network as slow is one thing, but designing it to work that way is another. OakDOT is aiming for a 15 mph design speed not through closure but through traffic calming. OakDOT planners have acknowledged publicly they learned lessons about barricades "the hard way": closures and diverters can still be a tool where volumes and speeds exceed targets but will only be implemented through robust planning.[76] Everywhere else, OakDOT would reduce speed and volume through traffic-calming devices and subtle cues like signage and markings (Figure 13). Patton admitted the challenges of strengthening a distributional approach with better community engagement. Citywide planning identifies where needs are but not necessarily how to meet them, which requires engaging people "where the needs are and what are the solutions that meet those grounded needs."[77] OakDOT continues to try and find a sweet spot between the efficiency of plan-based, standardized approaches and local engagement, connecting with neighbors more directly in the permanent Slow Streets program to get broader input and let local residents know what to expect.

Ultimately Oakland's Slow Streets program may have been launched with a big splash, but in our interview Patton expressed the value of incremental change that "gives people time to adjust their views and their social patterns as we go along. That kind of incremental change with space for social adjustments along the way is a really important point for keeping a constituency pointed in the right direction and not create a counter constituency." In the process, OakDOT is trying to build coalitions of interest. "We really want to harness that progressive transportation advocate vision," Patton suggested, while helping to "leverage that NIMBY mindset to a progressive end," linking neighborhood desire to slow their local streets with citywide bike planning goals without just diverting traffic to antagonize neighbors one street over. Patton hopes that Slow Streets might ultimately transform not only the

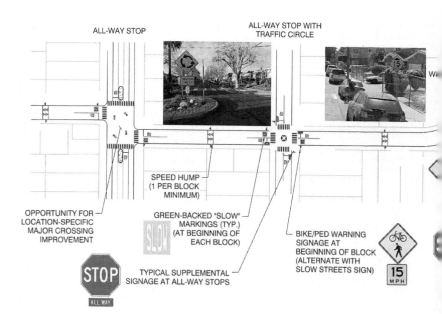

transportation network but also the public realm: "Designed for slowness, these streets also become places within a neighborhood.... The immediacy of the street for informal and unplanned activities makes it available to everyday life in an easier manner than a nearby park." Thus, Slow Streets could thereby help support travel between neighborhoods as well as "shared life" within them.[78]

Oakland's Slow Streets program is perhaps ultimately notable for its ambition, the complex equity issues it revealed, and the ways planners are working through them. It represented an unprecedented rethinking of public streets as both safer transportation spaces and shared public places, but it revealed stark differences in perception and usage across the city's diverse neighborhoods, challenging Oakland planners to be careful in shifting from pop-up pandemic experiments to a permanent program. In the process, Oakland's Slow Streets program reveals the challenges of approximating intersectional mobility justice. Promoting a citywide approach to safety improvements through wider planning

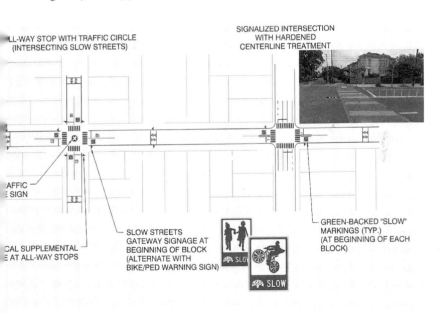

Figure 13. Oakland's permanent Slow Streets program adapts bicycle-boulevard techniques to prioritize pedestrians, cyclists, and neighborhood livability. Diagram courtesy of City of Oakland, California, Department of Transportation.

frameworks promoted distributional equity. At the street level, the program is explicitly multimodal, using traffic calming and reduced speeds to promote fair access and sharing among all users. In terms of social difference, however, the program struggled to recognize and engage diversity across neighborhoods. By trying to promote sustainable transportation and reduce future climate impacts, Slow Streets advanced intergenerational equity. Such improvements may not carry the same cultural freight as bike lanes, so they may raise fewer green gentrification concerns, though Patton acknowledges it's a matter of time before houses are marketed as being on a Slow Street. "Without dealing with basic income inequality, what we do will tend to reproduce the inequalities we already have," he admits, "and I don't know how to solve that."[79] What they can offer underserved neighborhoods is traffic safety, however, and a chance for diverse local voices to be better engaged with citywide planning.

Oakland's Slow Streets—in their ambitions, successes, and travails—reflect the complex equity issues involved in reclaiming roadways from cars. They highlight the need to confront these issues not as something incidental to a technocratic planning and design process but as integral to robust public discourse about who streets ought to serve. Achieving a perfectly intersectional street in Oakland may be impossible, given diverse and conflicting perspectives, but a network of 15 mph Slow Streets planned for citywide access with neighborhood input moves in that direction.

Traffic Calming, Slow Streets, and Neighborways in Pittsburgh

Pittsburgh is a hilly former industrial powerhouse that largely developed in the nineteenth century around walking and streetcars but whose narrow and steep streets became crowded with vehicles over the twentieth century. However, in recent decades Pittsburgh has increasingly committed to public safety, multimodal accessibility, and equity on its public streets. Given the geographical challenges of building new walking and biking infrastructure, planners and advocates have sought to reallocate existing street space through traffic calming, Neighborways, and pandemic Neighborhood Slow Streets programs.

Pittsburgh has been committed to Complete Streets since 2015, when then-mayor Bill Peduto issued an executive order in pursuit of "the vision of zero traffic fatalities." A year later, Pittsburgh adopted a Complete Streets policy that sought to "assure access to safe, non-motorized mobility options" and stated that "streets form nearly half of Pittsburgh's public space and therefore the City must consider the impact of right-of-way design on the public realm," particularly since many residents lack access to quality open space.[80] Recognizing the link between transportation and equity, the city created a new Department of Mobility and Infrastructure (DOMI) in 2017 with the mission "to provide the physical mobility necessary to enable the social and economic mobility of the people of Pittsburgh through the management, design, improvement, and operation of the public right-of-way."[81] Though Pittsburgh has, until recently, lacked strong traditions of comprehensive planning, the importance of the city's streets gained increasing prominence in related planning efforts like the OnePGH resilience strategy (2017) and its *Climate Action Plan* (2018).

These policies and plans emphasized new multimodal infrastructure like bike lanes and multiuse paths, but the city's narrow rights-of-way and reliance on on-street parking pushed planners to seek other solutions within neighborhoods. After some quick wins on key corridors, bike advocate Eric Boerer, advocacy director for BikePGH, realized that expanding bike infrastructure was going to be tough, so he began asking, "Now what?"[82] City staffers were arriving at the same conclusion, leading Kimberly Lucas, former deputy director and now DOMI director, and her colleagues to realize they needed to slow streets.[83]

After overcoming the initial misconception among city engineers that speed humps were illegal under state law, DOMI launched the Neighborhood Traffic Calming Program in 2019 to install speed humps on residential streets (Figure 14) and longer, flatter speed tables on commercial streets. The program was initially designed to be neighborhood driven, requiring more than 50 percent of property owners on a block to sign a petition requesting traffic calming. In the first and second years of the program, DOMI received only forty to fifty applications, however, leading DOMI project manager Sean Stephens to conclude by 2020 that this "weird caveat" requiring property-owner permission, favoring whiter and wealthier neighborhoods, was "inequitable" and the agency needed a different approach.[84]

At the same time, DOMI launched Neighborways, a related initiative to designate low-traffic residential streets as connections within

Figure 14. Pittsburgh's Neighborhood Traffic Calming Program helps make speed humps standard features on neighborhood roadways. Photo by author.

and between neighborhoods as safer, more comfortable alternatives to busy arterial streets. Though particularly oriented to expanding the bicycling network, Neighborways use traffic calming, in the words of the project's website, "to keep speeds slow and safe for all users."[85] They were limited to low-speed and low-volume streets and designed with context-sensitive tools, including speed humps, mini traffic circles, curb extensions, shared-use markings, and distinct signage to designate the corridor and to provide wayfinding for cyclists and pedestrians. Planned in 2019 to be constructed in 2020, Neighborway locations were guided by the bicycle and pedestrian planning process and were designed in consultation with local residents.

One of the first Neighborways to be planned traversed the Bloomfield and Friendship neighborhoods (also known as Coral-Comrie Neighborway for the streets it traversed), connecting a variety of the city's East End neighborhoods and linking them through existing bike infrastructure. DOMI planners consulted with local residents and bike-ped advocates, including Bruce Chan, founding member of Bloomfield Livable Streets, which already had experience advocating traffic calming. "We had already gotten speed humps," Chan recalled, and to celebrate "we had a party, a hump-viewing party." When the group learned of plans for a Neighborway, "we were excited. . . . We knew the general route, we wanted to give support but also wanted to give our input . . . and to reach out to the public and advocate, since change is a big thing." The Coral-Comrie Neighborway leveraged an already low-volume street frequented by cyclists and formalized it with signage, speed humps, neighborhood traffic circles, shared-use markings, and other intersection improvements (Figure 15). These weren't going to entirely remake the street, Chan admits, but these investments could build on what was already there to open the street to new users.[86] Neighborhood resident Julie Albright recounted:

> We were thrilled when we discovered that the Neighborway would be mere steps from our house. Coral was a street my family often traveled prior to this change, on foot, on bikes, and by car—but to know that it was designated as a Neighborway made me feel safer when I took my six-year-old on her bike or scooter. I had more confidence that drivers would be slower and more careful. My husband and daughter also took longer bike rides, following

Figure 15. Pittsburgh's Neighborways create low-speed, low-volume alternative routes for pedestrians and cyclists through simple techniques like signage and traffic calming. Photo by author.

the Neighborway as far as she could. The designated path was a motivator.[87]

The Neighborway designation changed her perception of the street in unanticipated ways. A neighborhood cat roams and sometimes sits in the middle of the street, but now she says "I'm not as worried that he'll be crushed by a car!" She has become more—even "disproportionately"—outraged when people speed on the Neighborway, but she admits, "I'm on a Neighborway high horse, I suppose."

These traffic-calming efforts were building steam in early 2020 when Covid-19 hit, providing a foundation for pandemic efforts. In mid-March 2020, Mayor Bill Peduto declared a state of emergency, closing schools, limiting large gatherings, and encouraging social distancing, followed by Pennsylvania Governor Tom Wolf's stay-at-home order limiting travel to only essential services. After the initial lockdown, the city sought ways to reopen safely. In early May of 2020, Pittsburgh created a Task Force on Streets and Mobility that was charged with identifying challenges facing the city's businesses and opportunities for using streets differently to support them. The task force and subcommittees met and within two weeks provided the *Street Life: Supporting the Vitality of PGH People and Places during COVID-19* report, which focused on supporting businesses with opportunities like curbside dining and finding ways for people of all ages to get outside in their neighborhoods. Looking to models like Oakland, the report suggested "either prohibiting vehicular traffic altogether or limiting it only to low speed local vehicles."[88] Though the pandemic was the immediate context, DOMI leader Kimberly Lucas told me that "reclaiming the streets is something that has been talked about for decades. This was our opportunity."[89]

Shortly thereafter, Pittsburgh announced a pandemic Neighborhood Slow Streets program enabling local residents to request that their low-volume residential streets be designated as safe places for socially distanced outdoor activity. Tosh Chambers, then policy analyst with DOMI (and now with the public-private partnership Move PGH), recalled the uncertain early weeks of the pandemic: "We didn't know how long exactly it would last; a few weeks in, we realized it was going to be around a while. . . . This changes how people interact with other people, especially in public space."[90] Concerned simultaneously about social distancing, mode choice, and activating public space, "we thought, we want to make public space more safe and welcoming, but for those who wanted to be socially distant." In contrast to existing traffic-calming and Neighborways programs, each of which involved systematic planning and design, Neighborhood Slow Streets were to be a more tactical intervention that could advance long-term goals. Chambers recalled, "We really believed in the Complete Streets vision for Pittsburgh and saw this as an opportunity. We believe streets can be more than a space for transportation, but also can be a place for play, community gathering . . . overall community enjoyment."

DOMI quickly issued *Neighborhood Slow Street Guidelines* suggesting that discouraging all nonlocal traffic and encouraging very low speeds could create "more places for our community to safely walk, run, bike, scoot, and roll." Like the traffic-calming program before it, pandemic Neighborhood Slow Streets were neighborhood driven, requiring sponsorship by at least one resident per block with preference given to those applications with widespread support among neighbors and neighborhood organizations. DOMI's selection process prioritized contiguous blocks to form a connected network and weighed proposals in relation to geographical and democratic criteria, street classifications and adopted planning priorities, the application's demonstrated outreach, and local capacity to maintain the barriers.[91]

Pandemic Neighborhood Slow Streets—like existing traffic calming and Neighborways—were not technically closures; they used signage, barriers, and cones to discourage through traffic and limit speeds. Sandwich-board signs were developed that read, "Neighborhood Slow Streets . . . Local Traffic Only," with images of pedestrians, cyclists, and a car (in order from left to right). They also stated, "Share this space safely! Wear face coverings, distance when possible, and drive slowly." Once Slow Street applications were approved, DOMI placed the barriers and signs, but they required applicants to maintain their condition and proper location. The program emphasized that these measures were merely pilots and could be canceled with the streets returning to prior operations if DOMI determined they were not producing the intended results.[92]

The thinking behind these pandemic responses reflected that of a new *Bike(+) Master Plan* already in the works and published in June 2020, which articulated a vision of a "safe, comfortable, and convenient bike network for all types of riders and all types of trips." Though specifically a bicycle plan, its primary object extended beyond bike infrastructure to rethink the public street. It offered a vision of the future in which "walking and bicycling are the most joyful modes for short distance trips." The plan proposed extending the Bike(+) Network through officially designated Neighborways managed to limit volume, slow traffic, and provide street spaces "comfortable for all ages and abilities."[93] The growing realization that neighborhood-driven improvements didn't produce spatially equitable results prompted planners to recommend a regular assessment to assure fair distribution citywide while prioritizing vulnerable populations. They also proposed regular engagement with groups representing people with disabilities to "ensure access for all, with particular attention to those with mobility impairments."[94]

Overlapping efforts to slow traffic and reclaim streets as public spaces accelerated during the pandemic to become increasingly embedded in long-term transportation planning. In September 2021, DOMI published a comprehensive transportation plan called *Envision 2070: Mobility in a Sustainable Pittsburgh* with a "vision for a connected, equitable, and sustainable city with livable and living streets." The plan is guided by ideas of mobility justice, arguing that "transportation is a human right. Achieving an equitable city requires equitable transportation access. . . . The Vision provides for dignified travel for all, irrespective of income, race, or ability." It argued for actively and effectively managing streets to maximize public benefit by creating "people-centered streets."[95] The plan recognized that "for the last century, cities have devoted the majority of the public [right-of-way] to moving and storing cars" but promised "over the next half-century, Pittsburgh will rebalance this equation. . . . The City will share street space more equitably among the many modes demanding movement" by approaching such public spaces more "holistically."[96]

As Covid-19 waned, Pittsburgh phased out the pandemic Neighborhood Slow Streets, removing barricades and signage. In its place, it announced an expanded, permanent Neighborhood Traffic Calming Program that solicits applications from neighborhoods but screens for eligibility, evaluates according to engineering criteria, and filters according to DOMI's equity index. The program has been very popular, with DOMI reporting 946 applications in its first two years. Of those, it evaluated 427 eligible applications and constructed 56. "At this point we're

142   Slowing the Street

a victim of our own success; people pretty universally want it," DOMI Director Lucas told me, leading the agency to consider making it an opt-out instead of an opt-in program and standardizing traffic calming in the design of neighborhood streets.[97]

Pittsburgh's Neighborways, Neighborhood Traffic Calming Program, and pandemic Slow Streets emerged from a growing commitment to multimodal equity, public safety, and climate action to become a successful pop-up and ultimately a key long-range transportation strategy. Catalyzed by the specific challenges of Covid-19, evolving thinking about mobility and infrastructure in Pittsburgh increasingly focuses on the role of roadways as public places that reflect community values and prioritize walking and biking over cars. All of this starts with the question of speed (and indirectly volume), answered through the simple but powerful tool of the speed hump.

To what degree do these traffic-calming strategies really reclaim Pittsburgh's streets? DOMI staff have documented reduced traffic speeds and increased bike ridership, but other changes, though less tangible, may be more socially significant. Stephens told me:

> It's one of those hard things to measure. I know that there are many locations where we've done speed humps where the neighbors are super grateful. A council member has likened traffic calming to something like winning the lottery. . . . One neighborhood celebrated with a block party. It changes how the street feels in many cases. It's not like we're adding street trees; it's a minor improvement, but it's a major change in how the street operates.[98]

Boerer agrees, noting of traffic calming, "It's pretty amazing how many people really want to see this," and while Neighborways "can seem like a half-assed approach to bicycle infrastructure, but done right it works pretty well."[99] Chan admits the changes to his already low-volume street weren't radical but signified to him that the "city cared about multimodal mobility," and formalizing the street as a multimodal space helped him as a cyclist to feel "more dignified on it. I belong here."[100] Pandemic-era Neighborhood Slow Streets may have been shorter-lived, but they did illustrate the potential to engage people with their street in new ways. "Some of the success really depended on the applicant, the resident on the actual street, how well they could socialize this idea on their street,"

Chambers recalls. Some places lacked consensus and the barriers eventually migrated to the wayside, but "in other cases those signs just took over more and more of the street. We had a lot of active utilization to try and sanction off the street to some extent. . . . It was taking on a life of its own."[101] Indeed, Lucas noted that some neighborhoods still maintain the Neighborhood Slow Streets signs and barricades years after the program formally ended.[102]

From a neighborhood perspective, slowing and calming streets goes beyond traffic safety to help shape a local sense of place. Albright has observed how the new Coral-Comrie Neighborway has changed her Friendship neighborhood for the better. The corridor is now a "lively place to be, especially after work and in warm weather," she told me, as the street corridor has become more popular with kids and people walking their dogs. Infrastructure improvements have also helped change neighborhood dynamics. "People have planted vegetables, herbs, and flowers in the roundabouts that were installed with the Neighborway, so that gives the street a pretty, communal feel," she continued.[103] Such placemaking potential prompted Chan to wonder if Neighborways "are just glorified bike routes, or are they a stepping stone . . . to rethink streets entirely?"[104]

As it rolled out these programs, DOMI increasingly sought to bolster its growing emphasis on equity in planning, policy, and design. For a decade, Pittsburgh has directly tackled the issue of multimodal equity through Complete Streets and Vision Zero, increasingly by taming speeding cars so that other modes might share the roadway. Though it has shied away from full closures or Shared Streets, its traffic-calming efforts—and especially pandemic Slow Streets—prioritized biking and walking over through traffic. Lucas admits the challenge of making transformative safety improvements at a wider scale to have a wider impact. For that, she told me, "It's gotta be more than speed humps."[105] Another challenge has been balancing the procedural equity of neighborhood initiative and input with a citywide view of spatial and distributional equity. Early on, DOMI relied exclusively on applications, but it has since increasingly screened and scored via its equity index to ensure a fair geographic distribution, with special emphasis on disadvantaged neighborhoods.

Such planning has defined equity primarily in terms of transport-related social differences and inequities (e.g., age, ability, access to a car) and not explicitly made an effort to reduce racial inequality, but its emphasis on the most vulnerable users and economically disadvantaged neighborhoods nonetheless addresses social justice. Lucas notes that Pittsburgh elected its first Black mayor, Ed Gainey, in 2021, so the city is "prioritizing engagement. . . . We're very intentionally focused on closing the racial disparity gaps." For DOMI, that means rethinking transportation planning and multimodal infrastructure—Lucas admits "bike lanes have been contentious." For example, the agency recently completed a pedestrian-focused mobility plan in Homewood, one of the city's historically Black neighborhoods, including one of the city's first complete neighborhood sidewalk inventories. "We've been intentional in selecting those places," Lucas said.[106] Though Pittsburgh has witnessed significant gentrification, the emphasis on traffic calming over major infrastructure may help foster greater livability and expand public spaces without involving the kind of major investments that could accelerate displacement.

However, speed humps, Neighborway signage and traffic circles, and pandemic Neighborhood Slow Street barricades don't fully reclaim Pittsburgh's streets for multimodal access or public space. Yet their relative simplicity belies a significant reordering of Pittsburgh's public right-of-way. Through basic traffic calming, the city hopes to slow vehicles and make walking and biking safe, convenient, and joyful. Viewing streets as more than multimodal transport space, Pittsburgh now seeks to reclaim streets as public places that "reflect the values of our community."[107]

A More Livable City, One Speed Hump at a Time

As efforts to reclaim streets go, traffic calming is hardly the most radical. By law and design, calmed streets remain transportation infrastructure with limited opportunities for social life. Yet seemingly modest changes to the form of roadways can significantly transform their function. Sharing streets among diverse modes of travel creates contested and often asymmetrical relationships. In such settings, speed—as a multiplier of mass and potential inducer of traffic volume—becomes the critical variable determining how safely the road can or cannot be shared. Thus, the growing movement to slow streets represents a fundamental challenge to the hegemony of vehicular speed and volume and a first and important step to making streets more equitable and livable.

These techniques are not new. For a century, even as cities remade roadways as high-velocity and high-volume piping systems for cars, they sought to balance circulation and livability on neighborhood streets. For the past fifty years, cities have experimented with adjustments to local streets in both horizontal and vertical dimensions to discourage speed and through traffic. Some have gone further to conceptualize shared or woonerf streets that substantially slow traffic enough to invite pedestrians to reclaim their historic place on the roadway.

The movement to slow streets, already underway before Covid-19, accelerated during the pandemic as people sought open-air transportation, recreation, and places to play. While some cities like Boston continued on with traditional traffic calming, others like Oakland and Pittsburgh suddenly installed barricades on local streets to close them to through traffic, encouraging walking and biking instead. These measures were temporary and not without controversy, and since the pandemic, most barricades and signs have come down. In each case study, however, the desire to enhance safety and quality of life on local streets that grew during the pandemic has endured in permanent traffic-calming programs, integrated with long-range transportation plans and regular paving programs, and focused on cost-effective and scalable techniques. Slower streets may not displace cars, but such measures can help return roadways to a greater balance between modes and their role as multipurpose transportation spaces. Though slow or calmed streets are not public spaces in the full sense, they shift streets toward more shared spaces at the heart of more livable neighborhoods.

Are traffic-calmed Slow Streets really equitable, though? The answer is complicated and only partially affirmative. Compared to the dangers, modal inequities, and poor quality of life of car-dominated streets, Slow Streets advance greater equity among modes, giving nondrivers a fighting chance to share the street. In these case-study cities, improvements have been situated within citywide plans toward a more equitable distribution of mobility and access, balanced against the procedural benefits of inviting neighborhood initiative and input. Planners have learned lessons from erring too far on either side of that spectrum, whether in Oakland's case by the political perils of top-down planning or the inequities seen in Pittsburgh and Boston of letting neighborhoods decide which communities should get these resources. These programs increasingly seek to address social disadvantage, defined primarily in terms of age and reliance on alternative modes, though they have become more attuned to social differences like race and income. Efforts to divert through traffic raise tough questions about who local streets belong to, especially since closures can signify a sense of neighborhood exclusion for some; thus, with the tapering off of the pandemic, barricade diverters have given way to traffic calming. While these public investments in livability and sustainability could play a role in urban change and gentrification, as they are increasingly engineered as standard features, such infrastructure could help avoid the controversy that sometimes surrounds bike lanes by fostering streets that are just green enough.

Calmed streets are still transportation spaces, but they reclaim them from heavy, speeding traffic, a first step toward shared public spaces. As simple as barricades and speed humps may seem, however, they raise complicated equity questions in theory and practice. Planners are working through them, if you pardon the pun, slowly.

5

OPENING THE STREET BY CLOSING IT

Calming streets makes them safer for cyclists, pedestrians, and neighbors, but even at slower speeds, it's hard for nondrivers to share the street with cars. Only by moving beyond calming to more aggressively limiting speeds and traffic can streets approximate shared transportation spaces and public spaces. In short, opening streets to nonmotorized travel and social life may take closing them to cars.

Closing streets is a tradition as old as the streets themselves. American cities have always made provisions for excluding vehicular traffic for holiday parades, festivals, or temporary markets, but these have been limited to occasional days and mere hours. Only within the past twenty years have cities experimented with regular events to close streets to cars for longer periods for active transportation and recreation, inspired by the international Ciclovía movement. Others have experimented with more regular, temporary closures focused on schools and children's play. With the onset of the Covid-19 pandemic, a number of cities expanded these concepts to more regular and ongoing closures.

This chapter recounts the evolution of so-called Open Streets from temporary events through pandemic-era closures to more permanent programs. What exactly constitutes an Open Street is a fairly open question. The nomenclature varies across cities: what some call "Open Streets" others call "Shared Streets," "Play Streets," "School Streets," etc. Their natures vary also in terms of both space (ranging from limited access at

147

148   Opening the Street by Closing It

very slow speeds to full pedestrianization) and time (from single-day events to permanent closures). Open Streets, like these efforts to reclaim roadways, exist on a spectrum. Yet all share the practice of at least partial closure to prioritize walking and biking while preserving the street's primary transportation function.

These evolving street closures—whether full or partial, labeled Open, Shared, or something else—reveal the power to transform transport infrastructure into a more fully public sphere, suggesting pathways for progressively reclaiming the roadway in both space and time. Controversies surround such changes and raise difficult equity issues. Their adoption and evolution have been uneven, laying bare the enduringly powerful hold of vehicles on the street. They also suggest the potential for reclaiming a more equitably shared street by simply closing it to cars.

From Parades to Guerrilla Takeovers to Open Streets
Historical Precedents for Closing Streets

For as long as American cities have opened streets to transportation flows, they have also periodically closed them to traffic.

American streets have long made space for commerce. The first farmers' market on record was established in Boston in 1634, and by the early years of the republic, nearly every town of any importance had one, often outdoors on the street.[1] This could create tensions between free circulation and market functions (and structures), but transport and commerce were often complementary, manifested in the wagons that transported goods and provided a place to do business. In the late nineteenth century, the relevance of street markets declined and Progressive Era reformers sought to push mobile vending (and with them immigrants and other groups associated with the so-called pushcart evil) off the street in favor of smoothly circulating traffic.[2] But farmers' markets, often on public streets, persisted and surged again in the late twentieth century.[3]

Streets have long hosted processions and parades that folklorist Susan G. Davis calls the "public dramas of social relations."[4] Their public ritual and festive culture can be "vital elements of political life."[5] Parades can be both patriotic affairs and ways for other groups to provide what urban geographer Sallie A. Marston calls "demonstrations of community power and solidarity."[6] These traditions continue today in events like Pride parades, which have provided "loud, colorful, and joyful celebrations of LGBT identity" since the 1970s, yet sociologist Katherine McFarland Bruce asserts they also "do the serious work of protest by challenging cultural meanings as marchers and spectators publicly revel in the joy of being themselves."[7]

Streets are natural venues for public protests. As soon as America's new Constitution was drafted in 1787, Pennsylvania farmers were blockading roads to protest governmental policy.[8] At nearly every historical juncture, Americans have taken to the streets, most recently in nationwide protests of George Floyd's murder by Minneapolis police. In reclaiming roadways from transportation, albeit temporarily, protesters ask important political questions accompanied by a call and response—heard from the Stonewall Inn in New York in 1969 to the Minneapolis Police Station in 2020—"Whose streets? Our streets!"

Streets also provide social space for neighborhoods to gather. Socializing on the roadway dates to colonial times and flourished in nineteenth-century cities. In 1923, the *New York Times* described how "New York foregathered in Summer in neighborhood streets and on its stoops." Such "jollification" surged during World War I but retreated with the following automobile era, only to be sustained by emerging neighborhood groups.[9] Amanda I. Seligman's research on Chicago's block clubs traces how neighbors, particularly in Black neighborhoods, used block parties to build networks seeking broader improvement efforts.[10] Other responses were more organic. Hip-hop, for example, is attributed to a 1973 high-school dance party overflowing onto the streets of New York's West Bronx.[11] The *New York Times* stated in 2019 that "New Yorkers, we live on top of one another, so it's only natural that sometimes we spill out onto the concrete . . . to enjoy the summer together. . . . No cars are allowed. . . . This is the New York City block party."[12]

Finally, streets have long been places for play, typically informal but sometimes organized. In 1914, New York police commissioner Arthur Woods, concerned about the effects of tenement life, sought to expand public places for children experiencing poverty to exercise. A new Police Athletic League closed streets on the Lower East Side, turning a normally bustling commercial corridor into a place for music, sport, and recreation.[13] Play Streets proved so popular that they immediately expanded across Manhattan and the outer boroughs by the 1920s and continued

150   Opening the Street by Closing It

to transform public streets through the twentieth century, leading the Police Athletic League to boast of a century's work that "fearlessly helped communities take back their streets."[14]

From Ciclovía to Free and Open Streets

More recently, cities have increasingly closed streets for events promoting active recreation and placemaking, often under the banner of Ciclovía or its variants.

Rooted in bicycle activism and traced to 1960s programs like Seattle Bicycle Sundays, the Ciclovía movement emerged with the 1974 closure of eighty blocks in Bogotá, Columbia, for *La Gran Manifestación del Pedal* (The Great Pedal Demonstration). From its beginning, the event looked beyond recreation to advocate multimodalism and public space, and its instant success inspired organizers and the city government to institutionalize Ciclovía as a transportation movement and policy tool. In the 1990s, this effort also came to be promoted internationally as a social strategy to combat urban violence through building a *cultura ciudadana* (citizens' culture). By the turn of the century, weekly events in Bogotá were attracting a million users over seventy-five miles of closed streets.[15]

Other cities across Latin America and the world took note, and a policy network emerged to promote a bilingual official Ciclovía manual.[16] In the United States, San Francisco created a Sunday Streets program in 2008 to transform streets "into car-free community spaces for all to enjoy."[17] That same year, New York City hosted its first Summer Streets, closing a 6.9-mile route through Manhattan. Oakland, California, created its own Oaklavía event in 2010. Simultaneously, Los Angeles inaugurated CicLAvia "to temporarily close streets to car traffic and open them to Angelenos to use as a public park."[18] Philadelphians instituted Philly Free Streets in 2016, closing a ten-mile route as a "people-powered initiative" to help reimagine streets as public spaces and use closures as catalysts for "reinforc[ing] community revitalization."[19]

What started as pop-up events quickly became a movement. In 2011, the new nonprofit Open Streets Project was founded and developed the *Open Streets Guide,* arguing that "by temporarily removing the danger of motor vehicles, open streets provide a novel type of public space that helps people make social connections and lets them view their city through a new lens."[20] It offered the "Open Streets Toolkit" to help in planning and operation, framing Open Streets as a way to reimagine streets as "paved parks" for diverse people: "We need to use our existing assets to their greatest potential. . . . We can get so much more from our streets!"[21]

By the end of the 2010s, more than ninety communities across the United States were periodically hosting Open, Sunday, Summer, and Free Streets events, ranging in size and frequency. They share a common goal of inviting people, in the words of cultural anthropologist and mobility justice advocate Adonia E. Lugo, "to come out into the street and reimagine life there through their own bodily practice."[22]

Green Alleys

As cities experimented with temporary roadway closures, they also explored the potential of transforming backyard service streets into Green Alleys to address environmental concerns like stormwater management and urban heat island effects while also creating shared public spaces. Alleys have traditionally served mundane functions, but they are an important part of cities' physical and social infrastructures and represent a significant portion of the roadway network. Cities seeking to reduce combined sewer overflows to comply with the Clean Water Act while avoiding massive infrastructure projects looked to alleys as green infrastructure to reduce runoff and promote infiltration.[23] Chicago pioneered these efforts as early as 2006, followed by others like Philadelphia, Seattle, and Washington, D.C.

Though Green Alleys were primarily a response to environmental challenges and driven more by sanitation and public works than transportation agencies, these roadways are reimagined for both slow transportation and public space. For example, the Los Angeles Department of Sanitation adopted *Green Streets and Green Alleys Design Guidelines Standards* in 2009 and partnered with the Trust for Public Land to develop neighborhood-scale Green Alley master plans. In the process of redesigning these roadways as green infrastructure, these entities also sought to increase access to quality open-space and recreation opportunities, especially in underserved areas.[24]

Drawing on such experiments, the National Association of City Transportation Officials (NACTO) included standards for Green Alleys in its 2013 *Urban Street Design Guide.* "The majority of residential alleys have low traffic and infrequent repaving cycles, resulting in back roads with potholes and puddling that are uninviting or unattractive," but the guide promoted the potential of sustainable materials, pervious pavements, and effective drainage not only to manage stormwater but also to "create an inviting public space for people to walk, play, and interact," through careful design and lighting.[25]

Pandemic Open Street Standards and Beyond

The success of temporary Ciclovía-style events and Shared Street and Green Alley retrofits provided models and a toolkit for cities to respond to the Covid-19 pandemic described in the case studies below. For national context, however, it's important to note efforts by NACTO to quickly promote street closures as a Covid-19 response in its 2020 *Streets for Pandemic Response and Recovery.*

As noted previously, NACTO has worked to develop multimodal street-design standards, with a growing emphasis on public placemaking. As urban officials confronted the challenges and opportunities of the pandemic, NACTO organized a Covid-19 Transportation Response Center to compile emerging and evolving practices to address immediate pandemic needs, but in the process they suggested that "as we recover, we must continue to align street design and recovery strategies to ensure that the existing inequalities and challenges that this virus is magnifying are not exacerbated."[26]

NACTO promoted street closures as a key strategy, including Open and Play Streets limiting traffic to essential services only to "provide safe space for physical activity, play, distant socializing, etc.," though they did not envision seating or structures on the roadway (Figure 16). Market Streets used barricades and signage to exclude vehicular traffic and to indicate vendor and customer zones and pathways. School Streets provided a "car-free on-street space for schools and care facilities" as well as "safe routes to schools."[27]

NACTO's pandemic guidance emerged from local experimentation to provide nationwide models for visualizing, planning, and implementing Open Streets closures. Though presented as temporary pandemic solutions, NACTO suggested that all these changes could be made permanent.

Opening the Street by Closing It   153

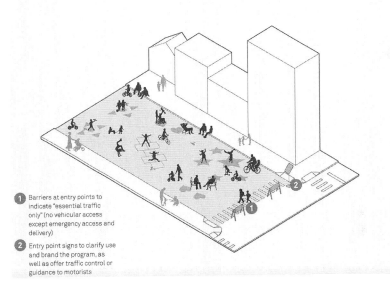

Figure 16. During the pandemic, NACTO produced guidance for closing roadways such as Open and Play Streets. National Association of City Transportation Officials, *Streets for Pandemic Response and Recovery* (Washington, D.C.: Island Press, 2020). Reproduced by permission of Island Press, Washington, D.C.

Case Studies in Opening (Closing) Streets

Prepandemic experiments in closing streets, particularly through short-term events, provided a foundation for more lasting Open and Shared Street closures in leading cities like New York, Denver, and Los Angeles. They reveal the power of something as simple as a barricade and signage for reclaiming the roadway, but the uneven and ongoing evolution of these programs highlights the complex opportunities and challenges of closing streets equitably.

Open Streets in New York City

New York City is America's densest and most walkable large city and has long-standing traditions of roadways shared among diverse modes of travel and social activities. Its pandemic Open Streets program was,

154 Opening the Street by Closing It

however, unprecedented in size and scope and has become a permanent strategy key to the city's plans of transforming "streets into public space open to all."[28]

Rethinking public streets has become ever more central to the city's general plans, strategic transportation plans, street-design manuals, and programs. The 2007 comprehensive *PlaNYC* emphasizes multimodal transportation and public-space goals to "re-imagine the public realm."[29] This was followed by the Plaza Program launched in 2008 to "transform underused streets into vibrant, social public spaces" within walking distance of residents.[30] New York Department of Transportation's (NY DOT) 2009 *Street Design Manual* provides detailed standards for converting streets into plazas to "create a vibrant public realm with high-quality public spaces," which the Bloomberg administration piloted most prominently in the progressive transformation of Times Square from a congested vehicle intersection through temporary closure with barricades, street furniture, and paint.[31] Based on the success of tactical strategies, the city hired Norwegian design firm Snøhetta to redesign the street as a public plaza, which was completed in 2017.

At the same time, the city increasingly experimented with shorter-duration street closures. In 2008, it announced a Summer Streets program to close roadways to traffic on three consecutive summer Saturdays for people to walk, run, bike, and play as a "celebration of New York City's most valuable public space—our streets."[32] The city also partnered with community organizations on Weekend Walks to temporarily pedestrianize neighborhood and commercial streets. When he announced these events, Bloomberg cited the example of Bogotá to tell local reporters that "cars are important, but streets are there for everybody."[33] The inaugural Summer Streets event in 2008 attracted fifty thousand pedestrians and bicyclists, and twice that many attended the following year. Local media called it "One Big, Car-Free Block Party."[34] Within five years, participation grew to 250,000 people over a 6.9-mile Summer Streets route and twenty-four neighborhood Weekend Walks.

These trends gained speed through the 2010s, advanced by the new de Blasio administration and updating of the *One New York* comprehensive plan, which maintained an emphasis on sustainability but also strengthened the commitment to social justice. The plan argued for street closures as a way to "expand the use of our streets as places to play, congregate, and be together" within an "integrated system" of interconnected parks, sidewalks, pedestrian plazas, and other open spaces.[35] The updating of NY DOT's *Street Design Manual* increasingly featured physical redesign strategies like Shared Streets alongside interim and permanent plazas and, for the first time, formalized programming strategies to activate roadways as public space.[36] Some closures were intended to be one-day events like Summer Streets. Others were multiday conversions like Summer Play Streets over the summer, School Play Streets during the school year, or Seasonal Streets to transform roadways into "pedestrian priority spaces that deliver public space" on weekends.

The Covid-19 pandemic presented a novel and historic challenge, but New York was already primed to rethink its streets. On March 12, 2020, Mayor de Blasio announced a state of emergency and later the closing of all nonessential businesses and gatherings, social distancing and masking guidelines, and the limitation of public transit and outdoor activity to solitary exercise. From the beginning, the city looked to roadways as a pandemic-response tool. Kyle Gorman, then a senior project manager in NY DOT's Public Space Unit (and now assistant director of public realm partnerships and programs), told me in our interview that the city's history "set us up for success to some degree. . . . There are hundreds of years of history oriented to walking, biking infrastructure." Building on the work of prior administrations, "there already was a lot of work happening related to pedestrian plazas, bike lanes, temporary closures. . . . We were lucky that infrastructure already existed."[37]

Within weeks, elected officials proposed closing New York roadways to cars and opening them for socially distanced transportation and recreation. However, there was little agreement on how to do so between the administration (and the New York Police Department) and the city council. Given concerns about public gathering and the perceived need to police social distancing, the administration limited initial Open Street pilots to 1.5 miles and four days per week to be managed by the New York Police Department.[38] Transportation advocates were openly critical of this limited response, and the city council—citing the experience of Oakland—argued for a light enforcement approach and crafted a bill to "allocate more street space to pedestrians and cyclists . . . with a city-wide target of 75 miles of streets."[39] The bill's sponsor, councillor Carlina Rivera, advocated for more trust in NY DOT and communities: "We should allow New Yorkers to have space available to them."[40] By the end of April, the mayor announced a compromise to create forty miles of car-free spaces toward a goal of one hundred miles, including sixty miles adjacent to parks, twenty miles in consultation with local precincts, and ten miles to be managed by local partners like business improvement districts.

From the outset, the Open Streets program was both a public-health strategy and a way to advance long-standing planning goals to promote walking and biking, provide open space, and advance equity. Gorman admits staff was primed for the unique opportunity of the "rolling back of the bureaucracy and the red tape that allowed us to do this."[41] Juan Restrepo, a community organizer with the nonprofit organization Transportation Alternatives, recalls, "We saw that the pandemic was an opportunity to radically rethink the role of streets in people's lives. . . . Any street can become part of the public good."[42] The first Open Streets were announced in early May of 2020 to span seven miles across five boroughs. Marking the event, city council Speaker Corey Johnson said, "Today is a great first step and an exciting day for an entire city starved of adequate open space."[43] Though the program was intended to be by neighborhood request, the city announced an initial set of closures that were mostly connected to parks.

New York's dynamic Open Streets emerged from creative interplay between city officials and community leaders. This is exemplified in the story of Thirty-Fourth Avenue in Queens, one of New York's largest and by many measures most successful Open Streets. Jim Burke, community activist and transportation advocate, recounts the early days of the pandemic in which their Jackson Heights neighborhood was "hit hardest with Covid and first."[44] Residents, many immigrants with lower incomes, were cooped up in crowded apartment buildings and intergenerational households and could not decamp from the city like wealthier residents. The neighborhood's narrow sidewalks and very limited open space also made outdoor social distancing hard. When the city started experimenting with Open Streets, it included just a few blocks in Jackson Heights adjacent to a park, managed by the New York Police Department. "When you came upon it, it looked like a crime scene," Burke recalls, and people diverted around. So locals decided to create their own "guerrilla Open Street" by installing a sandwich board that said "Local Traffic Only," and they put on their own orange vests to help manage it.

> We invited people out, literally from open windows, and people came out. The street filled up. Cars came up, they saw the sign and turned. Kids were playing, people were socializing. . . . We said to the city, "This is how you open a street. This is how you run it by the community, not through the police." . . . We said to the police, "We'll run it," and they said, "Great."[45]

Burke and others organized a new Thirty-Fourth Avenue Open Streets Coalition, which NY DOT ultimately entrusted to be the custodian of the Open Street. This was a novel challenge for the community, but from the outset the organization sought to go bigger. Instead of just a few blocks on Thirty-Fourth, "We said, no, the whole neighborhood," he recalls, leading to a twenty-six-block Open Street across the entirety of Jackson Heights. And they marshaled the many volunteers needed to set out and remove barricades on "every single street, every single morning and every single evening," and a cleanup crew to minimize complaints. With so many people helping, "a lot of people through that process became personally invested in the Open Street," he notes, and creatively "all those things kept building."[46]

Lessons learned from street-level experimentation were formalized in Open Streets policy. Limited Local Access Open Streets became standardized on NY DOT's website as "designated for pedestrian and cyclist use and enjoyment" but allowed for limited-use, local vehicular access like parking, picking up and dropping off, local deliveries, and emergency vehicles. No through traffic was permitted, and drivers were advised "to be extremely cautious and to drive 5 mph or slower." NY DOT provided a "typical setup" for Limited Local Access, including a graphic showing people walking, biking, and rolling down the center of the street, cars parked (but not circulating) on the street, and barricades with signage reading "Do not enter: Except pedestrians bicyclists & local vehicles" (Figure 17).[47]

Alternatively, NY DOT provided for Full Closure Open Streets to "allow for a range of car-free activities that support local businesses and neighborhoods, and create a safe place for New Yorkers to gather." These closures permitted no vehicular access or parking, but they did

Figure 17. New York City created more than eighty miles of Open Streets during the pandemic, designated as either Limited Local Access (*above*) or Full Closure (*below*). Image courtesy of City of New York, New York, Department of Transportation.

require a clear, fifteen-foot emergency lane. These closures went beyond slowing the street for active transportation and recreation to "support[ing] multiple uses, including outdoor dining and community programming." The typical setup diagram for Full Closures reflected this important distinction, depicting people of all ages walking, biking, and rolling on the street and sitting down at café tables on the roadway. In contrast to parklets or other full public-space conversions involving durable or permanent structures, everything about the Full Closure Open Streets could be moved or removed at a moment's notice. Later, NY DOT introduced a new Open Streets variant called Full Closure: Schools to support drop-off and pickup, recess, and outdoor learning. The program prohibited vehicular access and parking, but it required maintenance of a clear fifteen-foot lane for emergency vehicles.[48]

These barricades closed the streets, but transforming the roadway into a public space requires programming. Leslie Davol of Street Lab, a nonprofit dedicated to public-space design and programming, has long partnered with NY DOT. With the pandemic, she remembers that "the first response was to close the street for walking and biking, because you can't take the subway," but barricades were not enough to change the culture of the street: "If there's not constant use, the drivers plow right through."[49] Established organizations like Street Lab had the tools to do public placemaking, in part through programming to improve the urban environment, strengthen neighborhoods, and "bring New Yorkers together."[50] This was new for emerging groups like 34th Avenue Open Streets Coalition, however. Yet Burke recalls, "We immediately started programming, right from the first day," with games, English as a second language classes, yoga, etc. "I grew up in the Bronx. We played in the street. We owned the street, because that's where the room is," Burke recalls, "so for me, having this program was important to educate people 'the street belongs to us.'"[51]

By the end of summer 2020, NY DOT had expanded Open Streets over seven rounds to encompass eighty-three miles, more than any other city in the United States. At the same time, it permitted outdoor dining on closed streets through an Open Restaurants on Open Streets program—also referred to as Restaurant Piazzas—on 2.6 miles of roadway along twenty-two streets. And even as the pandemic led to the cancellation of popular annual Summer Streets and Weekend Walks,

160   Opening the Street by Closing It

NY DOT offered Open Streets as one alternative. The city's program garnered nationwide attention and plaudits from diverse commentators. In June 2020, the *New York Times* op-ed writers cited the program as part of a "golden moment" for tactical urbanism: "A viral twist of fate has given us a chance to alter the balance, creating streets that work for everyone."[52] Planetizen blogger James Brasuell wondered in an editorial "if the car has finally met its match."[53] Transportation advocates were, however, disappointed that the program did not go further. In September of that year, Transportation Alternatives issued a progress report entitled "The Unrealized Potential of New York City's Open Streets" that commended NY DOT for its hard work but found a "disconnected network of public space islands with management challenges" and noted that, despite heightened awareness of racial equity, Open Streets were concentrated in wealthier, majority-white neighborhoods. Transportation Alternatives argued for reinforcement and expansion of Open Streets, making the program permanent, employing permanent materials, and locating new Open Streets in areas with the least open space and fewest transportation choices.[54]

Calls to make Open Streets permanent were echoed prominently on the pages of the *New York Times,* whose editorial board observed in late November 2020:

> It took a pandemic, but New York City is seeing more clearly than ever that its roadways can do more than move cars and trucks. In a year with so little solace, New York's streetscape has brought steady relief. It's just one example of the many opportunities before the city in the months and years ahead to reimagine how its residents can live, work, play and get around town.[55]

On December 18, the *New York Times* feature article "How New Yorkers Want to Change the Streetscape for Good," written by Matthew Haag, lauded the "organic takeover and reimagining of the city's streets" and suggested that "people reclaimed the pavement and are, by and large, unwilling to give it back."[56]

In response, de Blasio announced a permanent outdoor dining program in September 2020 and a permanent Open Streets program in April 2021. At the signing ceremony (on an Open Street), the bill's sponsor, councilwoman Carlina Rivera, argued that "Open Streets aren't

just a solution to social distancing challenges posed by the pandemic—
they are a successful model for pedestrian prioritization."[57] The mayor
echoed these sentiments: "Open Streets transformed our city and changed
the way we came together as communities. . . . COVID-19 is temporary, but getting the most out of life in New York City is permanent."
The permanent program formalized Temporary Limited Local Access
and Temporary Full Closures, incorporating pre-Covid-19 Weekend
Walks and Seasonal Streets. It applied these same standards to Full Closures: School with the difference that they could only operate during
school days.

The permanent Open Streets program remains neighborhood
driven and managed, though to assist underresourced communities NY
DOT offers funding assistance according to equity goals in the *NYC
Streets Plan,* including operations and maintenance services for high-
need locations. In partnership with organizations like Street Lab, NY
DOT placemaking staff can help bring "arts, culture, fitness, and educational experiences to neighborhoods in need."[58] NY DOT has opened
the door to mobile vending beyond dining to include sales of general
merchandise, arts and crafts, and ticketed events.

Open Streets are now part of New York's landscape and NY
DOT's long-range transportation planning. Gorman, reflecting on the
experience of the pandemic program, comments, "I think it was one of
the best examples, because of very dire circumstances, that if you build
it they will come."[59] Based on the success of Open Streets, the city's
2021 *NYC Streets Plan* emphasized the importance of "creating streets
that are pleasant not only for walking through but also experiencing in
other ways." After safety, equity was a top goal, defined in the plan as
"prioritizing resources for communities in need of greater transportation mobility and access." From public engagement, NY DOT learned
that respondents strongly supported Open Streets both as a Covid-19
response and as a way to invest in diverse places traditionally deprived
of public investment, and they recommended prioritizing Open Streets
in neighborhoods proximate to transit and commercial corridors that
lack green-space access.[60]

Though Open Streets have waxed and waned over the course of the
pandemic and beyond, what Gorman describes as "two steps forward,
fifty steps back," the commitment to rethinking streets as public spaces

162   Opening the Street by Closing It

has become firmly established in New York.[61] At its pandemic peak, the city had converted 274 streets over a total of eighty-three miles into car-free or car-limited spaces, but by 2021 they were reduced to 126 active street closures over forty miles. By the summer of 2022, Open Streets were further reduced to a mere twenty miles. Nonetheless, by summer of 2023 the city still maintained more than 192 Open Street closures across all five boroughs comprising 365 blocks: 191 blocks of Full Closures, 261 blocks of Full School Closures, and 112 blocks of Limited Local Access closures. The majority of these blocks are closed just a few days per week, but about 100 are full-time closures (mostly Limited Local Access).[62] While these reflect a reduction in the number of Open Streets over pandemic heights, advocates like Jackson Chabot and Emily Chingay of the nonprofit Open Plans suggest that this may not necessarily be a bad thing: "Sometimes it's almost tough to assess the success of the program because it's been a moving target," Chabot says, but they contend that today there are "fewer but higher quality."[63]

Some of the most successful Open Streets have begun to transition from temporary closures to permanent reconstruction. Gorman notes that "from our perspective, from DOT, we say 'places are not made, they are grown'" to suggest "we're trying to grow all Open Streets to become more permanent improvements of public space."[64] In Jackson Heights, Thirty-Fourth Avenue has been designated as a permanent Open Street, and local stakeholders are working with NY DOT on long-range plans, according to Burke, to "envision it, with a zillion hours of community input," and redesign the street "as a series of rooms" with context-sensitive designs to create distinct public spaces.[65]

All the while, Summer Street events have bounced back from the pandemic to grow into twenty miles of temporary closures over the course of five Saturdays by 2023, the most extensive span since its launch in 2008. For the first time, in 2023 Summer Streets were extended to all five boroughs as key elements in the public-space strategies in Mayor Eric Adams's "Working People's Agenda," alongside a commitment to hire a new director of the public realm to coordinate public and private investment "to create extraordinary public spaces across the entire city."[66]

The creation of these new Open Streets has not been without controversy, of course, particularly as some of these closures are made permanent through redesign. In the fall of 2023, police arrested a protester

Opening the Street by Closing It   163

disrupting a ribbon-cutting for improvements to Berry Open Street in Williamsburg (the taxi driver shouted, "You are selling out New York City!") and an Upper West Side resident for blocking NY DOT workers from installing traffic-calming infrastructure, leading *Streetsblog* to observe that the protester "gave up her freedom for a parking space."[67] Planners and advocacy groups recognize that these changes don't always come easily in neighborhoods. "Historically, we've had a lot of conflict on streets," Chabot admits, recounting the shift from messy shared streets with vendors to a more streamlined and traffic-focused street, and suggests that "we're moving towards more nuance and more complexity, which can lead to more conflict." Chingay adds, "People, they have grown up in the city, it's hard for them to picture something else. . . . But a year later they may end up loving it." So Open Plans views its role as one of change management and conflict resolution "trying to find a middle ground." Ultimately, Chabot and Chingay agree that "it becomes a value question: Do we value parking a metal box or safety for children?"[68]

Altogether, New York's embrace of Open Streets reflects America's most expansive experiment in rethinking the public right-of-way in both substance and geographic scope. Building on decades-long efforts to reclaim streets for multimodal accessibility and public spaces, Open Streets in New York continue to evolve. In the process, they fundamentally changed how New Yorkers experienced their public rights-of-way. Davol describes the power of closing streets and opening them to people, both in terms of process and outcome: "What's been so amazing . . . is this sense of possibility and sense of ownership, when you close a street to think of it as a blank canvas." She describes the experience of kids who start by sitting on the asphalt to create chalk art and then are tempted to lie "face down on the yellow line, the asphalt, one with the pavement . . . that sense of possibility is so powerful."[69] Burke observed similar things when Thirty-Fourth Avenue was closed and what started as a Covid-19 measure became something bigger:

> Suddenly you realize you see people leisurely walking down the street, you saw routines form, kids playing in front of their house. . . . There's a median where people sat, and you'd see people there, at first nodding, and then talking to them, and then suddenly you

engage them in conversation and you become friends with them. It was an amazing community-building tool that we kind of stumbled upon, not on purpose.[70]

Where once traffic circulated, now people can walk, bike, and even dance; where cars parked, now markets have emerged to connect small vendors with neighborhood customers (Figure 18). Restrepo likewise sees a new kind of street life emerging: "We're reshaping how streets work. This process has taken place. It takes a reeducation of an entire city.... There's the aspect of New Yorkers having to navigate a different public realm."[71]

More than just a new experience of public space and community, the closures helped forge community bonds. Gorman observes that a key outcome of the program is that it brought people together who might not have been otherwise: "That community organizing, that community building, has remained even after the pandemic." Gorman continues,

Figure 18. New York's Open Streets, like Thirty-Fourth Avenue in Jackson Heights, Queens, slow or prohibit vehicular traffic to encourage walking, biking, and curbside dining and vending. Photo by author.

"People are more engaged than ever before. I'm not saying everyone agrees about transportation or the public realm . . . but now people are very much in tune with what DOT is doing."[72] Restrepo reflects on this new community role: "It feels pretty new, and the model is pretty interesting, a combination of the logistical and maintenance aspects of Open Streets . . . and an emphasis on activating the space through events, . . . the idea being we can provide a community space as a public good," but he notes that "if you're a newer Open Street operator . . . you have to do a lot of work to build up a grassroots base that really depends on key volunteers" and unpaid labor.[73]

The enthusiasm and burdens of this neighborhood-supported model came through in interviews with local organizers. Brent Bovenzi, a resident of Brooklyn's Williamsburg neighborhood and a volunteer with the local Berry Open Street, got involved almost by accident: "I wanted to go for a walk. . . . I naturally gravitated towards the Open Street, . . . then I stumbled upon events" and volunteered with North Brooklyn Open Streets at a time when "a lot of those volunteers got burned out. I'm part of the second wave."[74] This core group helps to program the Open Street on summer weekends, and though for a long time it was just barricades, the group worked with NY DOT on more permanent improvements. Organizers aren't content to stop there, according to Bovenzi: "Now we're saying, 'What's the next phase of asks? . . . What's a bigger vision of what this could be?'" In the process, Bovenzi has watched Berry Street evolve as both a transportation space and a public place. For example, the barricades are encouraging parents to let their kids ride bikes on the street ("They feel safe doing that"). Boulders installed as part of curb extensions now provide a place to sit down, where Bovenzi has witnessed conversations including a couple breaking up. While outdoor dining is great, he continues, with this new redesign "you are allowed to exist in that space without paying." In the process, the neighborhood surrounding Berry Street has itself been transformed, helping build support for change in the community and buy-in from NY DOT. For many residents, "it's easy to imagine change is bad," Bovenzi suggests, "versus what are the positives and why change could be good."

On the Troutman Open Street in Brooklyn's Bushwick neighborhood, volunteer organizer Kevin Qiu shares similar thoughts on the

166   Opening the Street by Closing It

positive changes and organizing burdens. The area is mostly light industrial with some bars, "a work street almost" during the day; but when closed midday, he sees kids biking on the street, and later people are "sitting especially as it becomes night, young people who couldn't otherwise go into a bar, hang out." By volunteering, Qiu has also become more engaged with others: "I got to know a lot of people on the street through working on it; working on the Open Street you run into a lot of people. . . . You have more of those spontaneous interactions." Yet organizing and programming takes a toll on volunteers: "If it's just two or three people leading the charge, there is burnout. . . . It's cool that we're organizing around it, but many of us are thinking DOT should just do this," Qiu observes.[75]

For these reasons, achieving truly intersectional equity has been a challenge. A program driven by neighborhood request is potentially more procedurally equitable but has created an uneven distribution of Open Streets across the city, concentrating them in wealthier and whiter neighborhoods. This presents issues of both spatial-distributional equity and social justice. Balancing competing bottom-up versus top-down priorities has been a challenge, according to Gorman. New York is a "tale of two cities," he suggests, divided between "wealthy and glitzy" Manhattan, where neighborhoods wanted and were able to manage Open Streets, and other places that may not be asking for Open Streets because they're thinking in more basic terms of sidewalks and stop signs. He admits:

> Quite honestly, it's quite hard to strike that balance. NYC is the quintessential bureaucracy. . . . It's now up to us. Open Streets is now permanent. We're moving away from pandemic to business as usual. . . . We really want to empower community-based organizations, . . . but we recognized there isn't always going to be an organization in every neighborhood who can take this on.[76]

Gorman believes that "the city needs to take a universal approach . . . across the board" that balances an application-based program ("so we're not kind of coming into a place and foisting this onto a corridor") with providing underserved neighborhoods with the resources and funding to expand their capacities. The city has currently budgeted $27 million to provide contract services to maintain Open Streets especially in underserved communities, but Gorman admits this isn't a lot in the context of New York and suggests that at a certain point NY DOT will be asking, "Why aren't we doing this ourselves?"[77] And while Open Streets have been viewed as a pandemic and public-safety response, which aligns with broader goals to expand access to public space, these are public improvements that can contribute to neighborhood change (and gentrification). Many of the Open Streets, again, are in wealthy or gentrifying areas (like Brooklyn), though they have also succeeded in less affluent and diverse places like Jackson Heights. The limited and temporary nature of many of these closures makes them less of a green gentrification concern than other major investments, yet planners who believe in the transformative potential of these open-space improvements are also approaching them carefully through engagement with local partners.

A century ago, New York City led the transformation of urban streets from a public realm into transportation infrastructure—a process that took decades. Today, it's leading the way in progressively converting them back again. Imperfect and incremental as that process may be, it suggests a trajectory toward much more equitable streets in the city's future.

Shared Streets in Denver

Denver, Colorado, has largely been built in the automobile era, but the city's recent policy shifts related to mobility, sustainability, and equity place growing emphasis on reclaiming streets. The city's pandemic Shared Streets program was early and ambitious, gaining national attention for converting almost twenty miles of Denver roadways into car-light or car-free spaces. While the temporary program has ended, a permanent Shared Streets program is being developed, and car-free events continue to grow. Denver's pandemic Shared Streets involved partial closures, sharing much in common with Slow Streets, as well as full closure of fewer streets. These shifts illustrate the possibilities and challenges of truly sharing the public right-of-way.

Denver first adopted a Complete Streets policy in 2011 to accommodate the needs of all users "for a livable, connected, and sustainable city." Subsequently, Mayor Michael B. Hancock signed onto Vision Zero in 2016 through the *Denver Vision Zero Action Plan* committed to

"Build Safe Streets for Everyone."[78] Though focused primarily on safe and convenient access, it also addressed the disproportionate burdens of traffic violence experienced by low-income neighborhoods and communities of color. Simultaneously, the city developed *Denver's Mobility Action Plan,* which featured "reinventing our roadways into complete streets."[79] These shifting priorities are reflected in *Comprehensive Plan 2040,* updated in 2019, which seeks to "maximize the public right-of-way to create great places."[80] In a flurry of transportation-related innovation and planning, in 2019 voters approved a ballot measure creating a new Department of Transportation and Infrastructure (DOTI) from what had been a division within Public Works. That same year the new agency published the *Denver Moves Everyone 2050 Plan* whose theme of "Rethinking Our Streets" introduced concepts like Shared Streets to create "car-free public spaces by closing off streets to general traffic temporarily and permanently."[81] DOTI also began developing the *Complete Streets Design Guidelines* toward a "paradigm shift so that Denver's streets are designed from the outside in," which prioritized the pedestrian and considered "the uses and activities along the street edge in balance with travel demands."[82]

Thus Denver, deep into rethinking streets, was primed to employ roadways as a pandemic strategy. Colorado declared a statewide emergency on March 11, 2020, and the next day, Mayor Hancock issued a stay-at-home order closing most public facilities but leaving parks open for recreation. Denver city councillor Chris Hinds, who represents downtown and adjacent neighborhoods, observed firsthand the sudden need for additional public space: "In our city center, it's pretty dense. People are on top of one another, but you're supposed to be doing social distancing," and sidewalks are often narrow, he says, making it "hard to shoehorn six feet into four feet."[83] Hinds, a wheelchair user and self-described victim of traffic violence who was left paralyzed after a car hit him while cycling in 2008, called on the city to open the roadway so residents could "use an entire street and have physical distancing. . . . We could help people with their sanity." City planner Jay Decker, DOTI transportation and innovation manager, similarly recalls, "With the pandemic, we learned you can't lock people indoors for very long in Colorado," and "We scrambled really quickly in a week" to find solutions.[84] Following the model of other cities (e.g., Philadelphia), they proposed temporary, recreational street closures, which Mayor Hancock announced on Twitter on April 3, to "really encourage people to get outdoors and feel safe walking and biking and enjoying outdoors with the proper physical distancing."

Denver designated 5.5 miles of streets in residential and commercial areas as so-called Shared Streets and 10.2 miles of Open Streets in parks (an additional 2.5 miles were added later in June). Open Streets, limited to park roadways and commercial streets with little or no residential parking demand, were fully closed to traffic with barricades (known technically as type three) and Road Closed signs. On neighborhood streets, however, Decker and other planners "felt like we couldn't close them down. . . . Our intention was for these to be Shared Streets" that limited traffic and speeds.[85] On Shared Streets, DOTI installed barricades and signage reading "Road Closed to Thru Traffic" and "Slow Down: Shared Street" with icons of a pedestrian and cyclist above a vehicle. Though not technically closed, these prioritized walking and biking by limiting access and slowing speeds to 5 mph (much lower than traditional traffic calming). In a related program focused on supporting businesses, in May 2020 Denver followed up with a temporary outdoor dining program to "safely expand service capacity" during the height of the pandemic by expanding their operations to sidewalks, streets, and parking lots. It invited applications from businesses and local organizations and permitted private activities in the public right-of-way as long as the closure was done safely, managed people's ability to get around the closure by foot, bike, wheelchair, and car, and maintained emergency access.[86]

These closures put the city in the "lead" among American cities in creating Open Streets for Covid-19 response, according to the planning website Planetizen, second only to Minneapolis.[87] "The city moved incredibly fast," Jill Locantore of the local nonprofit advocacy group Denver Streets Partnership told me: "I've never seen them move so fast. They almost installed them overnight."[88] Though temporary, she suggested at the time in local media that such tactical interventions could show the public the value of "people-first streets" and said that "it's a great opportunity for people to think about whether some of these changes should be made more permanent."[89] Residents began to use the streets in new ways (Figure 19). Locantore and Hinds recall fondly how their neighbors not only came out to walk, bike, and play in the street but also pulled up chairs for conversation or an evening drink.

As summer progressed, people across Denver came to like and value their Shared and Open Streets. A June survey by the Denver Streets Partnership found that 85 percent of respondents had walked, biked, or rolled on a Shared Street and nearly 90 percent of respondents agreed that Denver should reallocate street space for people.[90] An August petition circulated by the partnership garnered thousands of signatures calling on Mayor Hancock to "make the open and shared streets permanent features of our community and expand the network so that they can be enjoyed by people across Denver."[91] Hinds likewise observes that "during the first iteration for a year, a lot of people were frolicking in the street. People would set up lawn chairs in the street. . . . We would have our own physically distanced but not socially distanced get together," so he called on the mayor to make the program permanent.[92]

Figure 19. Denver installed barricades during the Covid-19 pandemic to create Shared Streets that limited through traffic, providing a model for a permanent Shared Streets program. Image courtesy of the City and County of Denver, Colorado, Department of Transportation.

Businesses districts also took the opportunity to close local streets under a separate outdoor dining program, which enabled restaurants and bars to operate in outdoor patio settings adjacent to their businesses.[93] Downtown, two blocks of Larimer Street were closed: one in the historic Larimer Square shopping and entertainment district and another on the 2900 block in the River North (RiNo) Art District. What started as an emergency response with barricades evolved through interim design. The 1400 block at Larimer Square was transformed into a plaza-like space as restaurant seating expanded out beyond the curb, planters were placed along the street, pavement was painted with colorful patterns, and lights and flags were strung between building facades. In 2021, the transformation earned recognition through a Mayor's Design Award for projects based on the "imaginative and innovative way they enhance public spaces and support community."[94] Further north in the RiNo Art District, what started as metal barricades and temporary seating evolved to include planters, sheltered curbside dining, and lighting strung overhead.

Not all neighborhoods were equally enthused with street closures. DOTI had rolled out Shared Streets based on plans and geographic criteria rather than neighborhood requests, and it had done so quickly. In some neighborhoods they were "wildly popular," according to Locantore. In others populated by essential workers reliant on cars, rethinking streets was less of a priority. Without much community engagement, DOTI's top-down approach "kind of backfired in those neighborhoods," she observes; "people were saying, 'What is the city doing?'" She credits DOTI for its agility but observes that "whenever you work that fast, you sometimes leave something out, especially the equity piece."[95]

Building on widespread though not universally positive public feedback, DOTI announced that the Shared Streets program would continue through the fall of 2020. Looking back, Decker observes:

> The biggest thing we learned is that if we wouldn't have had the pandemic, and an emergency measure to do this kind of thing, we probably wouldn't have done it. . . . People would have come out and been negative. . . . We just did it, and people saw it every day, and they came to like it considerably. . . . It wasn't just users, it was neighbors. We learned people really do want us to be aggressive to reclaim street space to be people space.[96]

Planners also found that design really mattered. For example, because type-three barricades were light and easily moved, people moved them. In neighborhoods with split opinions, skeptics moved the barricades out of the street at night, while supporters moved them back during the day. This created a maintenance hassle for DOTI, so the agency switched to heavier, water-filled plastic barricades when they extended the program again in the fall of 2020.

With growing normalcy and resumption of traffic over the summer of 2021, DOTI engineers became increasingly uncomfortable with a temporary Shared Streets program, began to pull the barricades, and proposed planning for something permanent. According to Decker, this provided an opportunity to do more engagement than had been done during Covid-19 and "to figure out where we do want to have Shared Streets, . . . which will look very different from the temporary program."[97] Observers like Locantore express mixed feelings about the evolution of the pandemic-era experiment and disappointment with the decision to end it. In the local media, she expressed regrets that Shared Street implementation wasn't more aggressive "at truly restricting car traffic so that you truly felt it was a safe space to walk in the street."[98] Of the decision to pull the barricades, she was blunt: "They were working really well. . . . The city just removed all of the infrastructure. . . . It wasn't for a lack of interest from community members or use of them; it was the city's unilateral decision to remove them."[99] Hinds was similarly frustrated that Shared Streets had been watered down over the pandemic and "became more car friendly, or more specifically more fire-truck friendly," after which "people retreated to the sidewalk, drivers would exert their dominance." And when DOTI "took it down entirely, they didn't ask council, they just took it down," Hinds complains.[100]

As car traffic resumed on these streets, DOTI embarked on a yearlong process of public outreach to study successes and lessons learned toward guidelines for locating and designing permanent Shared Streets. A 2022 Temporary Shared Streets Survey found that over half of respondents lived on or adjacent to Shared Streets, 90 percent liked them, and 85 percent favored making them permanent. People liked the improved safety for walking, biking, and interactions with vehicles. They also liked the broader livability of these streets, which they considered "quieter and more pleasant" (83%) and provided more space to recreate. People had many ideas for improving the program, including making barriers more effective at controlling cars (or removing them altogether).[101] In a separate Shared Streets Design Preferences Survey, DOTI found that respondents—admittedly mostly white and from mid- to high-income households—wanted places to socialize as well as travel through, strengthened through trees and vegetation and reduced traffic speeds and volumes.[102] In commercial areas, respondents primarily wanted to experience Shared Streets for social reasons, though in neighborhoods they wanted a place for walking and biking, gathering with friends and neighbors, and attending community events. When asked what design elements would make them "want to linger," respondents emphasized vegetation, seating and dining areas, lighting, and social spaces. To improve safety, they asked for traffic-calming elements to reduce the speed and volume of cars rather than signage and barriers to divert traffic.[103]

From such input and citywide public meetings, DOTI proposed a permanent Shared Streets program aiming to "prioritize people through creation of comfortable spaces to move, interact, and play within the right-of-way."[104] It suggested that Shared Streets should be located on local streets or designated Neighborhood Bikeways (though not on bus routes or adjacent to regional land-use centers) and that resources should be allocated based on DOTI's equity index (which combines social variables like race, household characteristics, and measures of access). Though pandemic-era Shared Streets had been launched in a matter of weeks, the permanent program will be implemented through the slower wheels of annual capital planning and budgeting. For planners like Deckcr, this represents an opportunity to methodically transform a few streets per year, using so-called quick-build strategies—what they call "paint and post"—to redesign streets on an interim basis with the longer-term goal to "come back at some point and formalize them."[105] But Locantore regrets the shift from an experimental approach to the slower and more limited rollout and challenges the idea of quick build as "a misnomer. . . . It can take years for the city to do even just paint and post projects," and full capital projects might take five years to plan and another to construct. She wonders aloud, "How is this ever going to be a network of shared spaces? We're going to be lucky to get maybe half a mile of Shared Streets a year."[106] Hinds expresses similar disappointment: "We're wrestling pretty hard right now to make sure [the] pandemic is a change" and not just an event to be gotten through. With all the major challenges facing the city, including public-safety issues like pedestrian and cyclist deaths, climate change, and more, he laments, "If DOTI is going down the path of incremental change... that doesn't make the equity statement I'm looking for or the people are looking for."[107]

Other street closures in commercial areas have endured and are being formalized through a permanent Outdoor Places Program with standards for patio spaces on sidewalks, curbsides, and "full-street closure pilots." To fully close a street, applicants must go through a robust process including a mobility study, community outreach, and design that prioritizes accessibility for all ages and abilities and that reflects neighborhood

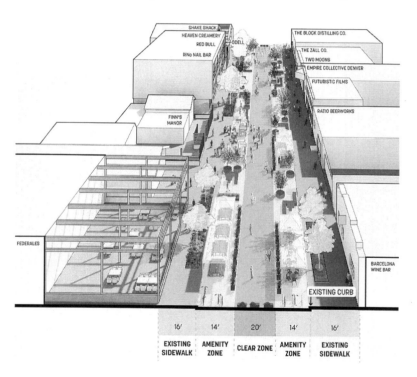

character to "facilitate safe, well designed, privately maintained outdoor spaces that enhance and activate the public realm for everyone."[108] The program is citywide, but closures and retrofits have been focused on downtown. The nonprofit RiNo Art District has applied for continued closure of the 2900 block of Larimer and has begun planning for its permanent transformation. During the pandemic, street-closure permits were "super easy to get," RiNo's co-executive director Sarah Cawrse told me, "but later the city said, 'We're going to develop some standards.'" In their permit process, the organization found that local businesses and residents viewed the changes positively and overwhelmingly (92.8 percent) supported keeping the street closed in 2024, though people asked for more amenities for public seating and mingling.[109] Looking to the future,

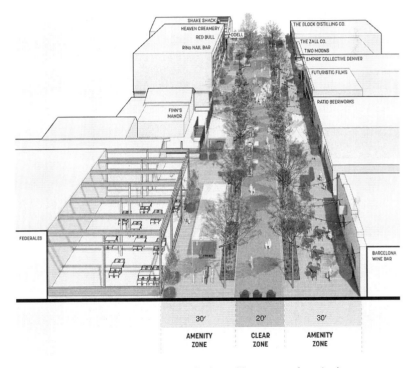

Figure 20. In Denver, the RiNo Art District is seeking to transform Larimer Avenue, which was closed during the pandemic, in phases starting with interim redesign and public engagement *(left)*. If studies support closure, RiNo envisions permanent new features to redesign the roadway as a public space and "vital community amenity" *(right)*. Image courtesy of RiNo Art District and Sasaki.

176 Opening the Street by Closing It

the organization has begun designing for the permanent conversion of the roadway as "a vital community amenity" with new features like furniture, planters, landscaping, and lighting. Business owners have created a nonprofit to maintain such improvements.[110]

Cawrse believes the neighborhood and city are both working toward the same goal, but the process has not been easy. "The city is looking for a much better balance between restaurant uses and true public spaces," she acknowledges, and she says this is RiNo's goal too: they want to build on existing improvements with additional chairs and tables toward more permanent redesign "so it functions as a true plaza."[111] But the permitting process involved with even pilot street closure has been onerous, reaching into the six figures. For Cawrse, this raises questions and equity issues. "I think it's a difficult conversation because it's the public right-of-way, which is ultimately owned by the city," she acknowledges, "but it's not really an equitable system the city has set up, since it takes grassroots organizing." This puts a heavy burden on local organizations, leading her to wonder, "What about those areas that don't have a BID [Business Improvement District]? What about those places in neighborhoods where they lack parks?" She wishes the city managed the process in partnership with local organizations. The city touts the program on its website, she observes, but in "putting it back on the community, that creates even more of a distance in equity and opportunity."

As Denver slowly embarks on permanent Shared Streets and Outdoor Places, these closures find common cause with other programs. Some are temporary, like Denver's own Ciclovía event, ¡Viva! Streets Denver. Organized by the Downtown Denver Partnership, the City of Denver, the Denver Streets Partnership, and others, the event "close[s] to cars and open[s] to people" along 3.5 miles of downtown streets, allowing participants to "experience the joys of being car-free."[112] And the city and the Downtown Denver Partnership are collaborating to create a new, multiuse 5280 Trail linking destinations and creating places, including fully Shared Street segments to become "Denver's Living Room." Hinds, in promoting the project, admits he is "trying to do revolution downtown" by promoting streets that are "fully open to the people, closed to cars, but open to the people."[113]

Like New York, Denver is a city whose growing traditions of multimodal planning positioned it to embrace the public street as a Covid-19 response tool, and the pandemic was an opportunity to advance long-range Vision Zero and Complete Street goals. Unlike New York, this western and more car-dependent city did not technically close most streets (despite its initial Road Closed to Thru Traffic signage) but limited through traffic and speeds on pandemic Shared Streets to approximate a space where pedestrians, bicyclists, and cars might safely coexist. Encouraging parity among modes of travel, exemplified by *woonerf*-like signage placing cars beneath pedestrians and bikes, Denver's Shared Streets advanced multimodal equity, even if shy of full pedestrianization. The top-down manner of its implementation can be critiqued on grounds of procedural equity, but it did seek a fair distribution of Shared Streets across the city, promoting spatial equity in access. As the program traditions from pandemic to permanent, planners are seeking a balance between universal public-safety values like Vision Zero and context sensitivity. They seek social and spatial justice by filtering public investments through a DOTI equity matrix and procedural equity through robust public participation while developing its Shared Streets policies and design guidelines. The outcomes of the permanent program are yet to be seen, and those I interviewed expressed frustration with the pace of change, but it nonetheless represents a new vision of public streets.

In their evolution from temporary pandemic responses to permanent program, Denver's Shared and Open Streets and Open Spaces have traded tactical creativity and expansive ambition for more durable but incremental transformation, linked to both structural innovations like new Shared Street design standards and events like ¡Viva! Streets Denver. These reflect a progressive reclamation of the city's streets—if limited in space and time—for car-light or car-free social life. In our interview, Hinds put these efforts in the context of a quote engraved on a downtown municipal office building named for Wellington Webb, Denver's first African American mayor. Echoing the quote, he asks, "What is the city but the people?" and answers by saying, "Shared Streets created a third space. . . . It really helped create part of that community. What is a community but its people?"[114]

Livable and Open Streets in Los Angeles

Los Angeles is known as a quintessential car city, but local policy and planning have come to increasingly prioritize pedestrian and bicycle

178   Opening the Street by Closing It

safety and accessibility while looking beyond multimodalism to reimagine public streets as places with a variety of initiatives. In addition to the Green Alleys program led by LA Sanitation and Environment to transform "uninviting alleys into walkable, bikeable, and beautiful public resources," the Los Angeles Department of Transportation (LADOT) argues that "streets can be more than just places to move people" and promotes diverse public-space programs.[115] The growth of CicLAvia events and the scaling up and down of pandemic street closures suggests both the potential and the challenges of closing roadways equitably in one of America's most car-centric major cities.

California adopted a statewide Complete Streets Act in 2008, which Los Angeles has advanced through transportation plan updates and the *2010 Bicycle Plan* committed to both Complete Streets and a transportation system that enabled street use by other modes and other public purposes.[116] Focused on creating a backbone network of bike infrastructure, it also introduced low-volume and slower Bicycle Friendly Streets (bike boulevards akin to Pittsburgh's Neighborways) and highlighted the importance of equity framed in terms of multimodal access.

Around the same time, local activists inspired by the success of Ciclovía events in Bogotá and elsewhere began discussing car-free events for Los Angeles. The origins of CicLAvia have been recounted in publications by Lugo, who, along with others, drew on a decade of bike advocacy to form a CicLAvia steering committee to propose a weekly city-run program demonstrating the diversity of the city's bike movement.[117] In scouting routes, however, organizers came to view the event as being about more than transportation. "Through our eyes, heavily congested, car-dominated stretches of Los Angeles became a series of potential sites for people on bike or on foot to see and sit," Lugo writes. "Each of us wondered, what would be the most transformative route that would allow people to see the same L.A. from a new perspective?"[118] The inaugural CicLAvia on October 10, 2010, closed 7.5 miles of streets to encourage residents to walk and bike through a route traversing Los Angeles's most densely populated and diverse neighborhoods. Thirty-thousand people participated and organizers like Lugo "saw nothing but smiles on the faces of people who may have never cycled before on the streets of Los Angeles."[119] Not only did CicLAvia open streets for use as a "public park . . . free for all," in the program's words, it also helped shape local and regional transportation policy as organizers gained strength to introduce CicLAvia as an element in the updated bicycle master plan. In the process, the event also revealed their limits as bike organizers and advocates to engage marginalized communities. "We assume that normalizing cycling will eliminate the gap between poverty and elite cycling," Lugo recalls, "without conceptualizing where these groups meet."[120]

In a separate but related initiative, concern for urban environmental issues like stormwater management and the effects of urban heating on public health prompted calls to reimagine backyard service alleys into Green Alleys. The 2008 *Transforming Alleys into Green Infrastructure for Los Angeles* report by local planners at the University of Southern California highlights disparities in open-space access and suggests alleys are "a valuable resource in land-scarce and park-poor communities throughout Los Angeles." Drawing from innovations in Chicago and elsewhere, the report recommends creating Green Alley plans and pilot projects.[121] In 2009, LA Sanitation published *Green Streets and Green Alleys Design Guidelines Standards* to highlight their "potential to be converted from impervious surfaces to permeable surfaces or Green Streets."[122] Though framed primarily in terms of stormwater, it recognized the potential of alleys for improving recreational opportunity, walkability, and neighborhood connectivity. To test these strategies, LA Sanitation (renamed to include "and Environment") collaborated with the Trust for Public Land to develop neighborhood-scale Green Alley plans and pilot installations. The program focused first on relatively lower-income and diverse neighborhoods, including North Hollywood and then South LA. In 2010, the Trust for Public Land developed the *South LA Green Alley Master Plan* to guide the transformation of alley segments across the city's historically Black but increasingly Hispanic South Side.[123] One of the first pilots was the Avalon Green Alley Network, which was opened in 2016 to treat stormwater and reduce urban heat but also to connect parks and schools through "valuable green space with features such as vines and trees and educational opportunities in the form of signage and artwork in the form of poetry."[124] The success of these pilots led to a permanent Green Alley program and installations elsewhere in the city.

Public discussion about the greater possibilities of the public right-of-way gained particular momentum with the election of Mayor Eric

Garcetti, whose very first executive order in 2013 was a Great Streets Initiative that argued that "neighborhoods begin with their streets, streets that are based on walkability, transit, and serve as community hubs." Beyond multimodal access, he also emphasized that "our streets and sidewalks are the largest open space resources that we have."[125] In 2015, Garcetti issued an executive directive launching a citywide Vision Zero initiative to reduce traffic fatalities to zero by 2035 and creating an inter-departmental Vision Zero steering committee to recommend short- and long-term actions. LADOT developed the *Mobility Plan 2035* in 2016 as an update to the city's general plan and as a policy foundation for achieving a transportation system balancing the needs of all road users, which called for "adaptive reuse of streets" for multimodal access and as public spaces that are "vibrant settings for social interaction."[126]

These policy and planning priorities are articulated in the 2015 *Complete Streets Design Guide,* which argues that "Los Angeles' streets serve a much larger purpose than just moving cars. . . . They can provide lively gathering places that foster community building and neighborhood identity."[127] The plan reimagined the roadway surface as neighborhood Shared Streets designed with traffic calming and landscaping (and an operating speed of 5 mph) to provide "a slow-speed environment where cars, bikes, pedestrians, and scooters are able to all comfortably utilize the same space" and as pedestrian plazas repurposing low-volume streets into "pedestrian-oriented public spaces."[128] LADOT formalized these in updated standard street dimensions in 2015 and later through the 2020 *City of Los Angeles Supplemental Street Design Guide,* which includes traffic-calming features like curb extensions, raised crosswalks, crossing islands, and traffic circles.[129]

At the same time, LADOT launched new programs to match this vision. Street plazas are one concrete example of infrastructure and pro-gramming to reclaim streets for public space. When she was working for LA County Health, Margot Ocañas (now director and supervis-ing transportation planner with LADOT) was interested to read about efforts in New York and Bogotá, "so I shut down a street with the police and three hundred people showed up."[130] This led to the Sunset Plaza pilot, which happened to be in Garcetti's district, and Ocañas being hired as the city's first pedestrian coordinator. In 2012, a new People St pro-gram was launched to transform streets into "active, accessible spaces for people."[131] These conversions were application driven and relied on community partners for funding and management. Though temporary, People St installations were designed according to NACTO standards, and LADOT expressed that they might "catalyze permanent roadway-to-plaza conversions."[132]

Simultaneously, LADOT developed a new Play Streets program to temporarily close roadways to create places for play, learning, and "fun for all ages." In partnership with the local nonprofit Kounkuey Design Initiative (KDI), it hosted demonstration events in five "park poor" neighborhoods. In its report on the initiative, KDI observes that in a city "where residents experience a dearth of accessible and safe public space, the 7,500 miles that make up our street network are in-fact the largest public space the City has to offer." Drawing inspiration from historical models like New York's 1914 Play Streets and more recent initiatives elsewhere, KDI defined Play Streets as:

> a neighborhood block, temporarily closed to vehicular traffic and transformed into a public space where residents of all ages are free to gather and play. Play streets can be held for one day only, but are more often recurring—transforming streets into semi-permanent public spaces and creating new spaces for recreation, learning, exercise, and culture.[133]

After initial pilots, the report recommended a second year of experimentation to work out issues like site selection and design guidelines, calling out the challenges of balancing a neighborhood-driven approach with a citywide perspective on "equitable, citywide access."[134]

These prepandemic efforts provided a foundation for Los Angeles's Covid-19 response. After California Governor Gavin Newsom declared a state of emergency, Mayor Garcetti issued a stay-at-home order and shuttered many parks. When it became clear that the pandemic would not pass quickly, many residents started taking to the streets. As other cities adopted Slow or Open Streets, community groups and the mayor's office looked to LADOT to act. Clare Eberle, LADOT transportation planning associate, recalls that "there was an official directive that DOT should launch this program. We were also hearing from community advocates. . . . There was a lot of dialogue. . . . Community members were kind of banging down our door to do something."[135] LADOT

182   Opening the Street by Closing It

prepared to launch pilots, but concern from public-health officials about the risks of mass gatherings led Mayor Garcetti to put the initiative on hold, leading local councilman Mike Bonin to tell reporters, "Folks are really disappointed, particularly, because so many other cities are doing this. . . . People here are saying, 'Why can't we do the same?'"[136]

After an initial delay, Garcetti announced a Slow Streets program in mid-May 2020, inspired by Oakland's efforts, saying, "This is an exciting moment for us to have a little bit of space in our neighborhoods, to do what we're already doing: walking."[137] LADOT's website justified the program as a response to the closure of recreational spaces and aimed "to create an opportunity for people to stay physically active while socially distant by reducing speeding on neighborhood streets."[138] Street-closure materials were designed to be a temporary fix to what LADOT anticipated would be a "short-term problem," including A-frame barricades placed within the roadway, such as Road Closed: Local Traffic Only signs alongside newly crafted signs reading, "Attention Drivers: Slow Down, This Is a Slow Street," with icons of a pedestrian, bicyclist, older adult, scooter, and wheelchair (and no icon of an automobile).

After a halting start, the program expanded rapidly to over fifty miles of streets across thirty different neighborhoods (Figure 21). The program proved popular in many parts of the city, and by the end of summer 2020, almost forty-three miles of streets remained closed as Slow Streets.[139] When Covid-19 caused CicLAvia to be canceled in 2020, the LA Metro Board voted to redirect these funds to longer-term and neighborhood-scale closures, which CicLAvia's executive director supported as part of its wider mission "to reimagine streets."[140] However, others expressed concerns about the program. Driver complaints and the constraints of California state law led LADOT to backtrack on calling Slow Streets "closures" and revised such signage to read only, "Attention Drivers: Slow Down." Others lamented this "watering down" and advocated strengthening the closures.[141]

Los Angeles's Slow Streets, like the pandemic itself, continued over 2020 and into 2021. As traffic increased with the easing of pandemic restrictions, some barricades were removed, but the program endured. As early as June 2020, a city councillor called for LADOT to study the feasibility of a permanent program. The agency quickly learned that strategies effective in the early days of the pandemic were

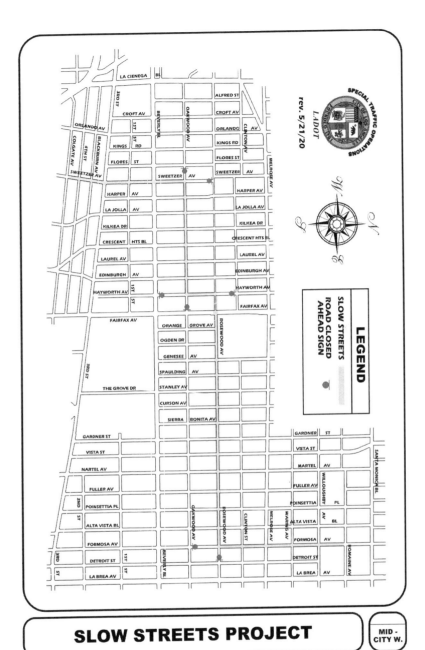

Figure 21. During the pandemic, Los Angeles invited neighborhoods to request their local roadways be designated as Slow Streets, but LADOT has shifted to citywide bike-boulevard planning. Image used courtesy of Los Angeles, California, Department of Transportation.

hard to manage over time. Eberle recalls, "There was a lot of neighborhood support," but "it was getting unsustainable to replace barricades." The agency began to develop an "engineering approach" that identified treatments and materials to reduce speeding while improving their durability. In collaboration with consultants, LADOT developed a tool kit that narrowed down an initially wide set of traffic-calming methods through internal review and community dialogue. "We started going out to community groups. . . . There was a lot of engagement," Eberle told me. "Meanwhile, our engineers were at work refining these and being tasked with creating standard plans" for tactical techniques like painted traffic circles. Though hoping for a standardized tool kit, LADOT staffers learned through the process that "creating a standard design is difficult."[142]

The challenges became even clearer as LADOT began implementing the interim version of what they called their "permanent" Slow Streets program. In 2022, LADOT redesigned and improved twelve Slow Streets in consultation with local communities through gateway treatments, sidewalk signage, and traffic-calming strategies that included mini traffic circles, speed humps, and roadway markings indicating a 15 mph speed limit. This improved local streets, but Eberle admits that "it ended up really looking like a neighborhood traffic management program, rather than an active mobility program. . . . And from DOT's standpoint, we're more interested really in fitting this framework around this goal of creating streets for people to walk and bike safely and take a network-based approach . . . rather than where homeowners would like to have them." They found that this neighborhood-based approach resulted in a fragmented geography of Slow Streets. "If you saw the map, it mostly looks pretty random," Eberle comments. LADOT had applied an equity framework to balance the selection of locations citywide but found it hard to equitably distribute resources like staff time.

> From a planning perspective, I saw very clearly that the neighborhoods . . . with a lot of resources spent a lot of time on their plans, . . . placing very high demand on staff times. . . . Neighborhoods without a lot of resources said, "Great, let us know when it's done." . . . There was a pretty dramatic discrepancy in the amount of resources those plans were getting.[143]

Eberle asked herself, "Did they get better results?" and concluded: "Probably . . . but the equity thing was very real."

While LADOT piloted Slow Streets, California Assembly Bill 773 helped make it easier for cities to close streets permanently, as long as closures were connected to citywide bicycle networks, walkable destinations, or green space; were necessary for public safety; involved outreach and engagement; and had streets clearly signed. Advocating for the passage of the bill, Mayor Garcetti cited "overwhelming demand" for continuing a program that has given "Angelenos access to safe spaces for fresh air . . . essential to mental and physical health," especially in lower-income communities "with dense housing and poor access to parks."[144] AB 773 was signed by the governor in October, and in November, the city council passed a motion directing LADOT to study how to make Slow Streets permanent.

Ultimately, however, LADOT decided to sunset Slow Streets as a neighborhood-driven program and instead develop something driven by a more comprehensive, data-based approach better aligned with the long-range *Mobility Plan 2035.* Ocañas states flatly, "The program is dead in the water . . . but elements have been absorbed by other programs."[145] "When you chase the shiny thing, whether that's for urgent need" without thinking through the long-term issues of resource allocation, Ebele concludes, "it has to burn out or turn into something else."[146] Guided by the department's commitment to "addressing inequities and creating a transportation system that treats everyone with dignity and supports vibrant communities," emphasized in LADOT's *2022 Annual Report,* the agency is trying to be more methodical in selecting and improving a network of slowed streets.[147] "We were using community feedback. It's powerful," Eberle admits, "but not really a citywide planning approach."[148] At the same time, Garcetti-era People St and Play Streets are similarly stalled. Ocañas observes the many challenges of street-to-plaza conversions, which include community demand:

> That whole vetting process is very intensive, and—even more importantly—when we get them installed, we're challenged, as with many things, with maintenance. . . . We'd like to reclaim spaces in areas of highest need, and if we want that to happen we need to go to those areas of highest need, educate the applicants,

186 Opening the Street by Closing It

often who are not of that background. . . . And the burden is, once we install a plaza, we've been required to ask the neighborhood to maintain it. . . . It's hard to find that fiscally strong partner.[149]

As a result, LADOT is moving away from a community-initiated street plaza model, but Ocañas suggests the agency would incorporate plazas when it builds greenways instead.

As pandemic-era closures and Slow Streets wind down or evolve into more limited programs, other longer-running programs like CicLAvia events continue to grow. More than 1.8 million people have experienced CicLAvia since its founding, making it the biggest of its kind in the United States. Over the years, the event's 280 miles of Open Streets have invited participation from 80 percent of the population of Los Angeles County. Framing the event more in terms of open space than transportation access, its website boasts that CicLAvia has "five times more people using its temporary park space during event days than are using all of the other parks in the city of Los Angeles combined."[150] While only a temporary closure, CicLAvia remains committed to the broader idea of rethinking and reclaiming streets. The event is the product of collaboration between the nonprofit CicLAvia and the city, but what was initially community led has become more institutionalized. Eberle, charged with CicLAvia among other Open Streets programs, notes that the agency had been asked to make the event weekly. Though it lacked the budget or capacity, the event has become a regular feature the agency hopes to expand. And whether frequent or periodic, temporary or permanent, for Eberle there is a through line that connects diverse efforts to reclaim roadway:

Whether it's an event or a space that has been repurposed, it really allows us to imagine what the city can be if we took more of that space back. That's the big-picture value. People don't necessarily connect it . . . but I think it works to help people think about it and to encourage us to collectively ask for better, ask for streets that work better for us.[151]

This was a common refrain among commentators celebrating the event's would-be tenth anniversary in October 2020, even though temporarily suspended because of Covid-19. Alissa Walker of *Curbed* magazine writes, "Ten years ago CicLAvia forever changed Los Angeles. . . . What CicLAvia has achieved goes beyond open streets. It has aligned one of the most diverse, inclusive, regional coalitions in LA history."[152] On *Medium*, Aaron Paley comments: "Each CicLAvia shows Angelenos what our streets can look like. For a day, Los Angeles becomes my dream city where the din of cars doesn't drown out conversation. . . . By helping to build and produce CicLAvia, the utopian city I imagined in my youth becomes a real place if only for a Sunday."[153] To the degree that the event has become integrated with other street-reclamation efforts in long-range transportation plans and policies, its impact appears less ephemeral and more enduring. Eberle admits that closing streets in Los Angeles can be challenging, but the success of Open Streets in New York and San Francisco provides inspiration for longer events and closures, and "there are hopes and dreams of reaching that in Los Angeles."[154]

The city's Green Alley network also continues to expand, albeit incrementally. In the San Fernando Valley neighborhood of Pacoima, a Bradley Alley/Plaza project has converted an unsafe and unattractive dead-end street and alley into a public plaza and green infrastructure. The women-led nonprofit Pacoima Beautiful has worked with LADOT, LA Sanitation and Environment, and community members to create "the first planned shared street in the City of Los Angeles, designed to slow traffic, create a safe place for residents to relax, meet up with neighbors, and walk and bike."[155] My interview with four of the organization's young planners and program managers reveals the evolving thinking and growing scope of the project. The predominantly Hispanic neighborhood has experienced historic redlining and underinvestment and has significantly less parkland per capita than the county average. At the same time, neighbors struggle with abandoned vehicles and quality-of-life issues. "Pacoima Beautiful hosted a block party to help clean up the area," recalls program coordinator Barbara Velasco, and this helped to "give people a sense of 'what if this space were for people and not cars?'"[156] This led the organization to work with LADOT's People St program toward more permanent redesign. Pacoima Beautiful's planning director Roxy Rivas adds, "In the beginning, the planners who were on the project were thinking about making the community safer by removing an area that was becoming a nuisance," but "part of the closure was also to create a greenspace that had simply not existed on

Van Nuys. . . . How do we create green space where there wasn't green space before?"[157] Unlike Green Alleys maintaining vehicular access for sanitation vehicles and resident parking, the Bradley Alley/Plaza was closed to traffic by bollards, resurfaced with colored pavements, and improved with some seating to become Bradley Plaza. The new space was successful, inviting new public uses like community gatherings and yoga classes.

The initial design's limited ability to create a welcoming public space soon became apparent, however, especially since it lacked shade and permanent seating. These needs aligned with a new emphasis on urban greening and stormwater through the *Pacoima Urban Greening Vision Plan* led by Pacoima Beautiful and the community organization LA Más. The plan recognized the neighborhood's transition from a suburban community to "a dense and vibrant enclave of newly arrived immigrants and longtime residents" in the face of "conditions detrimental to the health and quality of life of residents." The plan set goals to increase mobility through a network of adaptive greenways to provide public-space access and to create a sense of place.[158] Streets were central to the planning, including proposals for Green Streets, intersections, plazas, and alleys. Building on the success of its initial redesign as a People St, the plan helped inform a second iteration focused on capturing and infiltrating stormwater to improve water quality while increasing mobility for residents of the nearby San Fernando Gardens housing complex. Not simply designed as green infrastructure, the design process—according to Pacoima Beautiful—involved "meaningful engagement" with the community and design informed by resident and stakeholder feedback that includes native plants, a shaded area, and artwork that "showcases the local culture" by acknowledging the Indigenous importance of the land. The new project added new features to the existing plaza, including seating, a shade structure for gatherings or performances, and an outdoor classroom, and it extended the space to the adjacent alley, all installed with ample lighting to enable the 8,500 residents within a ten-minute walk "to have a safe, well-lit area to visit or walk through at night."[159]

The project has created a dynamic new public space while creating novel challenges for Pacoima Beautiful (Figure 22). Velasco sees how the project engages locals: "Community members take ownership of the space" not only during monthly cleanups but on a daily basis; "when the maintenance wasn't what it should have been, and the plants died, people planted their own."[160] The organization has taken a loose approach to management and permitting of the new public space, so it has also taken on a life of its own. "People will host their own meetings. . . . They don't have access to other spaces," Rivas tells me, and sometimes "people ask us if they can use it, and we say, 'Sure, that's what it's there for.'"[161] The planners and organizers in this environmental justice organization are happy with the transformation and believe it has made their neighborhood more equitable. This starts with transportation equity, helping make local streets safer and more comfortable for pedestrians, cyclists, transit riders, and people with disabilities. For project associate Rosa Ruiz, "When I think about Bradley Plaza, it comes to prioritizing the needs of pedestrians, which in LA is something we don't do. . . . These are the kinds of projects we need all over LA."[162] To design such projects in an informed and inclusive way, project lead Shance Taylor adds, takes "as many perspectives and understandings as possible. Someone coming from the outside is not going to have that same experience as the people in the community."[163] But that process constructs not only a public space but also an empowered community. "It takes a lot of community building" to get the space right, Ruiz continues, but "it's never just about the physical improvements; it's about the impacts on people's daily lives, advocacy, and capacity building." In the process, it helps people become empowered by seeing that "this is how you talk to LADOT . . . because it's your right. As someone who lives in LA, this is how you make the noise to get the projects you want done."[164]

In Los Angeles, efforts to rethink streets have been uneven, and their future beyond the pandemic emergency is uncertain but represents a fundamental shift in what has long been known as perhaps America's most quintessential car-centric city. Like the city itself, these policies and programs are somewhat sprawling. But they invite Los Angelenos to experience and lay claim to streets for equitable, multimodal mobility and as public spaces. The uneven and somewhat ephemeral nature of these efforts, which have shied away from both fully closing streets to cars and doing so on a long-term basis, has limited their ability to produce a truly Shared Street, much less create enduring public places. Yet they represent a substantial shift in public policy and discourse, which has produced tangible outcomes in the shape of walkable Green

Figure 22. Activists in Los Angeles's Pacoima neighborhood transformed an underutilized service way into the new Bradley Alley/Plaza through the city's Green Alley and People St programs. Image used courtesy of Pacoima Beautiful Staff.

Alleys, hugely popular CicLAvia events, and a popular pandemic-era Slow Streets program.

Los Angeles planners, as those elsewhere, struggled with how best to close streets equitably. All of these closures are limited in time or their ability to exclude vehicular traffic, but they have opened streets to more diverse users and uses, inspiring a different and more equitable vision of shared roadways. In the process, LADOT has emphasized citywide transportation planning toward spatial equity, guided by an equity matrix that prioritizes improvements in areas with the greatest needs. Experimentation with neighborhood-driven programs, while opening the door to greater community engagement, accentuated disparities in both the kinds of neighborhoods that requested projects and how much staff time they consumed. In a city like Los Angeles, LADOT has found it difficult to leverage pandemic programs to create lasting reclamations of street space. "It is more challenging for us to close streets here in LA than we see other cities doing," Eberle observes, given the scale of the city and its historical and cultural dynamics, which are "compounding and complex and intersectional." She asserts, "We're moving the needle for sure, but it's incremental."[165]

Open Streets from Events to Capital Improvements

Inspired by Ciclovía events, Open and Shared Streets closures surged during the pandemic and are now shifting to a more incremental, if more lasting, transformation of the American roadway. Open Streets challenge the traffic volume and violence of vehicular thoroughfares to advocate for a quieter and safer place for shared mobility. As deployed during the pandemic, roadways were still devoted to transportation but allowed the possibility of pause and play. Going beyond calming traffic to repositioning the car as equivalent or subordinate to other modes makes reclaiming their fair share of the roadway possible for smaller and slower forms of travel. Though Open Streets do not fully or permanently reclaim roadways for public life, they radically rebalance the circulation function of streets with their potential as the public realm. These initiatives may only convert a small portion of the roadway network, or do so temporarily, but they powerfully enable people to experience their streets as places for people and not for cars.

Open Streets are intersectional streets whose embodiment of mobility justice joins diverse axes of equity both substantive and procedural. By limiting cars and prioritizing those who walk, bike, or roll, Open and Shared Streets advance multimodal equity, at least by approaching parity among speeds and sometimes by excluding cars altogether. The location of Open and Shared Streets raises issues of distributional equity that planners hope to address by linking spatial analysis and long-range planning toward a network to provide fair access to all with a procedural-equity emphasis on bottom-up initiatives. They seek such balance through programs that invite neighborhood requests but allocate resources through equity matrixes that prioritize underserved communities. While some pandemic programs like Denver's were top-down, permanent programs emphasize local engagement yet increasingly incorporate these improvements in citywide infrastructure planning and capital budgeting. Open and Shared Streets have not raised the same kind of green gentrification concerns as other infrastructure measures (e.g., bike lanes), but planners and community members are cognizant of being sensitive to local communities and the potential risks of displacement that might result. Here a procedural-equity emphasis on a deliberative process engaging local people is viewed as key to achieving mobility justice without catalyzing unwanted neighborhood change.

These stories ultimately reveal, however, the enduring power of automobiles to lay a dominant claim to the street. The pandemic provided a unique moment to reverse that, which cities took advantage of to advance multimodal and placemaking aims. Yet the pressure for vehicular access is relentless, and only where there are strong counter-constituencies—including neighborhood groups, business associations, and advocates—can the barricades be held for very long. Nonetheless, having experienced the roadway as public space, if only for a day or a season, many people don't want to give it back. The methodical planning and capital improvement processes may not provide those spaces as quickly as the Covid-19 emergency did, but perhaps with time, these visions and experiences of Shared Streets may enduringly transform roadways one day of Ciclovía and one block of Shared Street at a time.

6

RECONSTRUCTING THE STREET AS PUBLIC PLACE

To slow or partially (or temporarily) close streets is a major change, yet more significant is the growing movement to durably reclaim the roadway as a public place. Cities have recently begun remaking portions of the roadway surface for outdoor dining and gathering. These incipient experiments, accelerated and vastly expanded during the pandemic, are increasingly becoming permanent. Where cars once parked are now parklets and streateries, and from traffic lanes emerge public plazas. These conversions may be limited in extent, but they represent a profound and perhaps lasting shift.

This chapter explores the physical remaking of American roadways as public spaces. It begins with a brief history of the nonvehicular—even the nonmobility—uses of public streets, from enduring pedestrian uses and pedestrianization experiments, to recent movements to transform public rights-of-way into places for social life. Tactical urbanist interventions like Park(ing) Day and local experimentation with public placemaking evolved into parklets and interim plazas and were standardized in National Association of City Transportation Officials (NACTO) guidelines, setting the stage for the sudden retrofitting of what NACTO calls "Streets for Pandemic Response and Recovery."[1] Against this backdrop, it helps to survey the current policy landscape across the United States and explore a set of in-depth case studies of cities that are remaking their streets for social life, including San

Francisco's Shared Spaces, Washington, D.C.'s streateries, and Portland's Public Street Plazas.

American streets are progressively being remade from pipes for cars into places for people, not simply for fleeting conversation among passersby but also as a destination where one can dwell a while. Emergency programs are being adopted permanently, and interim installations are paving the way for physical reconstruction. These changes, parking space by parking space, block by block, are transforming streets in ways more fundamental than perhaps any others discussed in this book. In the process, they raise an entirely distinct set of questions about what streets are for and how they might be most equitably shared.

The Reemergence of Public Life on the American Roadway

The Marginalized but Enduring Public Life on the Modern American Roadway

Despite their twentieth-century transformation into vehicular thoroughfares, streets were never completely given over to vehicular flow. Sidewalks maintained their complex mix of uses, including both pedestrian circulation and social activities like conversation, panhandling, street music, or even physical occupation by café tables or street vendors.[2] The road surface itself, despite having been paved as a conduit for cars, continued to host some static activities. Curbside parking, though an extension of the vehicular transport system, is actually a private occupation of public space. Cars typically sit empty, but they are occasionally used for conversation (or even necking, sleeping, and living), and food trucks have maintained traditions of curbside vending.

Though most twentieth-century cities gave their streets over to cars, others advocated a better balance. Many postwar cities, worried about downtown decline, embraced the strategy of pedestrianization. Some 140 American cities created downtown pedestrian malls between 1959 and 1985, though most were perceived as failures due in part to what planner Dave Amos suggests was a neglect of placemaking fundamentals.[3] Pedestrian-friendly cities had some success, however, like Santa Monica and its nationally recognized Third Street Promenade.[4] Other midcentury critics and urbanists sought a middle ground between streets as thoroughfares and pedestrianization through widening sidewalks, reducing vehicular traffic, and increasing the safety of street environments.

These efforts increasingly came under the banner of "livability," a term capturing the relationship between the street's function for transportation and neighborhood life. Building on the work of Kevin A. Lynch, planners Donald Appleyard, M. Sue Gerson, and Mark Lintell published their landmark 1981 book *Livable Streets,* which argues that streets could be "idyllic" if they engaged residents, enabled children to play (including on the street), and fostered social interaction, framing this as a choice between "on the one hand alienation, on the other friendliness and involvement."[5]

Such arguments aside, by the late twentieth century, streets were so dominated by cars that most multimodal advocates merely aspired to reintroduce safety and some degree of convenience for pedestrians and cyclists, limiting public placemaking aspirations to the sidewalk.

Park[ing] Day: Tactical Urbanism Takes to the Street

Perhaps because the car's hegemony was so complete and left few policy avenues to confront it, some advocates took a more activist approach. In 2005, San Francisco art and design studio Rebar converted a single metered parking space into a temporary public park. From their pop-up installation, a worldwide Park(ing) Day movement emerged to "call attention to the need for more urban open space, to generate critical debate around how public space is created and allocated, and to improve the quality of urban human habitat . . . at least until the meter runs out!"[6]

Rebar realized that 20 to 30 percent of San Francisco's land area was streets, and yet (minus sidewalks) 70 to 80 percent of that space was dedicated to vehicle movement and storage.[7] Brainstorming more "useful ways of occupying this precious part of San Francisco's public realm," they realized it wasn't illegal to put something other than a car in a parking space. Thus, on November 16, 2005, Rebar activists fed the meter and turned a downtown parking space into a small park with sod, potted trees and plants, and furniture. When the meter expired, they removed the park. More important than the park itself was its potential to "provoke a critical examination of the values that generate the form of urban public space."

These pop-ups inspired a movement. Rebar partnered with the Trust for Public Land to make Park(ing) Day an annual event "for people to reclaim urban space from cars, one parking space at a time." The idea spread to hundreds of cities worldwide, including variants like free health clinics, temporary urban farms, ecology demonstrations, political seminars, or free bike-repair shops. Rebar maintains a website that includes a Park(ing) Day DIY Planning Network, a manifesto, a how-to manual, and posters and graphics to support local efforts to reimagine and revalue the metered parking space as an "important part of the commons."[8] The resulting movement has become a "global experiment in reprogramming vehicular space for social exchange, artistic expression, and play."[9] From one parking spot in one city in 2005, the movement grew to 975 parks created in 162 cities in thirty-five counties by 2011.[10]

Rebar's *Park(ing) Day Manifesto,* informed by theories of how taken-for-granted societal beliefs and physical landscapes are mutually reinforcing, promotes Park(ing) Day as a tactic to "remix environmental signs and symbols." Though these installations were meant to be temporary, Rebar suggests they could become a "tactical turning point in the urban structure itself."[11] In its companion *Park(ing) Day Manual,* Rebar invites people to participate in this DIY movement and argues that "your installation is limited only by your imagination—and the future of this grassroots movement is in your hands."[12] It offers guidance on choosing a spot, building materials, seating, signage, and buffering. Because the events are designed to provide public discourse, the manual offers strategies to promote a positive message: "Remember: You are acting in the public interest to add to the health, comfort and vitality of your city." It also reminds people, "You are not protesting."[13]

Park(ing) Days remain transitory events, yet they invite profound questions about what public streets ought to be for and suggest the potential to durably transform them into places. The *Park(ing) Day Manual* concludes with "Next Steps: Catalyzing Lasting Change in Your City" by converting organizing momentum into political activism and parking spaces into permanent public plazas.[14]

Public Placemaking on the Road

Such experimentation aligned with a growing movement to promote public placemaking. Inspired by urbanist William H. Whyte, the Project for Public Spaces (PPS) was founded in the mid-1970s to advocate for the principle that "great public spaces strengthen communities."[15]

In 2000, the PPS published *How to Turn a Place Around: A Handbook for Creating Successful Public Places,* which argues for the importance of public spaces as "nexuses around which communities can come together."[16] Drawing upon Whyte's research, it offers design principles for building successful public spaces, starting with planning and outreach focused on grounded observation and bold vision, leading to strategies for translating ideas into action. Ultimately, it argues for a tactical approach of taking short-term actions to test ideas ("start with the petunias") and to give people confidence that "change is occurring—that their ideas matter."[17] While such placemaking highlights the importance of streets, it distinguishes them from traditional public places like parks. While the movement addressed issues like traffic speed, congestion, and impediments to walking or biking, its solutions were largely limited to traffic calming, and its arguments for placemaking mostly stopped at the curb.

By the twenty-first century, public placemaking increasingly came to encompass the roadway itself. Following the success of Park(ing) Day, the movement has increasingly advanced a bigger argument: the PPS website now states that "streets are themselves critical public spaces."[18] In a 2015 blog post, Annah MacKenzie of PPS argues, "Streets are our most fundamental shared public spaces, but they are also one of the most contested and overlooked." If "that's the bad news" she notes, the good news is that "it doesn't have to be this way! Streets can once again become thriving, livable environments for people, not just cars."[19] In 2015, PPS developed a "Streets as Places Toolkit" to redesign the entire right-of-way as public space "designed for lingering." Citing Appleyard and others, the PPS Streets as Place website advocates for helping people "begin to see streets in their entirety: not just their function in transporting people and goods, but the vital role they play in animating the social and economic life of communities."[20]

In 2019, these evolving ideas led to the joint PPS and Main Street America publication *Navigating Main Streets as Places: A People-First Transportation Toolkit,* which highlighted both traditional placemaking themes and environmental sustainability and equity, defined as "just and fair inclusion into a society in which all can participate, prosper, and reach their full potential."[21] The tool kit critiques the costs of car-oriented streets and argues for the equity benefits of people-oriented

198   Reconstructing the Street as Public Place

streets, only realizable when everyone has "equal access to all the benefits of Main Street."[22] More than just a statement of principles, it outlines how these can be materialized through programming and design.

From Tactical Pop-Ups to Interim Programs and Parklets

By the second decade of the twenty-first century, the placemaking movement was looking beyond parks and plazas or sidewalks to encompass the whole right-of-way and beyond tactical interventions to more structural change. Perhaps nothing exemplifies this more than the evolution from the performance art of Park(ing) Day into formalized parklets and interim plaza programs, which provided a model for scaling up during Covid-19.

San Francisco planners worked with Rebar to create a Pavement to Parks program in 2009. Andres Power, urban designer at the San Francisco Planning Department, explained at the time that the goal was "transforming a sea of asphalt" not through ambitious plans but through a tactical strategy that "fundamentally changes the old impasse of years of planning and just lets the space evolve over time."[23] The program introduced two primary tools: parklets and plazas. Parklets, like Park(ing) Day installations, occupy former vehicle-storage spaces in the parking lane and are funded by private sponsors. The program also envisioned more elaborate plazas created from underutilized portions of the right-of-way that had pedestrian safety issues, too much space allocated to cars, and the greatest need for public space, to be paid for with a combination of private and public funding. In its 2011 manual, Rebar excitedly notes the direct connection between Park(ing) Day and the emerging Parklet Program: "This movement has begun to catalyze structural change!"[24]

Simultaneously across the country, planners in New York City were undertaking bold experiments in transforming streets into interim public plazas. In 2008, transportation commissioner Janette Sadik-Khan and her colleagues launched a pilot Plaza Program to transform underutilized streets into "vibrant social public spaces" within walking distance of residents. These principles were articulated in the city's 2009 *Street Design Manual,* which defined plazas as "a place for people to enjoy the public realm," distinguished from sidewalks by becoming a "destination rather than a space to pass through."[25]

Based on early successes and developing standards, the city announced an ambitious pilot in 2009: pedestrianizing Broadway through Times Square. To reduce congestion, the city proposed that restructuring traffic patterns and redesigning streets would help revitalize an underperforming corridor and "get more people out on the street."[26] The project was strategically presented as a pilot built with temporary materials to enable careful study. Subsequent to its success, in 2010 the administration announced that these new pedestrian spaces would become permanent. To catch up with competing cities, Mayor Michael Bloomberg proposed the creation of "an enduring, world-class street" over a three-phase capital project between 2012 and 2016.[27] When pressed by skeptical reporters, he asked, "Are the roads for multiple uses—everybody, pedestrians, bicyclists, and motorists . . . or are they just for motorists?" The NYC Department of Transportation and the Times Square Alliance answered that question by working with the Scandinavian design firm Snøhetta to transform a busy vehicular intersection into a "world class piazza."[28]

New York, through its Plaza Program, street design guidelines, and ambitious transformation of Times Square, provided an early model of how traffic-choked thoroughfares could be transformed into public places and established a process for using interim experimentation to build support and design standards for making changes permanent.

Standardizing Parklets and Interim Plazas

Such local placemaking innovations were reflected in NACTO publications, including its 2013 *Urban Street Design Guide.* Though focused primarily on expanding multimodal access, it sets out strategies for transforming roadways into public places.

The guide introduces a set of "interim design strategies" for reclaiming asphalt by using pilots to build support toward more permanent construction. First and core among these strategies is to "move the curb . . . to host a wide variety of uses beyond parking," activate street life, and create "a new destination within the street."[29] The guide introduces parklets as public seating platforms that convert curbside parking spaces into vibrant community spaces and accommodate unmet demand for public space. Drawing inspiration directly from San Francisco's Pavement to Parks program, the guide provides criteria for location, arrangement, materials, and buffering from vehicular traffic, in addition to visual schematics for their possible design.

NACTO also introduces interim public plazas to transform underutilized areas of roadways into public spaces through low-cost and impermanent materials.[30] Its arguments are framed mainly in terms of transportation safety and apply only to "underutilized" spaces, suggesting the potential to "activate a public place" and "energize surrounding streets and public spaces."[31] Following the example of New York's Public Plazas, it specifies design materials to buffer parking and traffic flow, ensure ADA accessibility, provide public seating, and maintain drainage, while also offering procedural guidance to secure local community approval, "an essential milestone in realizing any plaza project."[32]

These strategies provided a foundation for local experimentation during Covid-19 and NACTO's own efforts to assist cities in dealing with the pandemic. In its 2020 *Streets for Pandemic Response and Recovery,* NACTO responds to the need for socially distanced mobility and access to essential services by reclaiming roadway space for public space purposes through outdoor dining, markets, school playgrounds, outdoor spaces for cultural gatherings, and even voting. Though designed to be temporary, the manual suggests that "it's the job of city and transportation leaders not to return to the inequitable, dangerous, unsustainable patterns of the past, but to help shape a better future."[33]

Case Studies in Reclaiming Roadways as Pedestrianized Public Spaces

This ongoing trend to reimagine the roadway as public space had been building slowly but was catalyzed and vastly scaled up during the pandemic. Local places, struggling to meet the need for socially distanced active transport and gathering and hoping to save restaurants and other businesses, came to reimagine and reclaim roadways in innovative ways.

From Park[ing] Day to Parklets to Shared Spaces in San Francisco

San Francisco was not only the birthplace of the Park(ing) Day movement; it has also been a test bed of evolving municipal programs, from its Pavement to Parks initiative to a more sweeping Covid-19-era Shared Spaces program and beyond. In the process, the city has become a national model for redesigning and sharing roadways as public places.

Interplay between experimentation and policy development has been a hallmark of parklets and similar efforts, according to San Francisco's director of shared spaces Robin Abad Ocubillo.[34] Abad Ocubillo, whose own master's thesis explores the relationships between urban design experimentation and formal planning, says that the program's evolution and iteration are rooted in tactical urbanism and reflect "something unique in the Bay Area and how people approach the public realm, origins in the social practice [of] art, the provocative, place-based installations . . . even a streak of transgressiveness."[35] From Rebar's Park(ing) Day in 2005 emerged the Pavement to Parks program in 2009, which led to the installation of the first public parklet in 2010. By 2013, San Francisco had thirty-five parklets, four plazas, and a goal to create an additional twenty parklets and two pedestrian plazas per year. In 2013, the city published the *San Francisco Parklet Manual* to guide the conversion of "utilitarian and often underused spaces in the street into publicly accessible open spaces available for all to enjoy" and add "beauty and whimsy to the City's streets."[36] The city established a permit approval process ("Parklet-o-matic") and specified location criteria, site planning guidelines, recommendations for building neighborhood support, and design specifications. The manual has been updated regularly to guide parklet development in the city and beyond.

The public street may invite experimentation, but it's also a bureaucratic space presenting barriers to implementation. Recognizing this, the San Francisco Board of Supervisors adopted a Places for People ordinance in 2016 to lower barriers to participation, facilitate greater equity (defined as geographic distribution), enable activation of streets space that is "frequent, diverse, and free to the public," and streamline review and permitting, while defining operational parameters.[37] Because parklets were intended to be public spaces, eligibility required public access and a full-time stewardship entity and was time-limited for up to twenty-four months. Though innovative, parklets and other Pavement to Parks installations expanded slowly, in part due to the program's noncommercial orientation.

With the onset of the Covid-19 pandemic, the program's character and scope changed dramatically. In March of 2020, the city issued a stay-at-home order that shuttered most nonessential businesses and limited restaurants to takeout and delivery. Streets emptied of traffic and many parked cars. To assist businesses and begin the transition to safe reopening, Mayor London Breed and Board of Supervisors president Norman Yee created a Covid-19 Economic Recovery Task Force in April 2020 with a spectrum of community and business leaders and a process of public engagement. One of its early actions was to create a new Shared Spaces program at the urging of business groups like the Golden Gate Restaurant Association, whose executive director Laurie Thomas recalls, "Like every other restaurant operator, I was forced with potentially losing my livelihood."[38] The city had a long tradition of sidewalk dining, but "that wasn't sufficient, we needed to take advantage of the outdoor space," Thomas argues. Public parklets, with their prohibition on full service and alcohol, didn't work for restaurants. In response, in late May, Mayor Breed announced expedited permits to share public spaces, including sidewalks, streets, and parking, to "promote public health, help struggling businesses survive, and contribute to a vibrant street life on our commercial corridors."[39]

For planners like Abad Ocubillo, named director of the new Shared Spaces program in July 2020, this was an unprecedented challenge and opportunity to rethink parklets. For a decade the focus had been solely on the "democratization of public space." He admits that reorienting toward commercial use was a big shift and that it took the pandemic to get them there.[40] The Parklet Program provided a useful precedent, but with the pandemic, a shift in culture enabled planners to take more license and risks. The city proposed a range of new Shared Spaces—curbside parklets, sidewalk spaces, Shared Streets, and off-street Open Lots to be opened for both noncommercial and commercial uses (including retail and dining) (Figure 23). For Abad Ocubillo, there were "so many reasons why the shift in public policy was necessary and right." Compared with curbside parking, he considers commercial parklets to represent a higher and better use, though he admits there was a "lot of robust discourse . . . on how do we balance these things."

From the outset, the program was concerned about access and equity. The city quickly adapted parklet rules to ensure accessibility for persons with disabilities, emergency services, and transit boarding. To address geographical distribution and social equity, the city administered an equity grants program prioritizing neighborhoods hardest hit by

Figure 23. During the pandemic, San Francisco expanded its public parklets into a broader Shared Spaces program, converting curbside parking into outdoor gathering and dining. San Francisco Planning Department (via Flickr, https://www.flickr.com/photos/sfplanning/50568740497/in/album-72157715102556516/), licensed under CC BY 2.0.

Covid-19 and those labeled as "areas of vulnerability" (based on residents who were people of color, older adults, youth, people with disabilities, linguistically isolated households, and people experiencing poverty). The program also targeted businesses that were small, legacy, or located in cultural districts.

By the fall of 2020, San Francisco had approved 1,600 Shared Space permits. The Covid-19 Economic Recovery Task Force's final report highlights these successes and recommends extending and supporting the Shared Spaces program. The report also, however, laments uneven adoption and recommends making the program "more equitable, effective, and better poised" to support long-term recovery. It suggests simplifying the approval process, helping businesses and artists defray costs, and promoting the program's "uptake" in neighborhoods with modest participation.[41] The report argues that the city should encourage the conversion of roadways, whether curbside parking or the entire street, rather than sidewalks. Finally, it suggests engaging artists in the process of designing outdoor dining spaces.

Though initially a temporary emergency measure, the mayor extended the program in October 2020 until the end of 2023 to give businesses incentive and certainty to invest in attractive spaces. The success of the Shared Spaces program became the restaurant association's top priority, according to Thomas. Given San Francisco's "extensive, hardcore shutdown," she believes that without federal assistance and parklets, "we would have lost our restaurant industry."[42] After this period of rapid experimentation, in summer 2021 the Shared Spaces program began a two-year transition from what its website calls "an emergency lifeline to a permanent program." This included tightening rules to ensure access for people with disabilities and first responders and resizing or moving parklets to improve visibility at high-injury intersections.[43] A 2022 expiration date was set for parklets, but those in good standing were extended to March of 2023. At the same time, the equity grant program was reopened and focused on providing ADA and safety improvements. In March 2023, the city opened applications for postpandemic permits, requiring site plans, neighborhood consent, review and inspection, public noticing, and permit approval.

To guide the permanent program, planners developed and published the updated *Shared Spaces Manual* in December 2022 (Figure 24). The manual's goals emphasize equity and inclusion, defined as focusing resources on "communities most impacted by historical disparities" and ensuring access for people with disabilities; balancing curbside functions in alignment with Vision Zero and Transit First policies; making sure some public seating is always available and the space is publicly accessible when not in commercial use. The manual also advances community development goals; encourages arts, culture, and entertainment; and highlights the importance of maintaining the street as a place for movement "fully accessible to, and useable by, all people with disabilities," while remaining accessible for public and emergency services.[44]

San Francisco's Shared Streets program has transformed public roadways, institutions, and the politics surrounding them. Abad Ocubillo recalls that when he first started with the Parklet Program, "every single parklet was a pitched battle," but "we're operating in a completely

Reconstructing the Street as Public Place 205

Figure 24. San Francisco's newly updated *Shared Spaces Manual* seeks to balance the commercial activation of streets with public and emergency access. City and County of San Francisco, *Shared Spaces Manual Version 2.4* (San Francisco, 2022).

different environment now."[45] Merchants' associations that resisted the loss of parking now support parklets and even closing whole streets as economic-development strategies. People "have completely reoriented what they think the public right-of-way can be for," he continues. Though the program led with economic stabilization for the small business community, Abad Ocubillo believes it was able to deliver on many other things—like climate action, Complete Streets, multimodal mobility, neighborhood resilience, and arts and culture strategies—to provide "multiple, manifold benefits." Within the city's bureaucracy, the program also helped to "permanently rewire how we do business" by creating lasting connections across silos.

The evolution of these programs continues to reflect the dynamic interplay between local initiative and city planning. This is particularly the case downtown, where the pandemic and the loss of office traffic forced the Downtown SF Partnership "to reimagine downtown," according to Deputy Director Claude Imbault: "We needed to go big and go bold."[46] In a district with no parks and only privately owned public spaces, "we look naturally to the street" as a place to activate. In 2022, the Downtown SF Partnership commissioned the *Public Realm Action Plan for a Reimagined Downtown San Francisco* to address "demands for a high-quality public realm" and transform downtown from a business center to a social destination and "pedestrian paradise."[47] Imbault, who led the planning effort, argued to "amplify our assets . . . make downtown as a canvas," with streets key to that effort. The partnership's plan, in turn, provided a model for the city's own 2023 *Roadmap to Downtown San Francisco's Future* that aimed to enhance public spaces. This included the $6 million Powell Street Promenade project to revitalize a key connection between the cable car turnaround and Union Square by replacing metallic sidewalk extensions, which have been in the interim phase for almost a decade, with "elegant new sidewalk treatments to create a unified widened sidewalk."[48] While Imbault appreciates the partnership's ability to innovate the city's willingness to advance those strategies, he laments enduring bureaucratic hurdles: "The vision is there, the product is there, but the mindset of city staff to think cross-functionally is a challenge," particularly when public safety issues like fire access are involved; "issues of life and limb are important, but there must be a balance."[49]

Thus, the city's *Shared Spaces Manual* reflects tensions between different priorities and "years of fighting and back and forth," according to Thomas; "Robin [Abad Ocubillo] can tell you, we fought like cats and dogs."[50] Tensions centered on dining and seating versus a clear path for pedestrian travel, how best to assure ADA accessibility, design standards for platforms and other structures, and how to meet fire department demands for emergency access. "I lost hours of my life on this," Thomas recalls, particularly around thorny issues of fire and emergency access, "but I think it resulted—with the exception of fire—in a fair outcome." On streets historically controlled by municipal agencies, it was new for business owners to have such a direct stake in the roadway surface beyond parking. For Abad Ocubillo, this engagement with business owners was critical: "They're helping all of us shift our thinking, helping bend the long arc, getting us to a better Complete Street design."[51]

Another novel and complex issue is what to charge for leasing curbside parking. Commercial parklets were free during the pandemic, but the city has since worked to determine fair annual fees for permit application (proposed to be $3,000 for the first parklet, $1,500 for the second) and licensing ($2,000 per year). Thomas thinks these fees are too high, especially in addition to the costs of building and maintaining parklets. During the pandemic, it was a matter of survival, but moving forward businesses will now need to analyze these economically in terms of return on investment, leading Thomas to ponder, "Is it worth it for eight feet?"[52]

Since curbside and street space are limited, there are also territorial public versus private issues. Thomas admits that there are public concerns about a "land grab" by businesses, but under the new program, restaurants will be limited to two parklets, and the city is clawing back any additional installed during the pandemic. Thomas acknowledges public versus private debates are perhaps the greatest tension within the program, but she pushes back: "I call bullshit on that. . . . Parking has always been a private use. There was a lot of hypocrisy there."[53] Though the Shared Spaces program values the commercial activation of the curbside over parking, San Francisco remains committed to their accessibility as public spaces. It requires new commercial parklets to install one public bench for each parking space converted and seating opportunities during daytime hours and evenings. It also incentivizes creating public seating through a tiered fee structure: fully public parklets are priced low (20 percent of the regular cost) and step up depending on the level of commercial control; to support small businesses, it halves fees for those with annual gross receipts less than $2 million. "We're trying to meet in the middle and evolve a new paradigm. . . . We'll see how it works," Abad Ocubillo argues, suggesting these incentives are "an expression of values . . . trying to keep this typology [the public parklet] at the front of people's minds."[54] Simon Bertrang, who works with the nonprofit SF New Deal, which seeks to support small and minority-owned businesses, shares this belief in the power of parklets to help under-resourced communities: "On the corridor level . . . we want the business owners to be able to operate outdoors dining, but at the street level the people in the neighborhood can benefit."[55]

Retrofitting streets for public space does affect transportation, however, and not just involving cars. For example, curbside parklets make that roadway space unavailable for bike lanes. Multimodal planners and advocates have to strike a balance among priorities, tensions exemplified in key transportation and business corridors like Valencia Street in the Mission District. During the pandemic, Valencia's parklets and street closures brought what local business owners described to reporters as "joy . . . during such a dark period in our city."[56] Yet the corridor is also one of the city's busiest and most dangerous, particularly for cyclists. In 2022, San Francisco Municipal Transportation Agency (SFMTA) undertook the Valencia Bikeway Improvements Project to increase safety, as part of the city's Vision Zero program, while also preserving the street's economic vitality and balancing competing demands for curb access.[57] New curbside uses "added a layer of complexity for all users," making side-running bike lanes less feasible, so SFMTA approved and is piloting a new, protected bikeway running down the center of Valencia.[58] This has been controversial among cyclists who prefer the comfort and access of side-running bike lanes. Advocate Janelle Wong of the San Francisco Bicycle Coalition acknowledges that parklets present a novel challenge, further complicating the mix of uses to accommodate within street space.[59] Wong suggests, however, that these complexities are worth navigating because "we want to promote public spaces that put people first . . . not storing cars." Wong admits that with the Valencia quick-build, "we don't know what that will mean for people biking. . . . We understand and hear the criticism," but she hopes that these new compromises will reduce traffic volumes, make it safer for pedestrians, give more visibility to cyclists, and "overall make it calmer for everyone."

What do these new Shared Spaces mean for mobility justice on San Francisco's streets? The answer is, unsurprisingly, intersectional. Remaking streets as multimodal infrastructure and fully fledged public places shifts the point of intersection among different equity axes too. From a citywide perspective, the voluntary nature of the Shared Spaces program, shaped not by spatial planning but by local initiative, has resulted in an uneven spatial distribution. San Francisco is trying to address this through incentives and support targeting underserved neighborhoods and minority-owned businesses. In terms of multimodal equity, the program fully reclaims streets for public space purposes while accommodating continued access to active transportation and public safety. This is a different kind of approach, according to Wong: "What placemaking is about now is to welcome all groups of people" and not simply a conversation about transportation equity or race "but bringing people together. . . . It's no longer about fighting for space. You have to share it. . . . It requires everybody in the community to slow down and be a little more aware."[60]

Shared Spaces clearly have potential to alter the trajectory of urban change. Abad Ocubillo acknowledges that there are green gentrification concerns in San Francisco, relating both to public infrastructure and public–private partnerships: "This is something that is bandied about, and depending on how you're situated, sentiment and perception skews." However, he claims that these arguments are "specious" and that issues of neighborhood stability are more a matter of global capitalism than street design, countering that "we can't not continue to deliver on safer infrastructure, innovative public–private partnership programs that are going to create a civic enterprise around the public realm."[61] Bertrang frames the issue of green gentrification in a different way:

> If you're working with small business owners to support their business . . . and you're thinking about the benefits to the residents, you're automatically going in the direction of equity. . . . Commercial corridors are places where people connect. It's not just for business[es] employing people. There are places where people come together and bond. . . . When you go down and patronize small businesses, it's a place of connection.[62]

From this perspective, Bertrang believes the Shared Spaces program can provide tangible benefits to existing residents.

Shared Spaces has also begun to transform decision-making around streets, making them procedurally more equitable. The program seeks transparency in decision-making, simplified for applicants, to encourage a bottom-up and community-driven approach, with extra support for smaller businesses and communities. For Wong, these changes suggest a "good pivot," giving people a growing voice in shaping the public street: "There are more people at the table, and for good reasons."[63]

The Shared Spaces program presents novel opportunities and challenges, in both theory and practice, but its tactical nature offers an opportunity to work these issues out. In this regard, Abad Ocubillo sees the program's power as "both an end unto themselves and a really critical strategy for achieving these long-term goals relative to Complete

210   Reconstructing the Street as Public Place

Streets design and implementation. . . . They're operating at both levels." Street conversions that began as a "novel, joyous experiment" have evolved through an "ephemeral festival phase into 24/7, long-term installations . . . from ornament to become part of our vernacular."[64] These interim strategies are now paving the way for permanent sidewalk widening and roadway narrowing. "I credit conversations about parklets with enabling us to radically narrow streets," Abad Ocubillo continues, suggesting that "the discussion of Complete Streets, dare I say car-free streets, is in a completely different place" thanks to the parklet as a vehicle for changing streets and shifting the mentality around them.

Curbside Streateries in Washington, D.C.

The nation's capital, Washington, D.C., was designed to emphasize streets both as axes focusing on monumental public spaces and as expansive public spaces themselves. After becoming dominated by vehicles over the twentieth century, planners have recently begun to reclaim roadway space for multimodal access and public uses. Limited experiments with public parklets ramped up during the pandemic within the district's robust Streatery Program to reclaim curbside parking for dining, walking, and public seating, which has become a permanent feature of life in Washington.

The politics of public streets are always complicated, but in a federal district, the *public* in *public streets* refers not only to the city's residents and many commuters but also to the American people. The city has long valued its street culture, and since the 1970s it has permitted sidewalk cafés through its public space permit program. Yet until recently, roadways have remained the domain of traffic and parking, often prioritizing suburban commuters. In 2015, the district, inspired by Park(ing) Day, began to experiment with parklets as a strategy for "exchanging curbside road space for additional public gathering space."[65] District Department of Transportation (DDOT) planners developed design guidelines to take the concept of "pop-up public park, transformed from an on-street parking space, and [turn] it into something more permanent."[66] Unlike other public improvements guided by municipal plans and funded publicly, the Parklet Program invited participation from eligible applicants like business and property owners, business improvement districts, and community organizations. The district provided guidelines specifying minimum dimensions, buffering from traffic, ADA accessibility, and other structural details. However, implementation depended on local initiative, and five years into the program, only three parklets had been developed. Transportation planner Kimberly Vacca was hired in early 2020 to support DDOT's growing focus on public placemaking but felt that the program was hampered by high permitting fees linked to hourly parking rates and a limited focus on public space uses.[67]

Covid-19 radically changed that situation. In March of 2020, Mayor Muriel Bowser declared a state of emergency, shuttering businesses and emptying streets of traffic. In May, the District Council adopted the Coronavirus Support Temporary Amendment Act of 2020, limiting indoor occupancy of restaurants and bars but also expanding outdoor dining. A new Streatery Program expanded activities already permitted on sidewalks to the roadway—free of charge—as long as eligible applicants registered with DDOT, obtained written approval from private property owners, and abided by district laws and rules around social distancing and spacing, masking, and hours of operation. Fixing the Parklet Program had already been on DDOT's agenda, according to Vacca, but "until Covid, there was little political will to confront the car."[68] Covid-19 changed Vacca's role "drastically," as she was suddenly charged with overseeing the new and vastly expanded Streatery Program.

The novelty of the program opened the field for rapid local experimentation. A leading force was the Georgetown Business Improvement District (BID), a private nonprofit representing property owners and merchants in one of D.C.'s core and most elite neighborhoods. Already dedicated to protecting and enhancing the "accessibility, attractiveness and appeal" of its commercial district, in the summer of 2020 the BID responded to the pandemic by helping merchants shift dining outdoors. Early streateries were ad hoc and temporary, with café tables set out on roads behind traffic barriers. While Georgetown is renowned for its historical character, it is also bisected by busy thoroughfares like M Street. For Nat Cannon, placemaking manager for the Georgetown BID, the new streateries met a need but were not very attractive: "It felt like you were in a construction zone."[69] In addition, the racial justice protests in June of 2020 had left many businesses boarded up and the streets devoid of furniture. Reactivating neighborhood streets was a key challenge for the BID, as well as an opportunity for Cannon to pursue a long-range vision for the neighborhood's streets, including the M Street corridor and its busy traffic and undersized sidewalks. "We were very open about our goals from the beginning," Cannon admits; "we knew even before the pandemic that M Street should be one of America's great streets. . . . We had that in mind, that was the end goal."[70]

Designing and implementing new streateries, especially in a community with such high design standards, posed an unprecedented challenge. Georgetown's BID wanted a more durable solution than café tables behind jersey barriers and ultimately hoped to extend sidewalks into the street. Constructing in the public right-of-way raised novel permitting and logistic issues, however, including what Cannon describes as the "utility nightmare underneath our roads."[71] Sidewalk extensions had to facilitate stormwater flow in the gutter, mark the locations of utilities like manhole covers, and be removable for utility repairs. Given the scale and scope of its project, rather than go through the streatery process, the BID directly applied for a construction permit, requiring coordination with DDOT and twenty-six other agencies.

In the spring and summer of 2021, the Georgetown BID installed 4,500 linear feet of plastic sidewalk extensions it dubbed the "Georgetown Decks." Though focused on serving over thirty restaurants with outdoor dining, the decks looked beyond dining to include street furniture and seating for general public use. And the BID sought more than single parklets to make the decks continuous, spanning entire blocks to support pedestrian traffic and public space uses, while also incorporating other transportation functions like delivery, bus drop-off, bike racks, and scooter parking.

In the process, the Georgetown Decks came to be "not just a transformation of a corridor, it was a transformation of a whole community," according to Stephanie Bothwell, a local consulting urban designer and board member with the nonprofit Citizens Association of Georgetown.[72] As both resident and urban designer, Bothwell has a personal and professional interest in the sustainability and equity of the street as a public realm, sharing with the Georgetown BID and others the desire to make local streets more hospitable by widening sidewalks. "In our community, we had too many lanes of traffic for it to function as a place,"

Bothwell observes. The installation of Georgetown Decks fundamentally altered the conception of the street from circulation space to destination: the "perception that people have of the street is changing, and I'm not sure it's going to go back."

Such major changes to the streetscape would have been "nonstarters" without Covid-19, Cannon readily admits, which opened up the district from bureaucratic rigidity to creative flexibility. Political leaders on the District Council extended the Streatery Program until the end of 2021 and again through most of 2022 to assure restaurants that investing in these spaces would be worthwhile. Public planners and engineers helped neighborhoods innovate. Georgetown's initiative put it, in Cannon's words, "out ahead of DDOT," but she credits successful implementation to "very careful collaboration" with diverse agencies, especially champions at DDOT. Though everyone was nervous with these new changes, Cannon admits, they shared the same vision: "They get it, right? We need less space for vehicle uses and more for other uses."[73]

Based on such collaborative experimentation, DDOT published its first interim *Reimagining Outdoor Space: Restaurants and Retail; Guidelines for Expanded and New Outdoor Seating* in 2021. Addressing the continued need for safe open-air dining, the guidelines enabled restaurants to convert curbside parking and alleys into parklets and allowed community organizations like BIDs or advisory neighborhood commissions to convert entire blocks, alleys, and even travel lanes into streateries and "dining plazas."[74] DDOT waived permit fees but set minimum design and public safety standards, including a clear pedestrian path on the sidewalk, planters or other buffering from traffic, and ADA accessibility for any new curbside decks. Because these new installations were, in effect, structures, DDOT also introduced safety standards for heating, furniture, and any enclosures. And though the program was temporary, DDOT assured readers that new guidance would be forthcoming for "continued use and treatments of public space."

The program invited businesses and communities to rethink roadways, but it didn't happen overnight. One example is the Logan Circle Neighborhood, whose Main Street program is managed by the nonprofit organization District Bridges (analogous to a BID but focused on merchants). The program's director, Michele Molotsky, recounts how the pandemic prompted their neighborhood, with little experience in parklets, to suddenly get into the business of streateries.[75] In her role providing technical assistance, she approached business owners with the invitation to pursue streateries, but many were skeptical. One of those was John Guggenmos, longtime neighborhood resident, community leader, and owner of LGBTIQIA clubs Number Nine and Trade: "I originally thought it was a crazy idea," Guggenmos tells me, "I hadn't really envisioned what that space could be. . . . Okay, here's a parking space, and we're going to put some tables there, with the dust and the buses?" When Molotsky offered to help him apply for a streatery and he considered the choice between doing it and laying off staff, Guggenmos thought, "'Why not?'"[76]

Though Guggenmos didn't see the vision at first, the more he thought about the importance of café culture to the district, the more he realized having people linger outside was a "perfect fit" and embraced the challenge of thinking creatively about ways to transform the street space. Thanks to Covid-19 relief funds, he extended indoor seating and design elements onto the roadway and added umbrellas and other outdoor furniture, which he credits with saving jobs during the pandemic. As life returned to normal, he relinquished one of the streateries on a busy street but kept the other. The outdoor seats are the first to fill up, he tells me; it's "what every business wants, people sitting out front." Reflecting on the impact of the streatery on his business, Guggenmos says, "I couldn't quantify it, but I sure would hate to see it go. . . . It's part of the signature of the space" (Figure 25).

By the summer of 2022, there were 385 streateries across the District of Columbia. This historic transformation of the public right-of-way came with new opportunities but also with tensions and trade-offs. An early and consistent issue was the loss of parking, though interviewees generally viewed this trade-off as worth it. Molotsky pointedly reminds me that on streets dominated by traffic and parking, "It's kind of baked into the cake that it's inequitable from the start."[77] And while streateries imply a new privatization of the street's public space, so too is metered parking. Guggenmos, noting the affordability issues surrounding car ownership and parking, admits, "I'm not sure we were equitably sharing the streets to begin with."[78] Similarly, Cannon asks rhetorically, "Isn't parking really just private vehicle storage? . . . Doesn't a streatery . . .

Reconstructing the Street as Public Place 215

Figure 25. Washington, D.C.'s Streatery Program expanded rapidly during the pandemic to become a durable feature, as people like club owner John Guggenmos expanded their businesses onto the roadway. Image courtesy of District Bridges.

provide more for the public good than a parked car?"[79] Bothwell, though sharing in the critique of parking, is less sure about these new public uses: "To pave the sidewalk with bricks, that's not a land grab. But to occupy the street with temporary stuff over a long period of time, that's a land grab . . . no matter how you pay it or play it."[80]

Streateries raised new public issues beyond just parking. Non-transportation uses like café tables can encroach on pedestrian space. When enforcement was lax during the pandemic, Vacca saw a lot of businesses encroaching on the minimum five-foot circulation space,

216   Reconstructing the Street as Public Place

which vulnerable users "struggled to access."[81] People in Georgetown witnessed this firsthand: Bothwell notes that "there's a creeping that goes on" when businesses take more than their allocated space or move fixtures around.[82] Cannon admits that "everyone starts to get greedy. You give them an inch and they'll take a mile."[83] Thus, keeping pedestrian paths clear became a key priority for DDOT and neighborhood organizations. Streateries also created new barriers between sidewalks and the street, making it a challenge for pedestrians to reach ride-hailing services and for drivers to make deliveries. In response, Georgetown's BID took care to plan their decks so as not to block bus stops, and they believe it has improved transit access. These issues are increasingly incorporated in design and approval, but streateries ultimately change the flow of the public street, trading vehicular uses for pedestrian flow in ways that both enhance accessibility and present new obstacles. While Bothwell believes the changes have been good for diners and transit riders, she notes that there have been trade-offs: "What was kind of a quasi-bike route on M Street is now gone."[84]

Streateries have also transformed the district's streets and the neighborhoods surrounding them. Streateries buffer sidewalks and businesses from the roadway, trading vehicular parking to enhance the pedestrian experience and livability. Where there were parked cars, there are now new places of social activity for people to eat and drink, even if these changes are not welcomed by all. Molotsky personally believes in mixing uses and "the more the merrier," but neighborhood opposition to noise led some restaurants to pull streateries back from quieter streets to concentrate on the busier frontage.[85] As new streetscape elements, streatery installations can prompt criticism in neighborhoods with high aesthetic standards like Georgetown. Indeed, aesthetic concerns about the plastic decks were a primary reason that the Georgetown BID reduced their extent in 2022, Cannon admits, especially those public spaces perceived to be "empty" because they lacked merchant tenants. The future of sidewalk extensions in the neighborhood likely hinges on the ability to design something with permanent-looking elements (e.g., curbing) that can remain officially "temporary" awaiting traffic study. Despite some concerns about parking, noise, and aesthetic issues, however, Cannon thinks the community has embraced the change overall: "We've created a new atmosphere for outdoor dining in Georgetown, and people love it. . . . We want to preserve that."[86]

The district and neighborhoods are trying to work out these issues in a permanent Streatery Program. Citing a survey from the winter of 2020–2021, in which 89 percent of respondents expressed interest in making the program permanent, DDOT has developed draft *Streatery Guidelines* to meet two goals: to support food establishments and to "ensure Streateries are designed to be safe and accessible to all users of public space."[87] For a planner like Vacca, the best way to balance competing claims to street space is through public standards: "We realized early on that prescriptive guidelines would be helpful," developed through coordination among public services, community organizations, and businesses "to understand what those competing needs are . . . beyond our DOT perspective."[88] After intense research on user need, DDOT has tried to codify these in a permanent program.

One big policy question with limited precedent for DDOT is what to charge for renting street space. Streatery permits were free during the Covid-19 emergency, and some businesses got used to that. For Vacca, "the entitlement some of these businesses have to the space is . . . almost shocking," and though outdoor dining provides higher public value than vehicle storage, it ranks below other public safety accommodations.[89] DDOT is proposing a twenty-dollar-per-square-foot yearly rental fee, higher than typical sidewalk permits but lower than hourly parking rates (and a fraction of commercial lease rates). This spurred Cannon to wonder, "Why are we valuing curb lane space more than sidewalk space?"[90] Guggenmos took these proposed new fees in stride, saying, "If you have a thriving business . . . it's not a big deal to pay that."[91] Whatever the rates are, they represent a new kind of private leasing of public space, akin to a concession in a public park. In some ways, this merely represents a substitution of one private use (vehicular storage) for another (business use). While the privatization of public travel lanes and alleys is more unprecedented, trading circulation for forms of dwelling, such trade-offs are nothing new to the pedestrian space of the sidewalk.

All told, streateries are a significant change to the district's streets, affecting the balance among different users and raising equity issues.

The Streatery Program, and stakeholder views of it, reflects changing understandings of the street and who has a right to it. At one level, the program is explicitly about equity, transcending the district's growing commitment to multimodalism to articulate a goal of safety and accessibility for all users of public space. For Vacca, an equitable street means "anyone can safely access it—the businesses, the amenities—without fearing for their safety. . . . It needs to be safe for everyone."[92] This implies rebalancing street spaces from a focus on vehicular access for parking and travel to pedestrian access for walking and gathering, with greater transportation equity and a broader mobility justice. Interviewees agree that streateries have enhanced access to the public space of the roadway, making the public right-of-way and surrounding places more livable. Because streateries are implemented from the bottom up through a public process, they embody a kind of procedural justice, emphasizing for planners like Vacca the importance of balancing community input and administrative efficiency.

In many ways, streateries improve the inequities of car-dominated streets but raise new mobility justice issues. From a distributive and spatial viewpoint, a bottom-up program has led to a very uneven geography of streateries. The enduring legacy of geographical and racial divisions means that underserved communities may lack the basic physical infrastructure or the capacity of strong business districts and community organizations. Streateries are sparse in the Black and Brown communities on the eastern side of the district. Achieving a more equitable distribution of these features is a longer-term planning challenge. Vacca muses, "How do we fix the infrastructure discrepancies first and then think about these improvements?"[93] Georgetown residents like Bothwell wonder how low-income neighborhoods that lacked BIDs could take on this challenge.

And though streateries contribute to the public realm in the district, the program's success reflects a private-sector interest in the real estate of the roadway. These new spaces are more publicly accessible than parking, but many are not actually public. Bothwell worries about the growing role of business improvement districts in the public realm: "There are a lot of heavy-hitting developers who are deciding how these dollars are spent. . . . There's a real chance for it to go sideways."[94] This raises unresolved and thorny questions about who has a right to shape and access streets. Finally, while streateries improve neighborhood life by supporting local businesses, their impact on livability and affordability is less clear. They have generated noise and aesthetic concerns in some places and raised concerns about gentrification for some. Bothwell describes this conundrum: "I think there is a tipping point from vibrant, happy, sustainable main street into complete, chaos party town. . . . I don't know where that tipping is."[95]

The District of Columbia Streatery Program reflects public street pandemic innovations that are likely to become enduring features. Through experimentation and innovation, planners, community stakeholders, and businesses have developed new policies and design strategies that are increasingly permanent. The experience has been geographically uneven and their future remains uncertain. Even so, it's clear that people have rethought and reclaimed the district's streets in ways not thought possible even just a few years ago, overall making the city's streets more accessible, vibrant, and equitable. Putting these changes in historical perspective, Molotsky says: "Streets were designed at a certain point in time, and we tried to shoehorn in the cars. Now we're trying to make space for walkers and bikes and now streateries." While this raises new tensions between cars and bikes, transportation and outdoor dining, she is encouraged that "people are working those through."[96]

Portland Public Street Plazas

Portland, Oregon, has long been a national leader in promoting alternative transportation through Complete Streets and Vision Zero programs, and in recent years it has expanded curbside dining and a Public Street Plazas program to "give right-of-way space back to pedestrians."[97] Developed over the past decade and accelerated rapidly during the pandemic, these have become permanent programs and features of Portland's streets.

In 2012, the Portland Bureau of Transportation (PBOT) launched an experimental Street Seats program, modeled on similar initiatives in San Francisco and New York, to permit businesses to build a temporary platform in the parking lane "to allow Portlanders to enjoy a meal or a drink outdoors, while enhancing street vitality and supporting local business."[98] A pilot with three restaurants was followed by evaluation, which revealed strong business and resident support for positive impacts on commerce and street vitality though also found concerns about privatization of the right-of-way.[99] In 2013, PBOT formally instituted both commercial and public Street Seats and provided basic design guidelines. Because such facilities took up parking, operators had to pay lost meter revenue in addition to other permitting fees.

Implementation proceeded unevenly. Early on, downtown business interests, worried about the loss of parking, lobbied successfully to keep the program out of the urban core, with editorial board support from the *Oregonian*.[100] When some groups did develop Street Seats, like a team of Portland State faculty members and students who installed the first one downtown in 2014, they encountered permitting hurdles and the daunting costs of replacing meter revenue.[101] Prior to 2020, PBOT was only permitting at most fifteen Street Seats annually. PBOT senior transportation planner Nick Falbo says that "every one of those was a beautiful and unique snowflake. . . . It was a boutique program" due to permitting costs and bureaucratic review. "It couldn't be scaled," he continues, but "we need scalable solutions."[102]

The Covid-19 pandemic thus presented PBOT with both a challenge and an opportunity. After a period of lockdown, in late April 2020 the agency announced a Safe Streets program to "reconfigure streets" by closing them to vehicular through traffic in an effort to support physical distancing, active and alternative mobility, and business reopening. That May, PBOT detailed the program in the *Safe Streets: Adapting Portland's Streets for Restarting Public Life* plan, framed in the context of the Covid-19 emergency but also looking beyond the pandemic. In her introduction, PBOT Commissioner Chloe Eudaly writes: "PBOT is carefully considering how transportation behavior has changed and how it needs to change, not just as we recover from this crisis, but to support a sustainable future."[103] City leaders, initially cautious about not taking advantage of the crisis, came around to the idea of PBOT's role. This "really opened the floodgates," according to Falbo.[104]

The Safe Streets program emphasized three strategies: Slow Streets limiting through traffic on low-volume neighborhood roads, Busy Streets to convert curbside parking for additional room for socially distanced pedestrian traffic, and a Healthy Business Program enabling enterprises and organizations to adapt to social distancing by operating outdoors.[105] All reclaimed roadway space for pedestrian traffic, but only the Healthy

Business Program enabled nontransportation uses like outdoor dining, which were reflected in schematic diagrams for new Mini Neighborhood Plazas on portions of side streets converted from parking, Neighborhood Plazas closing the entire width of a portion of side streets, and even Full Main Street Closures on key corridors. Portland opened these closures to other commercial uses, including retail and merchandise displays, but it specified evaluation criteria to prioritize public projects, favor careful and creative design, and have neighborhood support. Design guidance mandated temporary installation, a clear path for pedestrian circulation, ADA accessibility, and sufficient buffering from streets. The program reflected PBOT's strong traditions of multimodal planning and belief that streets can be changed, according to Falbo, but it took Covid-19 to shift many businesses and neighborhoods from worrying over lost parking to wider "recognition that the space can be used for something else." He adds, "They were getting direct benefits. They could connect the dots."[106]

This temporary program proved enormously popular: 1,184 Healthy Business Permits were issued by the end of 2020, creating not only new street spaces but also new roles for PBOT. Henry Latourette Miller of the Street Trust, a nonprofit advocating for multimodal transportation, acknowledges that while the city had some history of street closures (e.g., farmers' markets), the pandemic "supercharged it."[107] Latourette Miller suggests that many businesses never thought they might turn to PBOT for support, but the fact that so many plazas were created so fast suggested a collaborative "moment of many people working hard to put this online, towards success," which opened minds to a different way of thinking about streets. Latourette Miller suggests these new Public Street Plazas created from roadways a "sense of traditional, almost medieval square, where there is life of all sorts." In the process, business groups, even conservative ones, Latourette Miller adds, came to "love this program, for all the reasons an urban planner would love this program."

The program was also popular among the general public. In its surveys, PBOT found that 92 percent of respondents had visited a business operating in the public right-of-way and 94 percent believed street space should remain open for business use through the pandemic. Looking ahead to program extensions into 2021, PBOT officials note that

222 Reconstructing the Street as Public Place

Portland's dense street network—constituting 40 percent of land—is "our largest public space," and ask: "What if, instead of streets like this . . . we had streets for Community . . . streets for Play . . . streets for Family . . . Streets Centering Equity?"[108] In public announcements of the program's renewal, PBOT director Chris Warner states that the program had "reshaped the way Portlanders think about how we use our streets," which transportation commissioner Jo Ann Hardesty suggests was "leading to broader conversations about community building in our right-of-way."[109]

From the beginning, PBOT was explicitly concerned not only with socially distanced movement and business support but also with how to best and most equitably share streets. It mandated clear passage for pedestrians and ADA compliance, as well as a twelve-foot emergency-access lane across each plaza. Recognizing conflicts with utilities, it required that installations be movable. Explicitly acknowledging the disproportionate risks of Covid-19 to vulnerable populations, PBOT created a grant program supporting BIPOC-owned businesses to help offset the costs of traffic-control devices and outdoor dining equipment. In the summer of 2020, it wove these within a broader, two-year Transportation Justice Partnership Program "to build PBOT's capacity to strengthen our service to and engagement of communities that have historically been underserved by our Bureau and Portland's transportation system."[110]

After more than a year of rapid experimentation and growth, PBOT used American Recovery Act funding to begin to formalize a Vibrant and Inclusive Community Spaces program to support businesses, community confidence in outdoor public spaces, community participation, and neighborhood-built environments while "providing places to gather to reconnect people."[111] In presenting the program to policymakers, PBOT planners admitted publicly that prior efforts had been done in "a real scrappy fashion" and expressed excitement to "turn this into something a little more intentional and real" by moving beyond the emergency program, driven by permit holders, toward something better integrated with the city's Transportation System Plan.[112]

These new public spaces—both Healthy Business parklets and Public Street Plazas—have endured beyond the pandemic. As of summer 2023, Portland had eleven public plazas, ten business plazas (basically extended curbside parklets), and eight hundred curbside Healthy Business permits. These spaces have been accompanied, however, by persistent and complicated questions about the proper use of streets, which are even more complicated with full street closures than parklets, that PBOT has tried to resolve in its long-term programs. "It's hard. Streets are contested spaces," Falbo notes. "There is an understanding of what streets are for. . . . You make changes to that, and people have big feelings. . . . What is the purpose of a street?" Answering these complicated questions "becomes a community conversation about public space," he adds.[113]

PBOT is trying to facilitate that conversation and distill something like consensus within its permanent program and design standards. In annual Portland Street Plaza evaluation reports, PBOT emphasizes the value of "streets as places" and the pandemic's unique opportunity to experiment with public space to better serve the community beyond parking alone.[114] Survey data revealed the success of plazas in encouraging alternative transportation, building community, promoting public safety and vibrance, and enabling free circulation. Yet, it also highlighted challenges posed by the privatized uses of these public spaces: 28 percent did not feel comfortable using the plaza without spending money.[115] Based on careful analysis of pedestrian counts and patterns, PBOT has prioritized designs that promote smooth, active mobility and encourage people to linger, reflected in a working design tool kit. Recognizing that not all parts of the city are suitable for street plazas, the agency has advocated for focusing on those neighborhood centers identified in the city's Comprehensive Plan.

These conversations informed PBOT's new *Outdoor Dining Program Design Guidelines* to formalize restaurant and bar uses of the public right-of-way while seeking to ensure access for people with disabilities, emergency response, public transit operations, and loading zones in addition to addressing street safety hazards (Figure 26).[116] Setting out four key design principles—"accessible for all, design for maintenance, keep it simple, easily removed"—the guidelines distinguish between sidewalk-only permits and curbside installations, both seasonal and year-round.[117] Having been surprised by what he calls the "robustness" of restaurant structures in the right-of-way, Falbo describes how planners have created detailed standards for siting and location, spatial arrangement to balance seating areas and access (for pedestrians, emergency services), materials and design of structures, furniture, and even lighting and electrical, in addition to requirements for operation and maintenance.[118] The need for such guidelines represents a subtle but important shift for a transportation agency, whose purview now includes not only roadway infrastructure but also the structures upon it. It's important to note that these new features are only "for temporary use of public space," cannot be affixed to the street, and must be removable within forty-eight hours for roadway or utility maintenance. And while they permit new nontransportation uses, guidelines prioritize accessible pedestrian circulation over seating. The agency is currently formalizing similar guidelines for Portland's Public Street Plazas.

These new plazas involve new forms of collaboration between PBOT and communities on both design and programming. The agency

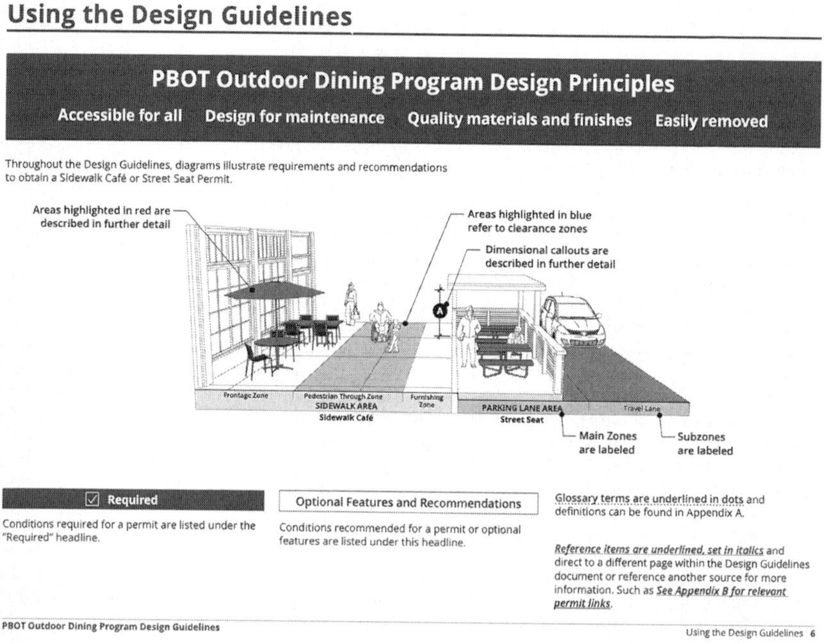

Using the Design Guidelines

PBOT Outdoor Dining Program Design Principles

Accessible for all **Design for maintenance** **Quality materials and finishes** **Easily removed**

Throughout the Design Guidelines, diagrams illustrate requirements and recommendations to obtain a Sidewalk Café or Street Seat Permit.

☑ Required

Conditions required for a permit are listed under the "Required" headline.

Optional Features and Recommendations

Conditions recommended for a permit or optional features are listed under this headline.

Glossary terms are underlined in dots and definitions can be found in Appendix A.

Reference items are underlined, set in italics and direct to a different page within the Design Guidelines document or reference another source for more information. Such as *See Appendix B for relevant permit links*.

PBOT Outdoor Dining Program Design Guidelines

Using the Design Guidelines 6

Figure 26. PBOT's *Outdoor Dining Program Design Guidelines* seek to ensure that new curbside parklets (and associated structures) are accessible, safe, and well built. Portland Bureau of Transportation, *Outdoor Dining Program Design Guidelines (Draft)* (Portland, Ore., 2023), 6.

had some experience with such engagement dating to the 1970s, but Covid-19 pushed this to new levels.[119] A good example of these new relationships is the Montavilla neighborhood on Portland's East Side, which has a vibrant business district on Stark Street but until recently lacked public spaces. Neil Mattson, the owner of a guitar studio and the president of the Montavilla East Tabor Business Association, laments how the 1920s street was "designed for cars. There's no place to pause. . . . We're starved for a place to sit and not have to purchase something to sit there."[120] When PBOT planners proposed a Public Street Plaza in 2020, locals seized the opportunity. In contrast to other street plazas attached to businesses, from the beginning PBOT and the neighborhood focused on making this a public plaza rather than a commercial space. "We had a say in making that determination," Mattson says. "It was basically PBOT proposed, 'This is going to be 100 percent public,' and we were like, 'Great!'" After initial difficulty securing consensus about the right site, PBOT closed a side street with planters in July 2021, provided public seating, and supplied paint for volunteers to create a road mural to transform the asphalt into a community space. "Our community naturally moved into that space," Mattson observes, and in the process he thinks the plaza has become "such a valued space. . . . I love the Montavilla Plaza. If it went away, there would be a sense of loss, a real sense of loss."

Interim Public Street Plazas remain temporary, and making them permanent will require resolving some complicated issues. Falbo acknowledges the legal and technical difficulties of closing streets, which is why most have officially remained temporary. He also admits that PBOT relies on private partners "maybe too much," leading him to wonder when PBOT will "grow into the role" of maintaining these plazas like they do streets.[121] Mattson agrees: "This temporary use design is messy. . . . I think the temporary plazas need to transition into something more municipal and engineered." Mattson doesn't blame the temporary program; he says the broader issue is "that our design of our streets is inadequate to what we're trying to do as a community. . . . If you really want these to succeed as plazas, then design them that way, dammit."[122]

Despite the challenges, PBOT is moving ahead to transform a number of interim plazas into permanent public space. An interim Pride

Plaza downtown on Harvey Milk Street was first created in 2021 to celebrate and provide a safe gathering space for the LGBTQ+ community. In 2022, Portland received a $1.2 million grant to redevelop it as a permanent plaza, linked to a wider downtown plan that connected other plazas, including the city's Ankeny West Park and Darcelle XV Plaza, as part of a planned six-mile linear urban park called the Green Loop.

These changes to street spaces, whether temporary or permanent, raise complicated equity issues that operate at a variety of scales. At the local level, a "primary driver" in equity conversations is the balance between embracing private use while protecting public use, according to Falbo. From experience, however, PBOT knows the importance of private partners in activating and managing the public realm. "We don't want to push back on that private use. . . . But we just don't want it to be so overwhelmingly privatized," Falbo admits. "There's a fine line."[123]

Another ongoing question has been the spatial distribution of these plazas and parklets (Figure 27). In Portland, as elsewhere, these programs are voluntary and reflect business or community initiative rather than spatial planning. Data and anecdotal observations reveal an uneven distribution of these installations across the city. Latourette Miller notes that "most of the areas that saw the most permits are whiter. . . . It's harder to disentangle correlation or causation," whether walkable streets already happened to be in whiter areas or race was itself a driver. PBOT sought to address racial equity issues in the temporary program through targeted outreach and grants to businesses identifying as BIPOC owned and continues to engage such communities in the development of the permanent program. However, Latourette Miller thinks that "addressing racial equity in this program is tough. . . . It's going to take more than outdoor dining programs to address it."[124]

A strength of the program, especially in contrast to traditional transportation engineering, has been the emphasis on local decision-making. Procedurally, this is more equitable than a top-down planning approach, but it can still reinforce distributional equity issues, since these improvements have been focused on the already-gentrified urban core and are harder to adapt to lower-income and more diverse neighborhoods like East Portland, which are more autocentric. PBOT is trying to use the planning process to address these issues, proactively cultivating participation through education and building partnerships. "We

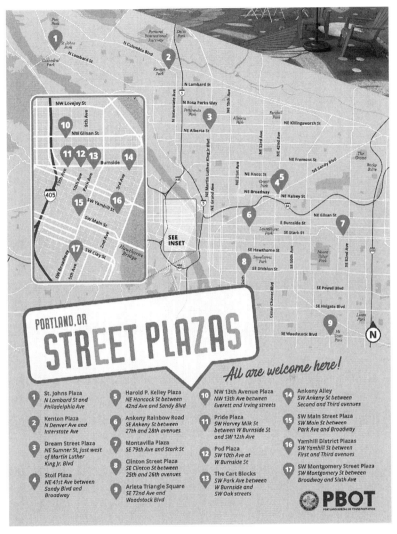

Figure 27. Portland Street Plazas have emerged across the city but remain concentrated in the more pedestrian-friendly (and gentrified) urban core, presenting equity challenges. "Public Street Plaza Directory," Portland Department of Transportation, accessed October 31, 2024, https://www.portland.gov/transportation/planning/plazas/plaza-directory.

require community partners to join us," Falbo admits, but he hopes PBOT gets to the point where these new public plazas become tools like bike lanes that are planned and funded like other infrastructure in support of the city's comprehensive plan to build town and community centers.[125]

Initially, there were concerns about the role that these improvements had on neighborhood change and gentrification, but Latourette Miller observes, "I think that conversation, which was such a big deal at the beginning, has fallen into the background."[126] Instead, the focus has shifted to bringing people downtown and successfully handling the messy life of Portland's streets within concurrent housing, drug, and mental health crises. In this context, Falbo notes, "it's hard to talk about public space when people have fears of what that public space will become. . . . It kind of poisons the conversation."[127]

Portland's efforts to reclaim streets for outdoor dining and plazas by rethinking roadways from simply transportation infrastructure into public spaces raise the myriad, complicated issues that surround public space anywhere. Planners and their partners are working hard to think them through, with balance and equity very much in mind. The programs and spaces are imperfect. Yet Latourette Miller, whose work with the Street Trust and as a local journalist connect him with diverse stakeholders, sees a bright spot: "There's so much sadness and trauma from 2020 and 2021. . . . It's so heartening to talk to folks who have never really worked with the city. . . . They all talked about this program as, 'It's good. It gives me hope for something. It's a very hopeful program.'" Though parklets took off more quickly, Latourette Miller suspects that the greater future potential may exist with the public plazas. Better balancing the public space of the street may not be easy, but he is optimistic: "Getting more use out of our streets, that's Portland's thing."[128]

Mobility Justice at Curbside and Beyond

Durable street conversions can take different forms and names, including parklets, Streateries, Shared Spaces, street patios, Public Street Plazas, and more, but they all share a fundamental and profound reorientation of the roadway surface from transportation space into the public realm. What were incipient and limited experiments prior to Covid-19 and then wildly expanded pilots during the pandemic have become commonplace across the United States. From these pop-ups and subsequent pilots, permanent programs and plaza reconstructions are emerging. The American street may never be the same again.

Such fundamental realignment recasts the conversation about mobility justice. It's still early in this paradigm shift, but the experiences of San Francisco, Washington, D.C., and Portland suggest an understanding of mobility justice that is more intersectional, introducing entirely new equity axes to those already colliding on the roadway. The basic lens of multimodal fairness still applies, demanding balance among people regardless of their modes of travel. In this sense, parklets, streateries, and public plazas are incontrovertibly more just, not only reconciling drivers and those who walk, bike, and roll but also displacing cars altogether in favor of those afoot. In the car-crazed United States, one can hardly imagine a more radical mobility equity project than a pedestrianized street.

The creation of new spaces through neighborhood or business initiatives, in contrast to traditional top-down transportation planning, has important equity implications. But this also results in an uneven—and potentially inequitable—spatial distribution. These new amenities have been located in whiter and wealthier neighborhoods with limited uptake in Black and Brown communities. Planners are aware of these issues and are working to address them, taking a proactive approach in encouraging broader neighborhood participation and providing grant support for minority businesses and underserved communities while increasingly integrating these improvements within broader transportation planning.

The social justice issues surrounding these new street spaces are complex. Though equity-minded programs seek to expand access to vulnerable neighborhoods, implementation still skews toward places with more resources. Transportation planners and urban designers, with their focus on infrastructure, have limited tools for promoting social diversity and equity among the individuals who use it. Ultimately, the most radically open strategy for inclusivity may be welcoming the public, whoever they are and however they may come, to the entire right-of-way. Additional requirements for public access and seating, even in commercial parklets, can help advance these goals, and the growing emphasis on public space programming within transportation agencies provides additional tools for proactively encouraging diversity and inclusion.

Perhaps the greatest challenge, however, is balancing the rights of the public against new private uses. Compared with parking, which is, in effect, a short-term private lease of public space, these new community uses—including private dining—represent a good change overall, yet they ultimately involve a swap of one private use for another. If we measure these new uses not against the status quo of parking but against the wider future potential of streets as fully public spaces, the question of fair access becomes more complicated.

Finally, by activating the right-of-way, these new parklets and plazas transform urban space, with outcomes that may be hard to predict. Making streets more livable and dynamic will be welcomed by many or most, especially along traffic-burdened arterials and vacant downtowns. Thus, cities are approaching these as improvements that ought to be shared across the city. Some have raised green gentrification concerns, but it's hard to assess the role of this new infrastructure in driving displacement. Whatever the impact, the changing character of local streets changes neighborhoods, so it ought to be considered carefully.

This reclaiming and remaking of the roadway surface may be spatially limited and continues to evolve, but it signifies something profound. The conversion of asphalt parking and travel lanes into community spaces represents a new way of thinking about the right-of-way as something truly public that ought to be shared by all and redesigned accordingly. A parklet seems an overly modest name for such a momentous change.

CONCLUSION
THE PROMISE AND CHALLENGE OF RECLAIMING STREETS EQUITABLY

Standing at the Intersection

The American street, centuries in the making, is at a crossroads. The past decade has seen unprecedented shifts in how we think about and design streets. People increasingly realize that public rights-of-way are our most extensive and integral public spaces. Though we've largely given them over to channeling and storing cars, people are starting to ask for something more from them (and something more equitable). The path our streets take—that we take—will help shape our urban future. A safer, more livable, sustainable, and equitable city can be found ahead, but getting there requires rethinking and reclaiming our roadways, from the curb in and centerline outward, toward an intersectional mobility justice and just streets for all.

Looking back, we're reminded that the idea of the entire street being a public space is nothing new. Until the early twentieth century, people recognized that roadways were transportation spaces, but they freely stepped into them as a public realm for walking, pausing, playing, and commerce. A century ago, drivers took over the street, and since then, roads have been regulated and engineered to marginalize everything but motorized traffic. Thus, it's hard for most of us to see them as anything but pipes for cars. If nondrivers forget their place, the street itself will remind them. Step onto most roadways and you'll at least be honked at, possibly ticketed for jaywalking, or even join the ranks of the

231

232   Conclusion

fourteen pedestrians killed every day by cars in the United States (a group disadvantaged not only by their transportation mode but typically also by their age, race, and income).

To stand in the middle of an intersection is to experience the nexus of forces that make roadways dangerous by design and inequitable in practice, rendering the least advantaged people most vulnerable to its manifold harms. There's hardly a better place to experience firsthand the colliding forces that make the contemporary city unjust.

However, that same vantage offers a glimpse of movements afoot to reframe streets as infrastructure accessible for diverse modes and to reclaim them as a public realm to be enjoyed by all. Decades of public discourse about complete and livable streets has increasingly become woven within transportation planning and translated through policy and design to accommodate alternative modes and to redefine streets as public spaces. These growing movements have provided the foundation for pandemic efforts to reclaim roadways, ostensibly for social distancing but often with a more ambitious agenda in mind. Cities have slowed their streets to reduce through traffic, opened them to walking, biking, and play, and converted them from transportation spaces into public places for gathering or dining. In the process, planners and communities have grappled with complex questions of what streets ought to be for, who they ought to serve, and how they can be shared equitably. This already-profound conversation has coincided with some of the most intense debates about racial and social justice in our nation's history. These swirling changes have spilled over the sidewalk, both figuratively and literally, to occupy the asphalt space of the American roadway in unprecedented ways.

Evolving approaches to American streets and mobility justice—through history, theory, and case studies of leading cities—offer a glimpse into a very different kind of urban future, which in many ways hearkens back to the past. Thinking historically, we realize that streets transformed from public places into vehicular thoroughfares a century ago could be remade for pedestrian-friendly civic life. Reconceptualizing mobility and mobility justice, particularly through the insights of social theory, helps us think more deeply about who streets should serve (and how). These historical and theoretical perspectives highlight the significance of recent, rapid, and perhaps fundamental shifts beyond multimodal

Complete Streets to reclaim the roadway through public placemaking. Creative experimentation and methodical planning by leading cities offer both inspiration and cautionary lessons. I happened to feature Boston, Oakland, Pittsburgh, New York, Denver, Los Angeles, San Francisco, Washington, D.C., and Portland, but these are only a few good examples. Across the United States, towns and cities offer stories of planners and communities reclaiming streets as public places, which suggests the unprecedented opportunities and challenges of remaking something as central, contested, and important as the public street, and doing so equitably.

Toward a More Intersectional Mobility Justice

To recount the history of the American street is to reveal the ways changing ideas about mobility and public space have manifested on the roadway. Even as the hegemony of motorists was literally cemented on twentieth-century streets, the claims of other users and uses endured. The critiques of urbanists and alternative-transportation advocates, often framed implicitly in terms of fairness, set the foundation for movements over recent decades for safer and more livable Complete Streets. The pursuit of multimodal access opened the way to a yet more profound realization (or perhaps recollection) that streets have been and could again serve diverse forms of transportation and public space uses. These evolving public discourses have paralleled dynamic scholarly conversations rethinking transportation, mobility, and the public street. These lenses bring into focus the street's potential as more than just a physical facility for "the purposes of vehicular travel" to see its role as a social space. What's more, they invite us to see public placemaking potential not only in parks, plazas, and sidewalks but also beyond the curb on the roadway itself. If we open our eyes and stretch our imaginations, what comes into view is the fuller potential of the American street as a public space where people can come together to claim their rights to space and access, to express themselves, and to forge relationships with others.

Claiming mobility as a right and contesting streets as public spaces raise complex questions that are easier asked than they are answered, however. What exactly do we mean by *mobility justice*? Navigating vibrant debates requires a careful theoretical synthesis of distinct approaches to equity: distributional, multimodal, social, place-based, intergenerational, and procedural. Because they view mobility justice from conceptually different perspectives, suggesting different strategies and remedies, they can at times seem—like traffic at an intersection—to collide. For this reason, I have argued for an intersectional mobility justice that carefully acknowledges intersectionality's feminist and antiracist roots yet extends the concept to see mobility and its experiences and politics— what Kimberlé Crenshaw calls the "complexities of compoundedness."[1] American streets and cities are, of course, impossible to understand apart from the social disadvantages experienced by women, people of color, and other oppressed groups. Yet disadvantage can take other forms too, as any child walking to school or cyclist navigating a busy intersection can attest. Intersectionality attunes us to individual experiences and social differences, but it inherently resists narrowing to any particular category and instead embraces the compoundedness of who we are and how we travel. It also helps to remind us that the experiences of mobility and equity (or its absence) are inseparable from societal structures and urban infrastructures. I therefore hope my effort to define *intersectional mobility justice* can be perceived as I intended it, not as cultural appropriation but as the logical extension of an idea of transcendent intellectual power.

Amid complex debates about mobility justice, in which people often talk past one another, an intersectional approach highlights distinct ways to approach equity and how they intersect within each of us and the streets we traverse. Like any intersection, however, we must somehow reconcile them. I've suggested that, ideally, our streets should be planned to fairly distribute the benefits of access and mobility across society and space, to ensure all transportation users would enjoy their fair share of safe and convenient access to street spaces, to provide an inclusive experience for diverse people, to catalyze inclusive and sustainable urban change without displacing existing residents, and to offer all users and affected residents a meaningful voice in decision-making. At times these approaches, axes, and priorities may appear to collide—for example, in presenting choices between installing bike lanes for today's cyclists (and tomorrow's planet) and preserving neighborhoods from the perceived threat of gentrification, between top-down spatial planning and empowering local control over streets, and myriad other balancing acts. An intersectional mobility justice does not automatically reconcile these approaches, but it attunes us to the challenge of articulating and weighing our values and applying them carefully through public decision-making toward a multifaceted vision and approach to just streets. Without a robust and intersectional theory of mobility justice, it's hard to reclaim streets equitably in practice.

From Multimodal Planning to Public Placemaking

Informed by values like sustainability and transportation equity, whether explicit or implicit, cities are increasingly reimagining their streets and reclaiming them through policy, design, and on-the-ground projects. Many are committed to slowing their streets not just for safety and livability but also to fundamentally reorder the relationship among different modes and between streets and surrounding neighborhoods. From maturing traditions of traffic calming and livable-street design, cities like Boston have embraced the basic traffic hump as a basic right of residents on all local streets. Oakland and Pittsburgh have drawn upon their experiences with bicycle planning to experiment with Covid-19 era Slow Streets, providing a model for permanent Slow Streets, Neighborways, and traffic-calming programs. By slowing streets, these cities have invited nondrivers to reoccupy the roadway for active mobility, conversation, and play. Even more ambitious are programs to close streets to vehicular traffic in order to open them for slow mobility and public space for days, weeks, or years on end. New York, Denver, and Los Angeles hastily installed barricades during the pandemic to convert local roadways into shared or *woonerf* streets. Though many of these roadways have been reopened to through traffic, these cities are applying lessons learned into planning and public improvements to promote multimodal safety and accessibility, expand open space in often park-poor neighborhoods, and help build community through the power of the public realm. Taking these ideas to their logical extreme, cities have increasingly and durably transformed roadways from transportation spaces into pedestrianized public places. San Francisco's early experiments with public parklets have evolved into a robust Shared Spaces program, Washington, D.C., has expanded streateries to extend sidewalk uses beyond the curb, and Portland increasingly looks beyond curbside dining to reclaim the entire public right-of-way as street plazas. Such pedestrianization of roadway space, often through the installation of features and structures, represents a major shift in the American streetscape,

236   Conclusion

some of which is shifting from interim to permanent. The nomenclature of such programs is complicated, and distinctions among them can be subtle. In this book, I have tried to categorize and classify these emerging approaches through a few case studies, but I cannot encompass all of the diverse experiments happening in American towns and cities. However, these broadening efforts share in common a radically ambitious goal: to remake streets from pipes for cars back into places for people.

In the process, these programs exemplify the opportunities and challenges of manifesting mobility justice on the street. How well do they measure up? They all seek a fair spatial distribution of accessibility and public improvements across the city's diverse neighborhoods and rely on transportation planning, mapping, and equity matrixes to guide decision-making. These cities increasingly go beyond multimodal accommodation at the margins to prioritize walking, biking, and public gathering, carefully balancing diverse uses through the details of policy and (especially) design. Planners have embraced the roadway's broader potential as public space, particularly for outdoor dining, but they nonetheless seek to maintain accessibility for nondrivers and emergency vehicles and to balance their public-realm value against the risks of privatizing public space. These programs, linked to sustainability goals, have an eye to future generations, but they are increasingly sensitive to the risks of displacement today. Procedurally, they endeavor to balance the benefits of top-down spatial planning with neighborhood input, purposefully engaging diverse and underserved neighborhoods through public processes whose level of democracy is unprecedented in the traditionally technocratic realm of traffic engineering. These programs are, of course, imperfect and must contend with the city's broader inequities. Compared with the status quo, however, they represent remarkable progress.

By welcoming nonmobility and broader public (and even private) uses onto the street, however, they substantially widen conversations about who the street should be for, which goes beyond equity among transportation users to more complex questions about sharing public space. Planners, advocates, and community members are grappling with these issues, showing careful thought about equity and mobility justice, defined in diverse yet remarkably similar ways. In their efforts to transform and manage the roadway as a public realm, however, they increasingly venture into novel territory for American transportation agencies. Not least of these challenges is how to balance vehicular access within pedestrianized public spaces. In this regard, European cities and their plazas could offer good lessons for American cities, but that would be another book entirely.

Where Might All This Lead?

In the broader scheme of things, these efforts to reclaim roadways remain marginal. They have been undertaken by only some cities, on only a certain number of streets, often for only limited periods of time. Many of the barricades and curbside gathering places that appeared during the pandemic have disappeared, and traffic has resurged in their place. Yet, this book highlights the important ways that new ideas about the roadway can become woven into policy, design, and thus the infrastructural DNA of everyday streets. The methodical institutionalization of Slow Streets, Open Streets, and curbside parklets and Public Street Plazas is perhaps less thrilling than dizzying pandemic rollouts, yet maybe it reflects an even more important and lasting shift. Like the pivot points of the mass manufacturing of autos and the influenza pandemic a century ago, we may be experiencing not a historical aberration but a watershed moment.

If we are indeed witnessing the beginnings of a longer-term transformation, they suggest a very different future ahead for the American public street and city. Look around and one sees opportunities abounding. Let's start with the neighborhood streets outside many of our houses or apartments, now likely dominated by cars. What if these were calmed with speed humps or transformed into Slow Streets or Neighborways, block by block, over the upcoming decades? This would be no more radical transformation than that effected a century ago, with no less radical consequences. Now let's imagine closing local streets—in our neighborhoods or downtown centers—to prioritize pedestrians, cyclists, and public gathering. Most of our towns and cities have innumerable candidate streets and potential people and businesses who might use them differently. Given the chance to stroll down the centerline of a downtown street, or to set up tables where cars typically park, one starts to see possibilities that are hard to unsee. This can lead to other realizations, like

238 Conclusion

the potential of curbside parking to become parklets or places to expand sidewalks and imagining how the entire right-of-way could become a plaza or park. Such visions are not only attractive to pedestrians, cyclists, and wheelchair users but can also appeal to neighboring residents and businesses. Transformations that start small with pop-up experiments can grow and become permanent, inspiring other places to take back their roadways too, now guided by the institutional power policy and design.

One doesn't have to look far to grasp the magnitude of the possibility: forty million miles of roadways in the United States, totaling more than twenty thousand square miles of land, often occupying more than 30 percent of our urban cores and 80 percent of municipal public space. Reclaim only a small portion of that and the transformation to our cities and planet would be astounding. Done properly, under the banner and principles of intersectional mobility justice, we could transform the very fabric of our lives and the societies of which we are part, helping us all share more fairly in all the mobility, social opportunities, and vibrance that a good street and city can offer. It's tempting to ponder.

The Journey Begins

These are exciting times to rethink mobility and the public roadway in the realms of theory and public space itself, inviting us to reimagine a very different street and city. In this sense, the everyday intersection provides an ideal material space and metaphor for conceiving a more comprehensive, compounded understanding of mobility justice that might guide efforts to create a more just city.

It's a remarkable moment when ideas and urban spaces simultaneously take great leaps forward, opening our minds to different understandings of something as fundamental as the street and suggesting pathways toward a better transportation system and a more just public realm. In something as simple as a speed hump or barricade, a café table, or a chalked hopscotch square on the asphalt roadway, we get a glimpse of both the past and possible futures.

We need to recognize that the public street, though integral to the social life of the city, has its limits. Making streets more equitable is necessary for making our cities more just, but it is hardly sufficient to address complex urban issues that transcend the public right-of-way.

Good policy and street design can only go so far to remake the city in the image of mobility justice. Because streets and roadways run through our cities and our lives, however, and their public spaces offer such vast, transformative potential, we can gain much by reclaiming them, and recognizing this project—ambitious as it is—can get us only part of the way.

Following the oft-quoted Chinese proverb attributed to philosopher Lao Tzu, we are reminded that "a journey of a thousand miles begins with a single footfall."[2] The project of defining equity and justice and creating equitable public streets for people is not new. Yet, thanks in part to the pandemic, this trajectory has accelerated markedly in recent years. Fully wresting our roads from cars will take unprecedented collaboration and entail new conflicts. If we are able to better realize the street's intersectional potential as a multimodal mobility space and public place, however, we will have moved much closer to a more just and vibrant city. Getting there can begin by stepping off the curb and onto the asphalt roadway to reclaim it one step at a time.

NOTES

Preface

1. "Public Road and Street Mileage in the United States by Type of Surface," Bureau of Transportation Statistics, accessed April 2, 2024, https://www.bts.gov/content/public-road-and-street-mileage-united-states-type-surfacea.

2. Michael Manville and Donald Shoup, "Parking, People, and Cities," *Journal of Urban Planning and Development* 131, no. 4 (2005): 233–45; National Association of City Transportation Officials, *Urban Street Design Guide* (New York, 2013).

3. Federal Highway Administration, *Summary of Travel Trends: 2022 National Household Travel Survey* (Washington, D.C.: United States Department of Transportation, 2023).

Introduction

1. Kenneth T. Jackson, *Crabgrass Frontier: The Suburbanization of the United States* (New York: Oxford University Press, 1985).

2. John M. Barry, "How the Horrific 1918 Flu Spread across America," *Smithsonian Magazine,* November 2017.

3. Francesco Aimone, "The 1918 Influenza Epidemic in New York City: A Review of the Public Health Response," *Public Health Reports* 125, supp. 3 (2010): 71–79.

4. Peter D. Norton, *Fighting Traffic: The Dawn of the Motor Age in the American City* (Cambridge, Mass.: MIT Press, 2008).

5. "About Black Lives Matter," Black Lives Matter, accessed March 7, 2024, https://blacklivesmatter.com/about.

6. "Complete Streets," Smart Growth America, accessed March 7, 2024, https://smartgrowthamerica.org/what-are-complete-streets/.

7. Tim Cresswell, "Towards a Politics of Mobility," *Environment and Planning D: Society and Space* 28, no. 1 (2010): 21; Kevin Hannam, Mimi Sheller, and John Urry, "Editorial: Mobilities, Immobilities and Moorings," *Mobilities* 1, no. 1 (2006): 1–22.

8. Robert D. Bullard and Glenn S. Johnson, *Just Transportation: Dismantling Race and Class Barriers to Mobility* (Gabriola Island, B.C.: New Society, 1997).

9. Karel Martens, *Transport Justice: Designing Fair Transportation Systems* (London: Routledge, 2017).

10. Mimi Sheller, *Mobility Justice: The Politics of Movement in an Age of Extremes* (London: Verso, 2018), 34.

11. Hannam, Sheller, and Urry, "Editorial," 15; Deborah Cowen, "Infrastructures of Empire and Resistance," *Verso Books Blog,* January 25, 2017, www.versobooks.com/blogs/news/3067-infrastructures-of-empire-and-resistance.

12. Andreas Marklund and Mogens Rüdiger, "Historicizing Infrastructure: After the Material Turn," in *Historicizing Infrastructure,* ed. Andreas Marklund and Mogens Rüdiger (Aalborg, Denmark: Aalborg University Press, 2017), 5–20; Alan Latham and Jack Layton, "Social Infrastructure and the Public Life of Cities: Studying Urban Sociality and Public Spaces," *Geography Compass* 13, no. 7 (2019): 3.

13. Regan Koch and Alan Latham, "Rethinking Urban Public Space: Accounts from a Junction in West London," *Transactions of the Institute of British Geographers* 37, no. 4 (2012): 521.

14. Jason W. Reece, "In Pursuit of a Twenty-First Century Just City: The Evolution of Equity Planning Theory and Practice," *Journal of Planning Literature* 33, no. 3 (2018): 300.

15. John G. Stehlin, *Cyclescapes of the Unequal City: Bicycle Infrastructure and Uneven Development* (Minneapolis: University of Minnesota Press, 2019), 11.

16. See, for example, Winnifred Curran and Trina Hamilton, introduction to *Just Green Enough: Urban Development and Environmental Gentrification,* ed. Winifred Curran and Trina Hamilton (New York: Routledge, 2017); Joerg Chet Tremmel, *A Theory of Intergenerational Justice* (London: Earthscan, 2009).

17. Susan S. Fainstein, "The Just City," *International Journal of Urban Sciences* 18, no. 1 (2014): 1.

18. "Complete Streets," Smart Growth America.

Notes to Chapter 1   243

19. "What Is Vision Zero?," Vision Zero Network, accessed December 1, 2023, https://visionzeronetwork.org/about/what-is-vision-zero/.

20. "About NACTO," National Association of City Transportation Officials, accessed February 2, 2023, https://nacto.org/about.

21. Kimberlé Crenshaw, "Demarginalizing the Intersection of Race and Sex: A Black Feminist Critique of Antidiscrimination Doctrine, Feminist Theory and Antiracist Politics," *University of Chicago Legal Forum* (1989): 149.

22. Kimberlé Crenshaw, Neil Gotanda, Gary Peller, and Kendall Thomas, introduction to *Critical Race Theory: The Key Writings That Formed the Movement,* ed. Kimberlé Crenshaw, Neil Gotanda, Gary Peller, and Kendall Thomas (New York: New Press), xiii.

23. Ange-Marie Hancock, *Intersectionality: An Intellectual History* (New York: Oxford University Press, 2016).

24. Hancock, *Intersectionality.*

25. Peter Hopkins, "Social Geography I: Intersectionality," *Progress in Human Geography* 43, no. 5 (2019): 941.

26. Lesley Murray, Kim Sawchuk, and Paola Jirón, "Comparative Mobilities in an Unequal World: Researching Intersections of Gender and Generation," *Mobilities* 11, no. 4 (2016): 542–52.

27. Crenshaw, "Demarginalizing the Intersection of Race and Sex," 167.

28. Norton, *Fighting Traffic*; David Prytherch, *Law, Engineering, and the American Right-of-Way: Imagining a More Just Street* (London: Palgrave Macmillan, 2018).

1. A Short History of the American Street

1. Geoffrey Hindley, *A History of Roads* (London: Peter Davies, 1971).

2. Lewis Mumford, *The City in History: Its Origins, Its Transformations, and Its Prospects* (New York: Harcourt, Brace & World, 1961), 72.

3. Mumford, *City in History,* 72.

4. John Gregory, *The Story of the Road: From the Beginning Down to A.D.* (London: Alexander Maclehose, 1931), 83.

5. Hindley, *History of Roads.*

6. Gregory, *Story of the Road,* 153.

7. Mumford, *City in History,* 368–69.

8. Mumford, 370.

9. John Reps, *Town Planning in Frontier America* (Columbia: University of Missouri Press, 1980).

10. Gregory, *Story of the Road,* 167.

11. Reps, *Town Planning in Frontier America,* 143.

Notes to Chapter 1

12. Clay McShane, *Down the Asphalt Path: The Automobile and the American City* (New York: Columbia University Press, 1994), 7.

13. McShane, *Down the Asphalt Path,* 51.

14. McShane, 62.

15. McShane, 80.

16. McShane, 62.

17. Peter D. Norton, *Fighting Traffic: The Dawn of the Motor Age in the American City* (Cambridge, Mass.: MIT Press, 2011), 7.

18. Kenneth T. Jackson, *Crabgrass Frontier: The Suburbanization of the United States* (New York: Oxford University Press, 1985), 162.

19. Norton, *Fighting Traffic,* 19.

20. Norton, 63.

21. McShane, *Down the Asphalt Path,* 173.

22. Nancy Tomes, "'Destroyer and Teacher': Managing the Masses during the 1918–1919 Influenza Pandemic," *Public Health Reports* 125, supp. 3 (2010): 48.

23. Miles C. Coleman and Will Mari, "Networks in Motion: The Alliances of Information Communication Technologies and Mobility Technologies during the 1918 Influenza Pandemic," *Mobile Media and Communication* 11, no. 2 (2023): 164.

24. John M. Barry, "How the Horrific 1918 Flu Spread across America," *Smithsonian Magazine,* November 2017.

25. Coleman and Mari, "Networks in Motion," 164.

26. Jackson, *Crabgrass Frontier,* 162.

27. McShane, *Down the Asphalt Path,* 173–74.

28. McShane, 174.

29. Stephen Robertson, Shane White, and Stephen Garton, "Harlem in Black and White: Mapping Race and Place in the 1920s," *Journal of Urban History* 39, no. 5 (2013): 871.

30. Norton, *Fighting Traffic.*

31. Norton, 17.

32. Norton, 52.

33. Norton, 52–53; David Prytherch, *Law, Engineering, and the American Right-of-Way: Imagining a More Just Street* (New York: Palgrave, 2018).

34. Norton, *Fighting Traffic,* 116.

35. McShane, *Down the Asphalt Path,* 216.

36. Jane Holtz Kay, *Asphalt Nation: How the Automobile Took Over America and How We Can Take It Back* (New York: Crown, 1997), 183.

37. Norton, *Fighting Traffic,* 140.

38. Norton, 140.

Notes to Chapter 1   245

39. Norton, 16.

40. Daniel H. Burnham and Edward H. Bennett, *Plan of Chicago* (Chicago: Commercial Club of Chicago, 1909).

41. Burnham and Bennett, *Plan of Chicago,* 39–41.

42. Cincinnati City Planning Commission, *The Official City Plan of Cincinnati, Ohio* (Cincinnati, Ohio: City Planning Commission, 1925), 97.

43. Norton, *Fighting Traffic,* 187.

44. Norton, 254.

45. National Committee on Uniform Traffic Laws and Ordinances, *Uniform Vehicle Code* (Washington, D.C.: National Committee on Uniform Traffic Laws and Ordinances, 2000), 1.

46. National Committee on Uniform Traffic Laws and Ordinances, *Uniform Vehicle Code,* 1.

47. National Committee on Uniform Traffic Laws and Ordinances, 7.

48. National Committee on Uniform Traffic Laws and Ordinances, 138.

49. Transportation Research Board, *Highway Capacity Manual: A Guide for Multimodal Mobility Analysis,* 6th ed. (Washington, D.C.: National Academies of Sciences, Engineering, and Medicine, 2016).

50. Jackson, *Crabgrass Frontier,* 250.

51. Ryan Reft, Amanda Phillips de Lucas, and Rebecca Retzlaff, "How Can a Highway Be Racist?," in *Justice and the Interstates: The Racist Truth about Urban Highways,* ed. Ryan Reft, Amanda K. Phillips de Lucas, and Rebecca C. Retzlaff (Washington, D.C.: Island Press, 2023), 3.

52. Reft, Phillips de Lucas, and Retzlaff, "How Can a Highway Be Racist?," 3; Rebecca Retzlaff and Jocelyn Zanzot, "The Interstates, Racism, and the Need for Truth and Reconciliation: The Case of Highway Routing in Alabama," in Reft, Phillips de Lucas, and Retzlaff, *Justice and the Interstates,* 35.

53. Richard F. Weingroff, "100th Anniversary: An Evolving Partnership," *Public Roads* 78, no. 3 (2014), www.highways.dot.gov/public-roads/november december-2014/100th-anniversary-evolving-partnership.

54. American Association of State Highway and Transportation Officials, *A Policy on Geometric Design of Highways and Streets,* 6th ed. (Washington, D.C., 2011), xlii.

55. American Association of State Highway and Transportation Officials, *A Policy on Geometric Design of Highways and Streets,* 7th ed. (Washington, D.C., 2017), 2.

56. Federal Highway Administration, *Manual on Uniform Traffic Control Devices for Streets and Highways* (Washington, D.C.: U.S. Department of Transportation, 2012), I-1.

57. Mumford, *City in History,* 507.

58. Jane Jacobs, *The Death and Life of Great American Cities* (New York: Vintage Books, 1961), 29.

59. Jacobs, *Death and Life of Great American Cities,* 50.

60. Jacobs, 364.

61. Amanda Phillips de Lucas, "The Perils of Civic Participation: Community Engagement and Interstate Planning in Baltimore," in Reft, Phillips de Lucas, and Retzlaff, *Justice and the Interstates,* 99.

62. Damon Scott, *The City Aroused: Queer Places and Urban Redevelopment in Postwar San Francisco* (Austin: University of Texas Press, 2023), 16.

63. Gilbert Estrada and Jerry González, "Latino Interchanges: Greater Los Angeles in the Freeway Era," in Reft, Phillips de Lucas, and Retzlaff, *Justice and the Interstates,* 140.

64. James Howard Kunstler, *The Geography of Nowhere: The Rise and Decline of America's Man-Made Landscape* (New York: Free Press, 1994), 113.

65. Kunstler, *Geography of Nowhere,* 124.

66. Andres Duany, Elizabeth Plater-Zyberk, and Jeff Speck, *Suburban Nation: The Rise of Sprawl and the Decline of the American Dream* (New York: North Point, 2000), 70.

67. Duany, Plater-Zyberk, and Speck, *Suburban Nation,* 195.

68. Robert D. Bullard, introduction to *Highway Robbery: Transportation Racism & New Routes to Equity,* ed. Robert D. Bullard, Glenn S. Johnson, and Angel O. Torres (Cambridge, Mass.: South End, 2004), 3, 11.

69. Michael Leccese and Kathleen McCormick, eds., *Charter of the New Urbanism* (New York: McGraw-Hill, 2000), 5.

70. Leccese and McCormick, *Charter of the New Urbanism,* 142, 145.

71. Bullard, introduction, 5.

72. Robin Smith, Sharlene Reed, and Shana Baker, "Street Design: Part 1. Complete Streets," *Public Roads* 74, no. 1 (2010): 1.

73. Barbara McCann, *Completing Our Streets: The Transition to Safe and Inclusive Transportation Networks* (Washington, D.C.: Island Press, 2013), 9.

74. McCann, *Completing Our Streets,* 22–23.

75. National Complete Streets Coalition, *Fact Sheet: Elements of an Ideal Complete Streets Policy* (Washington, D.C.: Smart Growth America, 2016), 1–2.

76. American Association of State Highway and Transportation Officials, *Guide for the Planning, Design, and Operation of Pedestrian Facilities,* 1st ed. (Washington, D.C., 2004), 2.

77. National Association of City Transportation Officials, "Our Mission," accessed October 18, 2024, https://nacto.org/about/.

78. "Park(ing) Day: The Origin Story," My Parking Day, accessed December 2, 2022, https://www.myparkingday.org/about.

Notes to Chapter 2   247

79. "Urban Street Design Guide," National Association of City Transportation Officials, accessed November 20, 2024, https://nacto.org/publication/urban-street-design-guide/.

80. Federal Highway Administration, *2017 National Household Transportation Survey* (Washington, DC: U.S. Department of Transportation, 2019).

81. United States Environmental Protection Agency, *Data Highlights Inventory of U.S. Greenhouse Gas Emissions and Sinks: 1990–2021* (Washington, D.C., 2023).

82. Smart Growth America, *Dangerous by Design 2021* (Washington, D.C.: Smart Growth America, 2021), 4.

83. Smart Growth America, *Dangerous by Design 2021,* 7.

84. Smart Growth America, 5.

85. Smart Growth America, *Dangerous by Design 2021,* 26.

86. Smart Growth America, *Dangerous by Design 2020* (Washington, D.C.: Smart Growth America, 2020).

87. Melina Druga, "AAA Report: Traffic Volume Plunged in Spring 2020," *Transportation Today,* July 21, 2021, https://transportationtodaynews.com/news/23344-aaa-report-traffic-volume-plunged-in-spring-2020/.

88. Michael Wilson, "Why Driving in New York City Now Feels 'Post-Apocalyptic,'" *New York Times,* May 17, 2020, https://www.nytimes.com/2020/05/17/nyregion/coronavirus-nyc-driving-traffic.html.

89. National Association of City Transportation Officials, *Streets for Pandemic Response & Recovery* (Washington, D.C.: National Association of City Transportation Officials, 2020).

90. National Association of City Transportation Officials, *Streets for Pandemic Response & Recovery,* 2.

91. "38th and Chicago," Meet Minneapolis, accessed November 20, 2024, https://www.minneapolis.org/support-black-lives/38th-and-chicago/.

92. Black Lives Matter, "About," accessed October 18, 2024, https://blacklivesmatter.com/about/.

93. Smart Growth America, "What Are Complete Streets?," accessed October 18, 2024, https://smartgrowthamerica.org/what-are-complete-streets/.

94. U.S. Department of Transportation, *U.S. DOT Strategic Plan FY 2022–2026* (Washington, D.C.: U.S. Department of Transportation, 2022), iv.

2. On the Road to Mobility Justice

1. Henri Lefebvre, "The Right to the City," in *Writings on Cities,* trans. and ed. Eleonore Kofman and Elizabeth Lebas (Cambridge, Mass.: Blackwell, 1996), 179.

2. Kimberlé Crenshaw, "Demarginalizing the Intersection of Race and Sex: A Black Feminist Critique of Antidiscrimination Doctrine, Feminist Theory and Antiracist Politics," *University of Chicago Legal Forum* (1989): 139–68.

3. Kimberlé Crenshaw, Neil Gotanda, Gary Peller, and Kendall Thomas, introduction to *Critical Race Theory: The Key Writings That Formed the Movement*, ed. Kimberlé Crenshaw, Neil Gotanda, Gary Peller, and Kendall Thomas (New York: New Press), xiii.

4. Peter Hopkins, "Social Geography I: Intersectionality," *Progress in Human Geography* 43, no. 5 (2019): 941.

5. Lesley Murray, Kim Sawchuk, and Paola Jirón, "Comparative Mobilities in an Unequal World: Researching Intersections of Gender and Generation," *Mobilities* 11, no. 4 (2016): 542–52.

6. Hopkins, "Social Geography I," 941.

7. Susan Hanson and Mei-Po Kwan, *Transport: Critical Essays in Human Geography* (New York: Routledge, 2009), xiii–xiv.

8. Tim Cresswell and Peter Merriman, eds., *Geographies of Mobilities: Practices, Spaces, Subjects* (Surry, U.K.: Ashgate, 2011), 110.

9. Weiqiang Lin, "Transport Provision and the Practice of Mobilities Production," *Progress in Human Geography* 42, no. 1 (2018): 92–111.

10. Tim Cresswell, "Towards a Politics of Mobility," *Environment and Planning D: Society and Space* 28, no. 1 (2010): 21.

11. Kevin Hannam, Mimi Sheller, and John Urry, "Editorial: Mobilities, Immobilities and Moorings," *Mobilities* 1, no. 1 (2006): 15.

12. Jason Henderson, *Street Fight: The Politics of Mobility in San Francisco* (Amherst: University of Massachusetts Press, 2013).

13. Jason W. Patton, "A Pedestrian World: Competing Rationalities and the Calculation of Transportation Change," *Environment and Planning A: Economy and Space* 39, no. 4 (2007): 928.

14. Hannam, Sheller, and Urry, "Editorial," 1.

15. Theresa Erin Enright, "Mass Transportation in the Neoliberal City: The Mobilizing Myths of the Grand Paris Express," *Environment and Planning A: Economy and Space* 45, no. 4 (2013): 797–813; Deborah Cowen, "Infrastructures of Empire and Resistance," *Verso Books Blog*, January 25, 2017, www.versobooks.com/blogs/news/3067-infrastructures-of-empire-and-resistance.

16. Henderson, *Street Fight*, 17–18.

17. Mimi Sheller, *Mobility Justice: The Politics of Movement in an Age of Extremes* (London: Verso, 2018), 261.

18. Lefebvre, "Right to the City," 179.

19. Kafui A. Attoh, "What *Kind* of Right Is the Right to the City?," *Progress in Human Geography* 35, no. 5 (2011): 664.

Notes to Chapter 2 249

20. *Oxford English Dictionary,* s.v. "infrastructure (*n.*)," July 2023, https://doi.org/10.1093/OED/1098763874.

21. Andreas Marklund and Mogens Rüdiger, "Historicizing Infrastructure: After the Material Turn," in *Historicizing Infrastructure,* ed. Andreas Marklund and Mogens Rüdiger (Aalborg, Denmark: Aalborg University Press, 2017), 1.

22. Alan Latham and Jack Layton, "Social Infrastructure and the Public Life of Cities: Studying Urban Sociality and Public Spaces," *Geography Compass* 13, no. 7 (2019): 3.

23. Marklund and Rüdiger, "Historicizing Infrastructure," 7.

24. Erik Swyngedouw, "Metabolic Urbanization: The Making of Cyborg Cities," in *In the Nature of Cities: Urban Political Ecology and the Politics of Urban Metabolism,* ed. Nik Heynen, Maria Kaika, and Erik Swyngedouw (New York: Routledge, 2006), 21.

25. Stephen Graham and Simon Marvin, *Splintering Urbanism: Networked Infrastructures, Technological Mobilities and the Urban Condition* (London: Routledge, 2001), 8.

26. Swyngedouw, "Metabolic Urbanization," 37.

27. Latham and Layton, "Social Infrastructure and the Public Life of Cities," 3.

28. Eric Klinenberg, *Palaces for the People: How Social Infrastructure Can Help Fight Inequality, Polarization, and the Decline of Civic Life* (New York: Crown, 2018), 16.

29. Latham and Layton, "Social Infrastructure and the Public Life of Cities," 9.

30. Regan Koch and Alan Latham, "Rethinking Urban Public Space: Accounts from a Junction in West London," *Transactions of the Institute of British Geographers* 37, no. 4 (2012): 515.

31. Marco te Brömmelstroet, Anna Nikolaeva, Meredith Glaser, Morten Skou Nicolaisen, and Carmen Chan, "Travelling Together Alone and Alone Together: Mobility and Potential Exposure to Diversity," *Applied Mobilities* 2, no. 1 (2017): 9.

32. Brömmelstroet et al., "Travelling Together Alone," 11.

33. John G. Stehlin, *Cyclescapes of the Unequal City: Bicycle Infrastructure and Uneven Development* (Minneapolis: University of Minnesota Press, 2019), 55.

34. Nicholas Blomley, *Rights of Passage: Sidewalks and the Regulation of Public Flow* (New York: Taylor and Francis, 2011).

35. *Oxford English Dictionary,* s.v. "public (*adj.*), sense 4.a," June 2024, https://doi.org/10.1093/OED/4949712546.

250 Notes to Chapter 2

36. Peter G. Goheen, "Public Space and the Geography of the Modern City," *Progress in Human Geography* 22, no. 4 (1998): 479–96.

37. Sharon Zukin, *The Cultures of Cities* (Cambridge, Mass.: Blackwell, 1995), 10.

38. Junxi Qian, "Geographies of Public Space: Variegated Publicness, Variegated Epistemologies," *Progress in Human Geography* 44, no. 1 (2020): 91.

39. Lefebvre, "Right to the City," 195.

40. Mark Purcell, "Excavating Lefebvre: The Right to the City and Its Urban Politics of the Inhabitant," *GeoJournal* 58, no. 2 (2002): 99–108.

41. Don Mitchell, *The Right to the City: Social Justice and the Fight for Public Space* (New York: Guilford, 2003), 190.

42. Zukin, *Cultures of Cities,* 11.

43. Darshan Vigneswaran, Kurt Iveson, and Setha Low, "Problems, Publicity and Public Space: A Resurgent Debate," *Environment and Planning A: Economy and Space* 49, no. 3 (2017): 496–502; Qian, "Geographies of Public Space," 78.

44. Lynn A. Staeheli and Don Mitchell, "Locating the Public in Research and Practice," *Progress in Human Geography* 31, no. 6 (2007): 792–811.

45. Qian, "Geographies of Public Space," 78.

46. Junjia Ye, "Re-orienting Geographies of Urban Diversity and Coexistence: Analyzing Inclusion and Difference in Public Space," *Progress in Human Geography* 43, no. 3 (2019): 490; Don Mitchell, "People's Park Again: On the End and Ends of Public Space," *Environment and Planning A: Economy and Space* 49, no. 3 (2017): 503–18.

47. Rafael H. M. Pereira, Tim Schwanen, and David Banister, "Distributive Justice and Equity in Transportation," *Transport Reviews* 37, no. 2 (2017): 170–91.

48. John Rawls, *A Theory of Justice* (Cambridge, Mass.: Harvard University Press, 1971), 4–7.

49. Rawls, *Theory of Justice,* 19.

50. David Harvey, *Social Justice and the City* (Baltimore: Johns Hopkins University Press, 1973), 98.

51. Edward W. Soja, *Seeking Spatial Justice* (Minneapolis: University of Minnesota Press, 2010), 74.

52. Karel Martens, Aaron Golub, and Glenn Robinson, "A Justice-Theoretic Approach to the Distribution of Transportation Benefits: Implications for Transportation Planning Practice in the United States," *Transportation Research Part A: Policy and Practice* 46, no. 4 (2012): 684–95.

53. Jonathan Levine, Joe Grengs, and Louis A. Merlin, *From Mobility to Accessibility: Transforming Urban Transportation and Land-Use Planning* (Ithaca, N.Y.: Cornell University Press, 2019).

Notes to Chapter 2   251

54. Karel Martens, *Transport Justice: Designing Fair Transportation Systems* (New York: Routledge, 2017).

55. Aaron Golub and Karel Martens, "Using Principles of Justice to Assess the Modal Equity of Regional Transportation Plans," *Journal of Transport Geography* 41 (2014): 18.

56. David Prytherch, *Law, Engineering, and the American Right-of-Way: Imagining a More Just Street* (New York: Palgrave Macmillan, 2018).

57. Eda Beyazit, "Evaluating Social Justice in Transport: Lessons to Be Learned from the Capability Approach," *Transport Reviews* 31, no. 1 (2011): 131.

58. Pereira, Schwanen, and Banister, "Distributive Justice and Equity in Transportation," 184.

59. Nancy Cook and David Butz, "Mobility Justice in the Context of Disaster," *Mobilities* 11, no. 3 (2016): 17.

60. Pereira, Schwanen, and Banister, "Distributive Justice and Equity in Transportation."

61. Martens, *Transport Justice*; Levine, Grengs, and Merlin, *From Mobility to Accessibility*.

62. Prytherch, *Law, Engineering, and the American Right-of-Way*.

63. Martens, *Transport Justice*.

64. Iris Marion Young, *Justice and the Politics of Difference* (Princeton, N.J.: Princeton University Press, 2022).

65. Audrey Kobayashi and Brian Ray, "Civil Risk and Landscapes of Marginality in Canada: A Pluralist Approach to Social Justice," *Canadian Geographies* 44, no. 4 (2000): 403, 414.

66. Linda Peake, "The Twenty-First-Century Quest for Feminism and the Global Urban," *International Journal of Urban and Regional Research* 40, no. 1 (2016): 224.

67. Lynda Johnston, "Gender and Sexuality II: Activism," *Progress in Human Geography* 41, no. 5 (2017): 654.

68. Ruth Wilson Gilmore, "Fatal Couplings of Power and Difference: Notes on Racism and Geography," *Professional Geographer* 54, no. 1 (2002): 15.

69. Susan Hanson, "Gender and Mobility: New Approaches for Informing Sustainability," *Gender, Place, and Culture* 17, no. 1 (2010): 15.

70. Caroline Criado Perez, *Invisible Women: Data Bias in a World Designed for Men* (New York: Abrams, 2019), 25.

71. Katarína Rišová and Michala Sládeková Madajová, "Gender Differences in a Walking Environment Safety Perception: A Case Study in a Small Town of Banská Bystrica (Slovakia)," *Journal of Transport Geography* 85 (2020): https://doi.org/10.1016/j.jtrangeo.2020.102723; Gabriele Prati, "Gender Equality and

Women's Participation in Transport Cycling," *Journal of Transport Geography* 66 (2018): 369–75.

72. Emilia Smeds, Enora Robin, and Jenny McArthur, "Night-Time Mobilities and (In)justice in London: Constructing Mobile Subjects and the Politics of Difference in Policy-Making," *Journal of Transport Geography* 82 (2020): 9.

73. Genevieve Carpio, *Collisions at the Crossroads: How Place and Mobility Make Race* (Berkeley: University of California Press, 2019), 14.

74. Robert D. Bullard, epilogue to *Just Transportation: Dismantling Race and Class Barriers to Mobility*, ed. Robert D. Bullard and Glenn S. Johnson (Gabriola Island, B.C.: New Society, 1997), 17.

75. Robert D. Bullard, introduction to "The Anatomy of Transportation Racism," in *Highway Robbery: Transportation Racism and New Routes to Equity*, ed. Robert D. Bullard, Glenn S. Johnson, and Angel O. Torres (Cambridge, Mass.: South End Press, 2004), 28.

76. Christopher A. Riddle, *Disability and Justice: The Capabilities Approach in Practice* (Lanham, Md.: Lexington Books, 2014), 3.

77. Aimi Hamraie, "Crip Mobility Justice: Ableism and Active Transportation Debates," *International Journal of Urban and Regional Research* (2021): https://www.ijurr.org/spotlight-on/disabling-city/crip-mobility-justice/.

78. Sheller, *Mobility Justice*, 14.

79. Sheller, 197.

80. Stephen Zavestoski and Julian Agyeman, "Complete Streets: What's Missing?," in *Incomplete Streets: Processes, Practices, and Possibilities*, ed. Stephen Zavestoski and Julian Agyeman (New York: Routledge, 2015), 4.

81. Zavestoski and Agyeman, "Complete Streets," 8.

82. Melody L. Hoffmann, *Bike Lanes Are White Lanes: Bicycle Advocacy and Urban Planning* (Lincoln: University of Nebraska Press, 2016), 20.

83. Hoffmann, *Bike Lanes Are White Lanes*, 159.

84. Kenneth Gould and Tammy Lewis, *Green Gentrification: Urban Sustainability and the Struggle for Environmental Justice* (New York: Routledge, 2017).

85. Julian Agyeman, *Introducing Just Sustainabilities: Policy, Planning, and Practice* (London: Zed Books, 2013).

86. Winnifred Curran and Trina Hamilton, introduction to *Just Green Enough: Urban Development and Environmental Gentrification*, ed. Winifred Curran and Trina Hamilton (New York: Routledge, 2017).

87. Stehlin, *Cyclescapes of the Unequal City*, 86.

88. Hoffmann, *Bike Lanes Are White Lanes*.

89. Erin Goodling and Cameron Herrington, "Reversing Complete Streets Disparities: Portland's Community Watershed Stewardship Program," in Zavestoski and Agyeman, *Incomplete Streets*, 176–202.

90. Bruce Appleyard and Donald Appleyard, *Livable Streets 2.0* (Cambridge, Mass.: Elsevier, 2021), 308–10.

91. United Nations, "Sustainability," accessed October 20, 2024, https://www.un.org/en/academic-impact/sustainability.

92. Joerg Chet Tremmel, *A Theory of Intergenerational Justice* (London: Earthscan, 2009), 204.

93. Young, *Justice and the Politics of Difference,* 22.

94. Bullard, introduction, 22.

95. Sheller, *Mobility Justice,* 185.

96. Martens, *Transport Justice.*

97. Henderson, *Street Fight.*

98. Prytherch, *Law, Engineering, and the American Right-of-Way.*

99. Crenshaw, "Demarginalizing the Intersection of Race and Sex," 149.

100. Kimberlé Crenshaw, "Mapping the Margins: Intersectionality, Identity Politics, and Violence against Women of Color," *Stanford Law Review* 43, no. 6 (1991): 1,297.

101. Crenshaw, "Mapping the Margins," 1,245.

102. Crenshaw, 1,249.

103. Crenshaw et al., introduction, xxv.

104. Crenshaw et al., xxix.

105. Kimberlé Williams Crenshaw, Luke Charles Harris, Daniel Martinez HoSang, and George Lipsitz, "Preface and Acknowledgements: Praying to the Disciplinary Gods with One Eye Open" in and introduction to *Seeing Race Again: Countering Colorblindness across the Disciplines,* ed. Kimberlé Williams Crenshaw, Luke Charles Harris, Daniel Martinez HoSang, and George Lipsitz (Berkeley: University of California Press, 2019), 13.

106. Alexander Styhre and Ulla Eriksson-Zetterquist, "Thinking the Multiple in Gender and Diversity Studies: Examining the Concept of Intersectionality," *Gender in Management* 23, no. 8 (2008): 568.

107. Ange-Marie Hancock, *Intersectionality: An Intellectual History* (New York: Oxford University Press, 2016), 16.

108. Gill Valentine, "Theorizing and Researching Intersectionality: A Challenge for Feminist Geography," *Professional Geographer* 59, no. 1 (2007): 10–21.

109. Hopkins, "Social Geography I," 941.

110. Hopkins, 942.

111. Monika Büscher, Mimi Sheller, and David Tyfield, "Mobility Intersections: Social Research, Social Futures," *Mobilities* 11, no. 4 (2016): 487.

112. Bonnie Das Neves, Carolyn Unsworth, and Colette Browning, "'Being Treated like an Actual Person': Attitudinal Accessibility on the Bus," *Mobilities* 18, no. 3 (2023): 426.

254   Notes to Chapter 2

113. Annelies Kusters, "Boarding Mumbai Trains: The Mutual Shaping of Intersectionality and Mobility," *Mobilities* 14, no. 6 (2019): 841–58.

114. Murray, Sawchuk, and Jirón, "Comparative Mobilities in an Unequal World," 549.

115. Smart Growth America, *Dangerous by Design 2024,* accessed October 20, 2024, https://smartgrowthamerica.org/dangerous-by-design/.

116. Crenshaw, "Demarginalizing the Intersection of Race and Sex," 167.

3. Multimodalism by Policy and Design

1. David Prytherch, *Law, Engineering, and the American Right-of-Way: Imagining a More Just Street* (New York: Palgrave, 2018).

2. "What Is Vision Zero," Vision Zero Network, accessed October 23, 2024, https://visionzeronetwork.org/about/what-is-vision-zero/.

3. Aimi Hamraie, *Building Access: Universal Design and the Politics of Disability* (Minneapolis: University of Minnesota Press, 2017).

4. National Council on Disability (formerly National Council on the Handicapped), *Toward Independence: An Assessment of Federal Laws and Programs Affecting Persons with Disabilities—With Legislative Recommendations: A Report to the President and to the Congress of the United States* (Washington, D.C., 1986).

5. "Testimony of the Honorable Lowell Weicker, Jr. on ADA," Disability Minnesota, ADA Legacy Project, accessed February 15, 2023, https://mn .gov/mnddc/ada-legacy/pdf/Weicker-ADA-Testimony.pdf.

6. "The Making of the ADA: Drafting and Introduction of the Original ADA Bill—Part 18," Burgdorf on Disability Rights, accessed February 15, 2023, https://adachronicles.org/making-the-americans-with-disabilities-act/.

7. Americans with Disabilities Act of 1990, As Amended, 42 U.S.C. § 12101 (1990), https://www.ada.gov/law-and-regs/ada.

8. Americans with Disabilities Act of 1990.

9. Hamraie, *Building Access,* 97.

10. Public Rights-of-Way Access Advisory Committee, *Building a True Community: Final Report Public Rights-of-Way Access Advisory Committee* (Washington, D.C.: Access Board, 2001), https://www.access-board.gov/prowag/ prowaac-report.html, 1.

11. Public Rights-of-Way Access Advisory Committee, *Building a True Community,* 1.

12. Public Rights-of-Way Access Advisory Committee, 1–2.

13. Hamraie, *Building Access,* 259.

Notes to Chapter 3   255

14. Barbara McCann, *Completing Our Streets: The Transition to Safe and Inclusive Transportation Networks* (Washington, D.C.: Island Press, 2013), 22.

15. McCann, *Completing Our Streets,* 4.

16. National Complete Streets Coalition, *The Best Complete Streets Policies of 2012* (Washington, D.C.: Smart Growth America, 2013), 1.

17. National Complete Streets Coalition, *The Best Complete Streets Policies of 2023* (Washington, D.C.: Smart Growth America, 2023), 3.

18. National Complete Streets Coalition, *Best Complete Streets Policies of 2023,* 4.

19. National Complete Streets Coalition, 4.

20. National Complete Streets Coalition, 19.

21. National Complete Streets Coalition, 8.

22. National Complete Streets Coalition, 25.

23. National Complete Streets Coalition.

24. "The Benefits of Complete Streets," National Complete Streets Coalition, accessed October 23, 2024, https://benefits.completestreets.org/.

25. Kimberlé Williams Crenshaw, "Color Blindness, History, and the Law," in *The House That Race Built: Original Essays by Toni Morrison, Angela Y. Davis, Cornell West, and Others on Black Americans and Politics in America Today,* ed. Wahneema Lubiano (New York: Vintage Books, 1997), 280–300; "Advancing Racial Equity," Smart Growth America, accessed October 24, 2024, https://smartgrowthamerica.org/our-work/racial-equity/.

26. "Demystifying the Safe Systems Approach," Vision Zero Network, accessed October 23, 2024, https://visionzeronetwork.org/resources/demystifying-the-safe-system-approach/.

27. "This Is Vision Zero," Trafikverket Swedish Transport Administration, accessed October 23, 2024, https://bransch.trafikverket.se/en/startpage/operations/Operations-road/vision-zero-academy/This-is-Vision-Zero/.

28. "Fundamentals of Vision Zero Action Planning," Vision Zero Network, accessed October 23, 2024, https://visionzeronetwork.org/building-a-strong-foundation-for-safe-mobility/.

29. "What Is Vision Zero?," Vision Zero Network.

30. Vision Zero Network, *Core Elements for Vision Zero Communities* (Washington, D.C., 2022), 1.

31. "What Is Vision Zero?," Vision Zero Network.

32. "9 Components of a Strong Vision Zero Commitment," Vision Zero Network, accessed October 24, 2024, https://visionzeronetwork.org/9-components-of-a-strong-vision-zero-commitment/.

33. "9 Components of a Strong Vision Zero Commitment," Vision Zero Network.

34. Vision Zero Network, *Factsheet: 9 Components of a Vision Zero Commitment* (Washington, D.C., 2022), 6.

35. "Transportation Research Board," U.S. Department of Transportation Federal Highway Administration, accessed February 27, 2024, highways.dot .gov/research/opportunities-partnerships/partnerships/transportation-research -board.

36. Transportation Research Board, *Highway Capacity Manual, 6th Edition: A Guide for Multimodal Mobility Analysis* (Washington, D.C.: National Academies Press, 2016).

37. Transportation Research Board, *Highway Capacity Manual,* 16-1.

38. American Association of State Highway and Transportation Officials, *A Policy on Geometric Design of Highways and Streets* (Washington, D.C., 2018), vi.

39. American Association of State Highway and Transportation Officials, *A Policy on Geometric Design of Highways and Streets* (Washington, D.C., 2011), xlii.

40. American Association of State Highway and Transportation Officials, *Policy on Geometric Design of Highways and Streets* (2018), 1–3.

41. American Association of State Highway and Transportation Officials, 1-26.

42. American Association of State Highway and Transportation Officials, 9-1.

43. Federal Highway Administration, *Manual on Uniform Traffic Control Devices* (Washington, D.C.: U.S. Department of Transportation, 2017), 1.

44. Federal Highway Administration, *Manual on Uniform Traffic Control Devices,* 384.

45. American Association of State Highway and Transportation Officials, *Guide for the Planning, Design, and Operation of Pedestrian Facilities* (Washington, D.C., 2021), 1-1.

46. American Association of State Highway and Transportation Officials, *Guide for the Planning, Design, and Operation of Pedestrian Facilities,* 3–7.

47. American Association of State Highway and Transportation Officials, *Guide for the Development of Bicycle Facilities* (Washington, D.C., 2012), 1-1.

48. American Association of State Highway and Transportation Officials, *Guide for the Development of Bicycle Facilities,* 4-1.

49. American Association of State Highway and Transportation Officials, *Guide for the Development of Bicycle Facilities,* 5-8.

50. American Association of State Highway and Transportation Officials, *Guide for Geometric Design of Transit Facilities on Highways and Streets,* 1st ed. (Washington, D.C., 2014), 1–2.

Notes to Chapter 3   257

51. Department of Justice, *ADA Standards for Accessible Design* (Washington, D.C., 2010).

52. "U.S. Access Board Issues Final Rule on Public Right-of-Way Accessibility Guidelines," August 8, 2023, https://www.access-board.gov/news/2023/08/08/u-s-access-board-issues-final-rule-on-public-right-of-way-accessibility-guidelines/.

53. "Accessibility Guidelines for Pedestrian Facilities in the Public Right-of-Way," 36 CFR Part 1190 (2023).

54. "U.S. Access Board Issues Final Rule."

55. "About NACTO," National Association of City Transportation Officials, accessed February 28, 2024, https://nacto.org/about/.

56. "Overview," *Urban Streets Design Guide,* National Association of City Transportation Officials, accessed October 25, 2024, https://nacto.org/publication/urban-street-design-guide/streets.

57. "Overview," *Urban Streets Design Guide.*

58. "Street Design Principles," *Urban Streets Design Guide,* National Association of City Transportation Officials, accessed October 25, 2024, https://nacto.org/publication/urban-street-design-guide/streets/street-design-principles.

59. "Street Design Elements," *Urban Streets Design Guide,* National Association of City Transportation Officials, accessed October 25, 2024, https://nacto.org/publication/urban-street-design-guide/street-design-elements/.

60. "Intersections," *Urban Streets Design Guide,* National Association of City Transportation Officials, accessed October 25, 2024, https://nacto.org/publication/urban-street-design-guide/intersections/.

61. "Streets," *Urban Streets Design Guide,* National Association of City Transportation Officials, accessed October 25, 2024, https://nacto.org/publication/urban-street-design-guide/streets/.

62. "Overview," *Urban Bikeway Design Guide,* National Association of City Transportation Officials, accessed October 24, 2024, https://nacto.org/publication/urban-bikeway-design-guide/.

63. "Bike Boulevards," *Urban Bikeway Design Guide,* National Association of City Transportation Officials, accessed October 24, 2024, https://nacto.org/publication/urban-bikeway-design-guide/bicycle-boulevards/.

64. National Association of City Transportation Officials, *Designing for All Ages & Abilities: Contextual Guidance for High-Comfort Bicycle Facilities* (Washington, D.C., 2017), 2.

65. "Rethinking Streets in a Time of Physical Distance," *Streets for Pandemic Response & Recovery,* National Association of City Transportation Officials, accessed June 25, 2024, https://nacto.org/publication/streets-for-pandemic-response-recovery/.

258 Notes to Chapter 3

66. "Emerging Street Strategies," *Streets for Pandemic Response & Recovery,* National Association of City Transportation Officials, accessed June 25, 2024, https://nacto.org/publication/streets-for-pandemic-response-recovery/.

4. Slowing the Street

1. National Highway Traffic Safety Administration, *National Traffic Speeds Survey III: 2015* (Washington, D.C.: U.S. Department of Transportation, 2018), 1.

2. State of New York, "Laws and Ordinances of New Netherland, 1638–1674, Compiled and Translated from the Original Dutch Records in the Office of the Secretary of State" (Albany, N.Y.: E. B. O'Callaghan, Albany, Weed, Parsons, 1868).

3. City of Boston, "Boston Town Records . . . [1631]–1822" (Boston: Municipal Printing Office, 1906).

4. State of Connecticut, *Resolves and Private Laws of the State of Connecticut, 1837–1857,* Vol. 1 (Hartford, Conn.: John. B. Eldredge, 1953).

5. Peter D. Norton, *Fighting Traffic: The Dawn of the Motor Age in the American City* (Cambridge, Mass.: MIT Press, 2008), 53.

6. National Conference on Street and Highway Safety, *Final Text of the Uniform Vehicle Code* (Washington, D.C., 1926).

7. Eric Charmes, "Cul-de-Sacs, Superblocks, and Environmental Areas as Supports of Residential Territorialisation," *Journal of Urban Design* 15 (2010): 357–74.

8. Bruce Appleyard and Donald Appleyard, *Livable Streets 2.0* (Amsterdam: Elsevier, 2020), 15–18.

9. Federal Highway Administration, *State of the Art: Residential Traffic Management* (Washington, D.C.: U.S. Department of Transportation, 1980), 14.

10. Reid H. Ewing, *Traffic Calming: State of the Practice* (Washington, D.C.: Institute of Transportation Engineers, 1999), 2.

11. Ewing, *Traffic Calming,* 509.

12. Jeff Gulden and Joe De La Garza, "Traffic Calming" in *Traffic Engineering Handbook,* 7th ed., ed. Anurag Pande and Brian Wolshon (New York: John Wiley & Sons, 2016), 522.

13. Lindsey Walker, Mike Tresidder, and Mia Birk, *Fundamentals of Bike Boulevard Planning and Design* (Portland, Ore.: Portland State University, 2009), 2.

14. Greg Krykewycz, "Introduction to Workshop: Neighborhood Greenways; Applications, Research, and Effectiveness" (presentation, Transportation Research Board 96th Annual Meeting, Washington, D.C., January 8, 2017).

15. Ewing, *Traffic Calming*, 10.

16. Natalia Collarte, "The American Woonerf: Creating Livable and Attractive Shared Streets" (master's thesis, Tufts University, 2014).

17. Ewing, *Traffic Calming*, 13.

18. National Association of City Transportation Officials, *Urban Streets Design Guide* (Washington, D.C.: Island Press, 2013), 3.

19. National Association of City Transportation Officials, *Urban Streets Design Guide*, 24–26.

20. National Association of City Transportation Officials, *Urban Bikeway Design Guide* (Washington, D.C.: Island Press, 2014), 147.

21. National Association of City Transportation Officials, *Streets for Pandemic Response and Recovery* (Washington, D.C., 2020), 2.

22. National Association of City Transportation Officials, *Streets for Pandemic Response and Recovery*, 26.

23. National Association of City Transportation Officials, 26.

24. City of Boston, *Boston Complete Streets Guidelines* (Boston, 2013), xiii.

25. City of Boston, *Boston Complete Streets Guidelines*, xiii.

26. City of Boston, 12.

27. City of Boston, *Vision Zero Boston Action Plan* (Boston, 2015), 12.

28. "Stonybrook," City of Boston, accessed July 20, 2023, https://www .boston.gov/stonybrook.

29. Vineet Gupta, remote interview by David Prytherch, September 15, 2023.

30. Conor Semler, remote interview by David Prytherch, July 20, 2023.

31. Senior Advisor for Community Safety, "Mayor Walsh Celebrates Ribbon Cutting of Boston's First Neighborhood Slow Streets Program," City of Boston, November 1, 2017, https://www.boston.gov/news/mayor-walsh-cele brates-ribbon-cutting-bostons-first-neighborhood-slow-streets-program.

32. Seth Daniel, "For Neighborhood with Slow Streets Pilot in Place, 'It Has Been a Blessing,'" *Dorchester Reporter*, September 9, 2021, www.dotnews .com/2021/neighborhood-slow-streets-pilot-place-it-has-been-blessing.

33. Laquisa Burke, remote interview by David Prytherch, February 14, 2024.

34. Boston Transportation Department, *Go Boston 2030* (Boston: City of Boston, 2017), 8.

35. Boston Transportation Department, *Go Boston 2030*, 150.

36. City of Boston, *Tactical Public Realm Guidelines* (Boston, 2018), 3.

37. Boston Transportation Department, "Five Neighborhoods Join the Slow Streets Program," City of Boston, July 20, 2017, www.boston.gov/news/ five-neighborhoods-join-slow-streets-program.

260 Notes to Chapter 4

38. Boston Transportation Department, *2017 Neighborhood Slow Streets: Scoring Methodology and Application Evaluation* (Boston: City of Boston, 2017).

39. Semler, interview.

40. Gupta, interview.

41. "Making Neighborhood Streets Safer," City of Boston, accessed July 26, 2023, https://www.boston.gov/departments/transportation/making-neighborhood-streets-safer.

42. Boston Transportation Department, "Street Upgrades to Enhance Mobility and Safety for Everyone," City of Boston, May 23, 2023, https://www.boston.gov/news/street-upgrades-enhance-mobility-and-safety-everyone.

43. Semler, interview.

44. Semler, interview.

45. Gupta, interview.

46. Boston Transportation Department, "City of Boston Speed Humps Policy and Design Directive" (City of Boston, May 10, 2023), 1.

47. Mandy Wilkens, remote interview by David Prytherch, September 8, 2023.

48. Gupta, interview.

49. Gupta, interview.

50. "Archive: Oakland's Slow Streets—Essential Places Program from April 2020 to February 2022," City of Oakland, accessed July 12, 2023, https://www.oaklandca.gov/projects/archive-oaklands-slow-streets-essential-places-program-during-covid-19.

51. Oakland Department of Transportation, *Strategic Plan* (Oakland, Calif.: City of Oakland, 2016), 16.

52. Oakland Department of Transportation, *Let's Bike Oakland: 2019 Oakland Bike Plan* (Oakland, Calif.: City of Oakland, 2019), 82.

53. Jason Patton, remote interview by David Prytherch, August 18, 2023.

54. "Oakland Mayor Announces 'Slow Streets' Measure to Limit Traffic in City," aired April 10, 2020, on KPIX/CBS News.

55. Laura Bliss, "Drivers Not Wanted on Oakland's 'Slow Streets,'" *Bloomberg CityLab,* April 17, 2020, https://www.bloomberg.com/news (page discontinued).

56. Patton, interview.

57. Justin Hu-Nguyen, remote interview by David Prytherch, August 4, 2023.

58. Patton, interview.

59. "Oakland Slow Streets Interim Findings Report, September 2020," City of Oakland, accessed August 1, 2023, https://www.oaklandca.gov/documents/oakland-slow-streets-interim-findings-report-september-2020-1.

Notes to Chapter 4   261

60. Oakland Department of Transportation, *Oakland Slow Streets Interim Findings Report* (Oakland, Calif.: City of Oakland, 2020).

61. Oakland Department of Transportation, *Oakland Slow Streets Interim Findings Report,* 39.

62. Oakland Department of Transportation, *Oakland Slow Streets Interim Findings Report,* 40.

63. Oakland Department of Transportation.

64. Anonymous Oakland resident, remote interview by David Prytherch, December 1, 2023.

65. Andrew Armstrong, remote interview by David Prytherch, October 13, 2023.

66. Armstrong, interview.

67. "Archive: Oakland's Slow Streets."

68. Oakland Department of Transportation, *Neighborhood Bike Route Implementation Guide* (Oakland, Calif.: City of Oakland, 2021), 11.

69. Oakland Department of Transportation, "Oakland's Slow Streets and Essential Places Program, Presentation" (City of Oakland, January 20, 2022).

70. Anonymous resident, interview.

71. Armstrong, interview.

72. "Archive: Oakland Slow Streets."

73. "Archive: Oakland Slow Streets."

74. Oakland Department of Transportation, "Oakland Slow Streets."

75. Oakland Department of Transportation.

76. Oakland Department of Transportation.

77. Patton, interview.

78. Patton.

79. Patton.

80. "Exhibit A: A Resolution Adopting the City of Pittsburgh Complete Streets Policy," City of Pittsburgh, file no. 2016-0935, accessed July 27, 2023, https://pittsburgh.legistar.com/LegislationDetail.aspx?ID=2876655&G UID=58D1D58A-BAA3-4C2A-B9A1-E040B0F44D64&Options=ID%7C Text%7C&Search=2016-0935, 1.

81. "Mobility and Infrastructure," City of Pittsburgh, accessed July 15, 2023, https://pittsburghpa.gov/domi.

82. Eric Boerer, remote interview by David Prytherch, September 6, 2023.

83. Kimberly Lucas, remote interview by David Prytherch, August 24, 2023.

84. Sean Stephens, remote interview by David Prytherch, September 1, 2023.

262   Notes to Chapter 4

85. "Neighborway Program," City of Pittsburgh Department of Mobility and Infrastructure, accessed August 1, 2023, https://pittsburghpa.gov/domi/neighborways.

86. Bruce Chan, remote interview by David Prytherch, October 5, 2023.

87. Julie Albright, personal communication, April 20, 2024.

88. City of Pittsburgh, *Street Life: Supporting the Vitality of PGH People and Places during COVID-19; Report of the Task Force on Streets + Mobility* (Pittsburgh, May 12, 2020), 54.

89. Lucas, interview.

90. Tosh Chambers, remote interview by David Prytherch, September 12, 2023.

91. Pittsburgh Department of Mobility and Infrastructure, *Neighborhood Slow Streets Guidelines* (Pittsburgh: City of Pittsburgh, 2020).

92. Pittsburgh Department of Mobility and Infrastructure, *Neighborhood Slow Streets Guidelines*.

93. Pittsburgh Department of Mobility and Infrastructure, *Bike(+) Master Plan* (Pittsburgh: City of Pittsburgh, 2020), 51.

94. Pittsburgh Department of Mobility and Infrastructure, *Bike(+) Master Plan*, 57.

95. Pittsburgh Department of Mobility and Infrastructure, *Envision 2070: Mobility in a Sustainable Pittsburgh* (Pittsburgh: City of Pittsburgh, 2021), 9–11.

96. Pittsburgh Department of Mobility and Infrastructure, *Envision 2070*, 30.

97. Lucas, interview.

98. Stephens, interview.

99. Boerer, interview.

100. Chan, interview.

101. Tosh Chambers, remote interview by David Prytherch, September 12, 2023.

102. Lucas, interview.

103. Albright, pers. comm.

104. Chan, interview.

105. Lucas.

106. Lucas.

107. Pittsburgh Department of Mobility and Infrastructure, *Envision 2070*, 8.

5. Opening the Street by Closing It

1. Jane Pyle, "Farmers' Markets in the United States: Functional Anachronisms," *Geographical Review* 61, no. 2 (1971): 167–97.

Notes to Chapter 5   263

2. Daniel M. Bluestone, "'The Pushcart Evil': Peddlers, Merchants, and New York City's Streets, 1890–1940," *Journal of Urban History* 18, no. 1 (1991): 69.

3. Allison Brown, "Counting Farmers Markets," *Geographical Review* 91, no. 4 (2001): 655–74.

4. Susan G. Davis, *Parades and Power: Street Theatre in Nineteenth-Century Philadelphia* (Philadelphia: University of Philadelphia Press, 1986), 6.

5. Simon P. Newman, *Parades and the Politics of the Street: Festive Culture in the Early American Republic* (Philadelphia: University of Pennsylvania Press, 1997), 5.

6. Sallie A. Marston, "Public Rituals and Community Power: St. Patrick's Day Parades in Lowell, Massachusetts, 1841–1874," *Political Geography Quarterly* 8, no. 3 (1989): 255.

7. Katherine McFarland Bruce, *Pride Parades: How a Parade Changed the World* (New York: New York University Press, 2016), 5.

8. Terry Bouton, "A Road Closed: Rural Insurgency in Post-Independence Pennsylvania," *Journal of American History* 87, no. 3 (2000): 855–87.

9. "Where Are the Block Parties of Yesterday? Social Institution That Promised Big Things Fails to Endure—People Move Too Often and Have Too Many Distractions for a New Version of the Barn Dance," *New York Times,* August 15, 1923.

10. Amanda I. Seligman, *Chicago's Block Clubs: How Neighbors Shape the City* (Chicago: University of Chicago Press, 2016).

11. Jeff Chang, *Can't Stop Won't Stop: A History of the Hip-Hop Generation* (New York: St. Martin's Press, 2005).

12. Sandra Garcia, "Welcome to the Party. The New York City Block Party," *New York Times,* September 14, 2019, https://www.nytimes.com/interactive/2019/09/15/nyregion/block-parties-nyc.html.

13. "A History of NYC's 'Play Streets,'" THIRTEEN, accessed September 22, 2023, www.thirteen.org/program-content/a-history-of-nycs-play-streets/.

14. "PAL Playstreets," Police Athletic League, accessed October 28, 2024, https://palnyc.org/playstreets.

15. Sergio Montero, "Worlding Bogotá's Ciclovía: From Urban Experiment to International 'Best Practice,'" *Latin American Perspectives* 44, no. 2 (2016): 111–31.

16. Montero, "Worlding Bogotá's Ciclovía."

17. "Sunday Streets," Sunday Streets SF, accessed August 2, 2023, https://www.sundaystreetssf.com/.

18. "What is CicLAvia?," CicLAvia, accessed August 2, 2023, https://www.ciclavia.org/about.

264   Notes to Chapter 5

19. "Philly Free Streets: Car Free Streets!," Philly Free Streets, accessed August 2, 2023, https://www.phillyfreestreets.com (site discontinued); Penn Praxis, *2016 Philly Free Streets: User and Business Response to the 2016 Philly Free Street Event* (Philadelphia: Open Streets PHL and the Knight Foundation, 2017).

20. Open Streets Project, *The Open Streets Guide: Opening Streets to People, Sharing Resources, Transforming Communities* (2012), accessed August 3, 2023, https://nacto.org/wp-content/uploads/2015/04/smaller_open_streets_guide_final_print_alliance_biking_walking_optimized.pdf, 7.

21. "Open Streets Toolkit," Open Streets Project, accessed August 2, 2023, https://openstreetsproject.org.

22. Adonia E. Lugo, "CicLAvia and Human Infrastructure in Los Angeles: Ethnographic Experiments in Equitable Bike Planning," *Journal of Transport Geography* 30 (2013): 207.

23. Arly Cassidy, Josh Newell, and Jennifer Wolch, *Transforming Alleys into Green Infrastructure for Los Angeles* (Los Angeles: USC Center for Sustainable Cities, 2008).

24. Trust for Public Land, Los Angeles, *Alleys Amplified: South Los Angeles Green Alley Master Plan* (Los Angeles: Prepared for the Los Angeles Bureau of Sanitation, 2012).

25. "Green Alley," National Association of City Transportation Officials, *Urban Street Design Guide* (2013), accessed October 28, 2024, https://nacto.org/publication/urban-street-design-guide/streets/green-alley/.

26. National Association of City Transportation Officials, *Streets for Pandemic Response and Recovery* (New York, 2020), 3.

27. National Association of City Transportation Officials, *Streets for Pandemic Response and Recovery,* 40.

28. "Open Streets," New York Department of Transportation, accessed January 25, 2024, https://www.nyc.gov/html/dot/html/pedestrians/openstreets.shtml.

29. City of New York, *PlaNYC: A Greener, Greater New York* (New York, 2007), 35.

30. "NYC Plaza Program," New York Department of Transportation, accessed August 15, 2023, https://www.nyc.gov/html/dot/html/pedestrians/nyc-plaza-program.shtml.

31. New York City Department of Transportation, *Street Design Manual* (New York, 2009).

32. "Summer Streets," New York Department of Transportation, accessed August 15, 2023, https://www.nyc.gov/html/dot/html/pedestrians/summerstreets.shtml.

Notes to Chapter 5   265

33. Sewell Chan, "Will Car-Free 'Summer Streets' Work?," *City Room* (blog), *New York Times,* August 8, 2008, https://archive.nytimes.com/city room.blogs.nytimes.com/2008/08/08/will-summer-streets-work-2/.

34. "Summer Streets 2009 = One Big, Car-Free Block Party," 4NewYork, accessed August 29, 2023, https://www.nbcnewyork.com/local/summer-streets -2009-one-big-car-free-block-party/2120474.

35. City of New York, *One New York: The Plan for a Strong and Just City* (New York, 2015).

36. New York City Department of Transportation, *Street Design Manual,* 3rd ed. (New York: City of New York, 2020), 256.

37. Kyle Gorman, remote interview by David Prytherch, October 6, 2023.

38. Gersh Kuntzman, "Here Are the Four Streets de Blasio Will Close to Cars—for Four Days," *Streetsblog NYC,* March 25, 2020, https://nyc.streets blog.org/2020/03/25/here-are-the-four-streets-de-blasio-will-close-to-cars -for-four-days.

39. Gersh Kuntzman, "UPDATE: Council Overrules De Blasio, Will Create Miles of Open Streets; Mayor Not Giving In," *Streetsblog NYC,* April 17, 2020, https://nyc.streetsblog.org/2020/04/17/breaking-council-big-dogs-de -blasio-will-create-miles-of-open-streets.

40. Dave Colon, "City Council's 'Open Streets' Bill Doesn't Say Much— but It Doesn't Have To," *Streetsblog NYC,* April 23, 2023, https://nyc.streets blog.org/2020/04/23/city-councils-open-streets-bill-doesnt-say-much-but-it -doesnt-have-to.

41. Gorman, interview.

42. Juan Restrepo, remote interview by David Prytherch, October 25, 2023.

43. Caroline Spivack, "NYC Opens 7 Miles of Streets in and Near Parks," *Curbed New York,* May 1, 2020, https://ny.curbed.com/2020/5/1/21244055/ new-york-open-streets-parks-social-distancing-coroanvirus.

44. Jim Burke, remote interview by David Prytherch, October 11, 2023.

45. Burke, interview.

46. Burke, interview.

47. "Open Streets."

48. "Open Streets."

49. Leslie Davol, remote interview by David Prytherch, October 18, 2023.

50. "About Street Lab," Street Lab, accessed March 25, 2024, https:// www.streetlab.org/about/.

51. Burke, interview.

52. Justin Gillis and Heather Thompson, "Take Back the Streets from the Automobile," opinion, *New York Times,* June 20, 2020, https://www.nytimes .com/2020/06/20/opinion/pandemic-automobile-cities.html.

266   Notes to Chapter 5

53. James Brasuell, "Cities Are Suddenly a Little Less Car-Centric," *Planetizen,* May 21, 2020, https://www.planetizen.com/features/109400-cities-are-suddenly-little-less-car-centric.

54. Transportation Alternatives, "The Unrealized Potential of New York City's Open Streets: A Four-Month Progress Report on the Open Streets Program in New York City," July 22, 2020, https://transalt.org/reports-list/the-unrealized-potential-of-new-york-citys-open-streets.

55. Editorial Board, "New York's Streets Have Brought Relief. Imagine Them Post-Pandemic," opinion, *New York Times,* November 30, 2020, https://www.nytimes.com/2020/11/30/opinion/new-york-city-coronavirus.html.

56. Matthew Haag, "How New Yorkers Want to Change the Streetscape for Good," *New York Times,* December 18, 2020, https://www.nytimes.com/interactive/2020/12/17/nyregion/nyc-open-streets.html.

57. City of New York, "Press Release: Streets Week! Mayor de Blasio Makes Open Streets Permanent Part of New York City's Urban Landscape," May 13, 2021, www.nyc.gov/office-of-the-mayor/news/361-21/streets-week-mayor-de-blasio-makes-open-streets-permanent-of-new-york-city-s-urban-landscape.

58. "Public Realm Programming," New York Department of Transportation, accessed October 28, 2024, https://www.nyc.gov/html/dot/html/pedestrians/activations.shtml.

59. Gorman, interview.

60. New York Department of Transportation, *NYCStreetsPlan* (New York: City of New York, 2021).

61. Gorman, interview.

62. "NYC Open Data," City of New York, accessed September 13, 2023, https://opendata.cityofnewyork.us/.

63. Jackson Chabot and Emily Chingay, remote interview by David Prytherch, December 8, 2023.

64. Gorman, interview.

65. Burke, interview.

66. "Mayor Adams Appoints Ya-Ting Liu as NYC's First-Ever Chief Public Realm Officer," City of New York, February 16, 2023, https://www.nyc.gov/office-of-the-mayor/news/115-23/mayor-adams-appoints-ya-ting-liu-nyc-s-first-ever-chief-public-realm-officer.

67. Craig McCarthy and Alex Oliveira, "Irate Protestor Shuts down NYC Press Conference for Berry Street Bike-Lane Completion," *New York Post,* November 21, 2023, https://nypost.com/2023/11/21/metro/irate-protestor-shuts-down-nyc-press-conference-for-berry-street-bike-lane-completion/; Julianne Cuba, "Upper West Sider Arrested for Attempt to Block DOT Open

Notes to Chapter 5   267

Street Project," *Streetsblog NYC,* October 16, 2023, https://nyc.streetsblog
.org/2023/10/16/upper-west-sider-arrested-for-attempt-to-block-dot-open
-street-project.

68. Chabot and Chingay, interview.

69. Davol, interview.

70. Burke, interview.

71. Restrepo, interview.

72. Gorman, interview.

73. Restrepo, interview.

74. Brent Bovenzi, remote interview by David Prytherch, December 8, 2023.

75. Kevin Qiu, remote interview by David Prytherch, December 4, 2023.

76. Gorman, interview.

77. Gorman, interview.

78. City and County of Denver, *Denver Vision Zero Action Plan* (Denver, 2017), 4.

79. City and County of Denver, *Denver's Mobility Action Plan* (Denver: City and County of Denver, 2017), 3.

80. City and County of Denver, *Comprehensive Plan 2040: Denver's Plan for the Future* (Denver, 2019).

81. City and County of Denver, *Denver Moves Everyone 2050 Plan* (Denver, 2019), 7.

82. Denver Department of Transportation and Infrastructure, *Complete Streets Design Guidelines* (Denver: City and County of Denver, 2020), 4.

83. Chris Hinds, remote interview by David Prytherch, October 2, 2023.

84. Jay Decker, remote interview by David Prytherch, September 19, 2023.

85. Decker, interview.

86. "Temporary Outdoor Dining Program," City of Denver, accessed March 6, 2024, https://www.denvergov.org/Government/Agencies-Depart
ments-Offices/Agencies-Departments-Offices-Directory/Community-Plan
ning-and-Development/Denver-Zoning-Code/Text-Amendments/Outdoor
-Places-Program/Temporary-Outdoor-Dining-Program.

87. James Brasuell, "Denver, Minneapolis Lead Nation in Open Streets for COVID Response," *Planetizen,* April 6, 2020, https://www.planetizen.com/
news/2020/04/108991-denver-minneapolis-lead-nation-open-streets-covid
-response.

88. Jill Locantore, remote interview by David Prytherch, September 20, 2023.

268   Notes to Chapter 5

89. Locantore quoted in David Sachs, "Some Denver Streets Will Close to Cars, Giving People Who Walk and Bike More Elbow Room during the Coronavirus Pandemic," *Denverite,* April 3, 2020, https://denverite.com/2020/04/03/some-denver-streets-will-go-car-free-giving-people-who-walk-and-bike-more-elbow-room-during-the-covid-19-pandemic/.

90. Denver Streets Partnership, "Shared and Open Streets," accessed September 15, 2023, https://denverstreetspartnership.org/what-we-do/shared-open-streets/.

91. Denver Streets Partnership, "Shared and Open Streets."

92. Hinds, interview.

93. "Temporary Outdoor Dining Program," City of Denver.

94. "Mayor's Design Awards," City and County of Denver, accessed March 6, 2024, https://denvergov.org/Government/Agencies-Departments-Offices/Agencies-Departments-Offices-Directory/Community-Planning-and-Development/Planning/Community-Engagement/Mayors-Design-Awards.

95. Locantore, interview.

96. Decker, interview.

97. Decker, interview.

98. Locantore quoted in David Sachs, "The Next Phase of Shared Streets Is to Get Rid of Some Shared Streets—and Plan for Permanent Ones," *Denverite,* August 5, 2021, https://denverite.com/2021/08/05/the-next-phase-of-shared-streets-is-to-get-rid-of-some-shared-streets-and-plan-for-permanent-ones/.

99. Locantore, interview.

100. Hinds, interview.

101. Denver Department of Transportation and Infrastructure, "Temporary Shared Streets Survey Summary," 2022, https://denvergov.org/files/assets/public/v/2/doti/documents/programsservices/shared-streets/shared-streets-survey-summary.pdf.

102. Denver Department of Transportation and Infrastructure, "Survey #2: Shared Streets Design Preferences," accessed September 25, 2023, https://denvergov.org/files/assets/public/v/2/doti/documents/programsservices/shared-streets/shared-streets-design-preferences.pdf, 2.

103. Denver Department of Transportation and Infrastructure, "Survey #2: Shared Streets Design Preferences," 1.

104. "Shared Streets Program," Denver Department of Transportation and Infrastructure, accessed September 20, 2023, https://denvergov.org/Government/Agencies-Departments-Offices/Agencies-Departments-Offices-Directory/Department-of-Transportation-and-Infrastructure/Programs-Services/Shared-Streets?lang_update=638657067124256902.

105. Decker, interview.

Notes to Chapter 5   269

106. Locantore, interview.

107. Hinds, interview.

108. "Denver Outdoor Places Program," City and County of Denver, accessed March 6, 2024, https://denvergov.org/Government/Agencies-Depart ments-Offices/Agencies-Departments-Offices-Directory/Community-Plan ning-and-Development/Denver-Zoning-Code/Text-Amendments/Outdoor -Places-Program.

109. RiNO Art District, *2900 Block Larimer Street Closure Initiative Community Feedback Summary Report* (Denver, December 2023), 17.

110. "2900 Block Larimer Street Closure," RiNo Art District, accessed March 2, 2024, https://rinoartdistrict.org/post/2900-block-larimer-street-clo sure.

111. Sarah Cawrse, remote interview by David Prytherch, March 7, 2024.

112. "FAQS," ¡Viva! Streets Denver, accessed November 20, 2024, https:// www.vivastreetsdenver.com/faqs.

113. Hinds, interview.

114. Hinds, interview.

115. "Green Alleys," Trust for Public Land, accessed March 20, 2024, https://www.tpl.org/our-work/green-alleys; "Livable Streets," LA Department of Transportation, accessed March 20, 2024, https://ladotlivablestreets.org/.

116. Los Angeles Department of City Planning, *2010 Bicycle Plan* (Los Angeles: City of Los Angeles, 2011), 9.

117. Lugo, "CicLAvia and Human Infrastructure in Los Angeles," 205.

118. Lugo, 205.

119. Lugo, 202.

120. Lugo, 207.

121. Cassidy, Newell, and Wolch, *Transforming Alleys into Green Infrastructure,* vii–viii.

122. LA Sanitation, *Green Streets and Green Alleys Design Guidelines Standards* (Los Angeles: City of Los Angeles, 2009), 1–2.

123. Trust for Public Land, *South LA Green Alley Master Plan* (Los Angeles: City of Los Angeles).

124. "Avalon Green Alley," LA Sanitation, accessed October 28, 2024, https://sanitation.lacity.gov/san/faces/home/portal/s-lsh-wwd?_adf.ctrl-state =19yhhox7f0_78&_afrLoop=46962169094633732#!.

125. City of Los Angeles, "Executive Order No. 1: Great Streets Initiative," October 10, 2013, https://lacity.gov/sites/g/files/wph2121/files/2021-04/ garcetti_ed01.pdf.

126. Los Angeles Department of Transportation, *Mobility Plan 2035: An Element of the General Plan* (Los Angeles: City of Los Angeles, 2015), 59.

270   Notes to Chapter 5

127. Los Angeles Department of Transportation, *Complete Streets Design Guide* (Los Angeles: City of Los Angeles, 2015), 3.

128. Los Angeles Department of Transportation, *Complete Streets Design Guide,* 29, 118.

129. Los Angeles Department of Transportation, Bureau of Engineering, *City of Los Angeles Supplemental Street Design Guide* (Los Angeles: City of Los Angeles, 2020).

130. Margot Ocañas, remote interview by David Prytherch, October 13, 2023.

131. "People St," LADOT Livable Streets, accessed April 1, 2024, https://ladotlivablestreets.org/programs/people-st.

132. Los Angeles Department of Transportation, *Complete Streets Design Guide,* 119.

133. Kounkuey Design Initiative, *Play Streets: Los Angeles Pilot Program Report* (Los Angeles: Los Angeles Department of Transportation, 2016), 7.

134. Kounkuey Design Initiative, *Play Streets,* 72.

135. Clare Eberle, remote interview by David Prytherch, October 6, 2023.

136. Bonin quoted in Dakota Smith and Laura J. Nelson, "Cities Are Opening Streets to Pedestrians during the Pandemic. L.A. Officials Say It's Risky," *Los Angeles Times,* May 3, 2020, https://www.latimes.com/california/story/2020-05-03/coronavirus-la-streets-pedestrians.

137. "Garcetti Announces Launch of 'Slow Streets' Program to Promote Social Distancing while Walking," KCAL News, May 16, 2020, https://www.cbsnews.com/losangeles/news/garcetti-announces-launch-of-slow-streets-program-to-promote-social-distancing-while-walking/.

138. "Learn about Slow Streets LA," City of Los Angeles, accessed September 22, 2023, https://ladot.lacity.gov/coronavirus/apply-slow-street-your-neighborhood.

139. Joe Linton, "Already Driver-Permissive L.A. City Slow Streets Being Watered Down Further," *Streetsblog CAL,* August 31, 2020, https://cal.streetsblog.org/2020/08/31/already-driver-permissive-l-a-city-slow-streets-being-watered-down-further.

140. Joe Linton, "So Cal covid-19 Street Repurposing: Slow Streets Expanding and Outdoor Dining Getting Underway," *Streetsblog LA,* May 29, 2020, https://la.streetsblog.org/2020/05/29/so-cal-covid-19-street-repurposing-slow-streets-expanding-and-outdoor-dining-getting-underway.

141. Linton, "Already Driver-Permissive L.A. City."

142. Eberle, interview.

143. Eberle, interview.

Notes to Chapter 6 271

144. Garcetti quoted in Elina Shatkin, "It Just Got Easier to Set Up 'Slow Streets' Programs in LA," *LAist,* October 11, 2021, https://laist.com/news/transportation/it-just-got-easier-to-set-up-slow-streets-programs-in-la-ab-773-givernor-newsom-signs-into-law-al-fresco-dining-boon.

145. Ocañas, interview.

146. Eberle, interview.

147. Los Angeles Department of Transportation, *2022 Annual Report* (Los Angeles: City of Los Angeles, 2023).

148. Eberle, interview.

149. Ocañas, interview.

150. "What Is CicLAvia?," CicLAvia, last accessed October 5, 2023, https://www.ciclavia.org/about.

151. Eberle, interview.

152. "Anniversary Accolades," CicLAvia, accessed October 1, 2023, https://www.ciclavia.org/10th_anniversary_accolades.

153. Aaron Paley, "CicLAvia—Reflections on Its Disruptive Power 10 Years After," *Medium,* October 6, 2020, https://medium.com/@aaronpaley/ciclavia-reflections-on-its-disruptive-power-10-years-after-6e2d3f3565f4.

154. Eberle, interview.

155. "Bradley Alley/Plaza," Pacoima Beautiful, February 20, 2024, https://www.pacoimabeautiful.org/programs/bradley-alley-plaza.

156. Barbara Velasco, remote interview by David Prytherch, February 28, 2024.

157. Roxy Rivas, remote interview by David Prytherch, February 28, 2024.

158. Pacoima Beautiful and LA Más, *Pacoima Urban Greening Vision Plan* (Los Angeles, 2016), 11.

159. "Bradley Alley/Plaza," Pacoima Beautiful.

160. Velasco, interview.

161. Rivas, interview.

162. Rosa Ruiz, remote interview by David Prytherch, February 28, 2024.

163. Shance Taylor, remote interview by David Prytherch, February 28, 2024.

164. Ruiz, interview.

165. Eberle, interview.

6. Reconstructing the Street as Public Place

1. "Streets for Pandemic Response & Recovery," National Association of City Transportation Officials, accessed October 28, 2024, https://nacto.org/publication/streets-for-pandemic-response-recovery/.

2. Nicholas Blomley, *Rights of Passage: Sidewalks and the Regulation of Public Flow* (New York: Routledge, 2011).

3. Dave Amos, "Understanding the Legacy of Pedestrian Malls," *Journal of the American Planning Association* 86, no. 1 (2020): 11–24.

4. Dorina Pojani, "Santa Monica's Third Street Promenade: The Failure and Resurgence of a Downtown Pedestrian Mall," *Urban Design International* 13 (2008): 141–55.

5. Donald Appleyard, M. Sue Gerson, and Mark Lintell, *Livable Streets* (Berkeley: University of California Press, 1981), 26.

6. "About," Park(ing) Day, accessed August 15, 2023, https://www.my parkingday.org.

7. "About," Park(ing) Day.

8. "About," Park(ing) Day.

9. "About," Park(ing) Day.

10. Krzysztof Herman and Maria Rodgers, "From Tactical Urbanism Action to Institutionalised Urban Planning and Educational Tool: The Evolution of Park(ing) Day," *land* 9, no. 7 (2020): 217.

11. Rebar Group, *The Park(ing) Day Manifesto: User-Generated Urbanism and Temporary Tactics for Improving the Public Realm* (San Francisco: Rebar Group, 2011), 9.

12. Rebar Group, *The Park(ing) Day Manual* (San Francisco: Rebar Group, 2011), 2.

13. Rebar Group, *Park(ing) Day Manual*, 11.

14. Rebar Group, 15.

15. "About," Project for Public Spaces, accessed October 28, 2024, https://www.pps.org/about.

16. Project for Public Spaces, *How to Turn a Place Around: A Handbook for Creating Successful Public Spaces* (New York: Project for Public Spaces, 2000), 10.

17. Project for Public Spaces, *How to Turn a Place Around*, 67.

18. "Streets as Spaces Toolkit," Project for Public Spaces, September 15, 2015, https://www.pps.org/article/streets-as-places.

19. Annah MacKenzie, "Reimagining Our Streets as Places: From Transit Routes to Community Roots," Project for Public Spaces, March 2, 2015, https://www.pps.org/article/reimagining-our-streets-as-places-from-transit -routes-to-community-roots.

20. "Streets as Places Toolkit," Project for Public Spaces, September 15, 2015, https://www.pps.org/article/streets-as-places.

21. Project for Public Spaces and Main Street America, *Navigating Main Streets as Places: A People-First Transportation Toolkit* (New York: Project for Public Spaces, 2019), 10–13.

Notes to Chapter 6　　273

22. Project for Public Spaces and Main Street America, *Navigating Main Streets as Places*, 13.

23. Power quoted in Allison Arieff, "Pavement to Parks," *Opinionator* (blog), *New York Times*, September 22, 2009, https://archive.nytimes.com/opinionator.blogs.nytimes.com/2009/09/22/pavement-to-parks/.

24. Rebar Group, *Park(ing) Day Manual*, 15.

25. New York City Department of Transportation, *Street Design Manual* (New York, 2009), 143.

26. Aaron Naparstek, "Bloomberg Puts Forward a Bold, Transformative New Vision for Broadway," *Streetsblog NYC*, February 26, 2009, https://nyc.streetsblog.org/2009/02/26/a-bold-and-transformative-new-vision-for-broadway.

27. Ben Fried, "Bloomberg, Sadik-Khan Commit to a World-Class, 21st Century Broadway," *Streetsblog NYC*, February 11, 2010, https://nyc.streetsblog.org/2010/02/11/bloomberg-sadik-khan-commit-to-a-world-class-21st-century-broadway.

28. "Times Square Transformation," Times Square Alliance, accessed April 1, 2024, https://www.timessquarenyc.org/times-square-transformation.

29. National Association of City Transportation Officials, *Urban Street Design Guide* (Washington, D.C.: Island Press, 2013), 74–75.

30. National Association of City Transportation Officials, *Urban Street Design Guide*, 85–86.

31. National Association of City Transportation Officials, 86.

32. National Association of City Transportation Officials, 88.

33. National Association of City Transportation Officials, *Streets for Pandemic Response and Recovery* (New York: National Association of City Transportation Officials, 2020), 6.

34. Robin Abad Ocubillo, remote interview by David Prytherch, May 19, 2023.

35. Robin Abad Ocubillo, "Experimenting with the Margin: Parklets and Plazas as Catalysts in Community and Government" (master's thesis, University of Southern California, 2012); Abad Ocubillo, interview.

36. City of San Francisco, *San Francisco Parklet Manual* (San Francisco, 2013), 1.

37. "Places for People," San Francisco Planning, accessed May 13, 2023, https://sfplanning.org/project/places-for-people.

38. Laurie Thomas, remote interview by David Prytherch, June 5, 2023.

39. City and County of San Francisco, *Economic Recovery Task Force Report* (San Francisco, 2020), 46.

40. Abad Ocubillo, interview.

274 Notes to Chapter 6

41. City and County of San Francisco, *Economic Recovery Task Force Report*, 46.

42. Thomas, interview.

43. "Shared Spaces Permit Transition Timeline," accessed May 15, 2023, https://www.sf.gov/step-by-step/shared-spaces-permit-transition-timeline.

44. City and County of San Francisco, *Shared Spaces Manual Version 2.3* (San Francisco, 2022), 8.

45. Abad Ocubillo, interview.

46. Claude Imbault, remote interview by David Prytherch, June 23, 2023.

47. Downtown SF Partnership, *Public Realm Action Plan for a Reimagined Downtown San Francisco* (San Francisco, 2022), 17.

48. "Roadmap to San Francisco's Future," accessed May 13, 2023, https://www.sf.gov/departments/roadmap-san-franciscos-future.

49. Imbault, interview.

50. Thomas, interview.

51. Abad Ocubillo, interview.

52. Thomas, interview.

53. Thomas, interview.

54. Abad Ocubillo, interview.

55. Simon Bertrang, remote interview by David Prytherch, July 17, 2023.

56. Kate Selig, "Three Blocks on Valencia Street to Become Pedestrian-Only Starting This Weekend," *Mission Local,* February 2, 2021, https://missionlocal.org/2021/02/three-blocks-on-valencia-street-to-become-pedestrian-only-starting-this-weekend/.

57. "Valencia Bikeway Improvements Evaluating Near-and-Long Term Safety Improvements for Valencia," San Francisco Municipal Transit Authority, accessed July 13, 2023, https://www.sfmta.com/projects/valencia-bikeway-improvements.

58. Garrett Leahy, "Controversial Bike Lane in Middle of SF's Valencia Street Approved by Transit Bosses," *San Francisco Standard,* April 4, 2023, https://sfstandard.com/2023/04/04/valencia-street-bike-lane-san-francisco-transit-approval/.

59. Janelle Wong, remote interview by David Prytherch, June 26, 2023.

60. Wong, interview.

61. Abad Ocubillo, interview.

62. Bertrang, interview.

63. Wong, interview.

64. Abad Ocubillo, interview.

65. "The Parklet Program," District Department of Transportation, accessed April 17, 2023, https://ddot.dc.gov/page/parklet-program.

66. District Department of Transportation, *Parklets: Program Guidelines* (Washington, D.C.: Government of the District of Columbia, 2020).

67. Kimberly Vacca, remote interview by David Prytherch, February 27, 2023.

68. Vacca, interview.

69. Nat Cannon, remote interview by David Prytherch, April 17, 2023.

70. Cannon, interview.

71. Cannon.

72. Stephanie Bothwell, remote interview by David Prytherch, June 23, 2023.

73. Cannon, interview.

74. District Department of Transportation, *Reimagining Outdoor Space: Restaurants and Retail; Guidelines for Expanded and New Outdoor Seating* (Washington, D.C.: Government of the District of Columbia, 2021).

75. Michele Molotsky, remote interview by David Prytherch, April 12, 2023.

76. John Guggenmos, remote interview by David Prytherch, April 20, 2023.

77. Molotsky, interview.

78. Guggenmos, interview.

79. Cannon, interview.

80. Bothwell, interview.

81. Vacca, interview.

82. Bothwell, interview.

83. Cannon, interview.

84. Bothwell, interview.

85. Molotksy, interview.

86. Cannon, interview.

87. District Department of Transportation, "Shifting to a Permanent Streatery Program," July 2022, https://www.georgetowndc.com/wp-content/uploads/2022/08/DDOT-Streatery-PRESENTATION-for-Draft-Permanent-Guidelines.pdf.

88. Vacca, interview.

89. Vacca.

90. Cannon, interview.

91. Guggenmos, interview.

92. Vacca, interview.

93. Vacca.

94. Bothwell, interview.

95. Bothwell.

276 Notes to Chapter 6

96. Molotsky, interview.

97. "Street Plaza Program," Portland Bureau of Transportation, accessed August 1, 2023, https://www.portland.gov/transportation/planning/plazas.

98. "Street Seat Program," Portland Bureau of Transportation, accessed July 15, 2023, www.portlandoregon.gov/sites/default/files/2020-09/ss-applica tion-packet-2017-03.01.2017-554743.pdf.

99. Sarah Mirk, "From Cars to Cafés: City Program Converts Parking Spots to Outdoor Dining," *Portland Mercury,* September 7, 2012, https://www.portlandmercury.com/news/2012/09/07/6966490/from-cars-to-cafan deacutes.

100. Jonathan Nettler, "Portland Parklets Program Gets Kicked to the Curb," *Planetizen,* April 17, 2013, https://www.planetizen.com/node/61933.

101. Mimi Zeiger, "Tactical Urbanism Takes Time: Architecture Students Build Downtown Portland's First Parklet Despite Regulatory Permitting Hurdles," *Architect's Newspaper,* July 29, 2015, www.archpaper.com/2015/07/new -portland-parklet-hard-lesson-tactical-urbanism/.

102. Nick Falbo, remote interview by David Prytherch, July 7, 2023.

103. Portland Bureau of Transportation, *Safe Streets: Adapting Portland's Streets for Restarting Public Life,* May 2020, https://www.portland.gov/sites/ default/files/2020-05/safe-streetspublicreview-draft052020a.pdf, 2.

104. Falbo, interview.

105. Portland Bureau of Transportation, *Safe Streets,* 16.

106. Falbo, interview.

107. Henry LaTourette Miller, remote interview by David Prytherch, August 3, 2023.

108. Portland Bureau of Transportation, *Summer Streets Activation Update,* accessed August 5, 2023, https://www.portland.gov/sites/default/files/2021/ summer-streets-plaza-program-update-action-table-5.17.2021.pdf, 10–14.

109. Portland Bureau of Transportation, "News Release: PBOT Continues Popular, Free Healthy Businesses Permit Program for Summer 2021," March 10, 2021, https://www.portland.gov/transportation/news/2021/3/10/ news-release-pbot-continues-popular-free-healthy-businesses-permit.

110. "PBOT Equity & Inclusion Community Partnerships," Portland Bureau of Transportation, accessed August 10, 2023, https://www.portland .gov/transportation/justice/pbot-equity-inclusion-community-partnerships.

111. "Vibrant and Inclusive Community Spaces," Portland Bureau of Transportation, accessed August 5, 2023, https://www.portland.gov/united/ vibrant-inclusive-community-spaces.

112. Jonathan Maus, "PBOT Readies Plan for 'New Era of Streets' as Plaza Program Matures," *Bike Portland,* November 3, 2021, https://bikeport

land.org/2021/11/03/pbot-readies-plan-for-new-era-of-streets-as-plaza-program-matures-340835.

113. Falbo, interview.

114. Portland Bureau of Transportation, *Portland Street Plazas: 2022 Evaluation Report,* accessed August 14, 2023, https://www.portland.gov/transportation/plazas/documents/portland-street-plaza-2022-evaluation-report/download.

115. Portland Bureau of Transportation, *Portland Street Plazas,* 23.

116. Portland Bureau of Transportation, *Outdoor Dining Program Design Guidelines (Draft)* (Portland, Ore., 2023), 1.

117. Portland Bureau of Transportation, *Outdoor Dining Program,* 6.

118. Falbo, interview.

119. Tonya Hartnett, remote interview by David Prytherch, July 18, 2023.

120. Neil Mattson, remote interview by David Prytherch, August 3, 2023.

121. Falbo, interview.

122. Mattson, interview.

123. Falbo, interview.

124. LaTourette Miller, interview.

125. Falbo, interview.

126. LaTourette Miller, interview.

127. Falbo, interview.

128. LaTourette Miller, interview.

Conclusion

1. Kimberlé Crenshaw, "Demarginalizing the Intersection of Race and Sex: A Black Feminist Critique of Antidiscrimination Doctrine, Feminist Theory and Antiracist Politics," *University of Chicago Legal Forum* (1989): 139–68.

2. Lao Tzu, *Dao de Jing,* trans. Robert Eno (2010), available at IU-ScholarWorks, Indiana University Libraries, https://hdl.handle.net/2022/23426, 30.

INDEX

AASHTO, 35–37, 40, 41, 94; *Guide for the Development of Bicycle Facilities,* 97–98; *Guide for the Geometric Design of Transit Facilities on Highways and Streets,* 98; *Guide for the Planning, Design, and Operation of Pedestrian Facilities,* 96–97; multimodal design, 96; *A Policy on Geometric Design of Highways and Streets,* 82, 93–95

activation: commercial, 205, 207; public space, 201

ADA. *See* Americans with Disabilities Act

alternative transportation. *See* multimodalism

American Association of State Highway Transportation Officials. *See* AASHTO

American Planning Association, 109

Americans with Disabilities Act, 9, 40, 83–87; civil rights discourses, 86; history of, 83–85;

as intersectional mobility justice, 86–87; *Public Rights-of-Way Accessibility Guidelines,* 82; roadway design, 85–86; *Standards for Accessible Design,* 82

Appleyard, Bruce, 66

Appleyard, Donald, 108

automobiles: and race, 28, 34, 74; as basis of roadway engineering, 31, 33–37; as basis of urban planning, 29–30; danger to pedestrians of, 2, 27–28, 42; early traffic controls of, 28–29; introduction of, 27; and the law, 31–33; takeover of street, 26–29

barricades, 144, 192, 235, 237, 238; and open streets, 152, 153, 157, 159, 165; operational challenges of, 157, 165; politics surrounding, 130, 131, 172, 182, 192; and public street plazas, 154, 171; and Slow/Shared Streets, 5, 106, 124, 125, 126, 130, 131, 141,

279

146, 169, 170, 172, 182; traffic calming and, 114

bicycle: activism, 65, 150; master planning for, 128–29, 129, 131, 178, 179, 235; roadway design for, 82, 96, 97–98, 102, 114. *See also* Ciclovía

bicycle boulevards, 10, 101, 111, 114, 128–29, 132, 137, 178

BIDs. *See* business improvement districts

bikes. *See* bicycle

Black communities. *See* communities of color

Black Indigenous People of Color (BIPOC). *See* communities of color

block parties, 142, 149, 187; Open Street events as a form of, 154

Bloomberg, Michael, 154, 199; role in creating NACTO, 41

Bogotá, Columbia, 150, 154, 178, 180

Boston: approaches to multimodal equity, 122; Complete Streets policy, 113; early speed limits, 107; multimodal design guidelines, 113–14, 118; Neighborhood Slow Streets program, 115–19; speed hump program, 114, 120–21, 235; transportation planning, 114, 118; Vision Zero commitment, 114

business improvement districts: equity issues surrounding, 176, 218; and merchants associations, 205, 213–14; in New York, 156; role in planning and placemaking, 205–6, 218–19; in San Francisco,

205–6; in Washington, D.C., 211–17

café tables. *See* furniture, street

capability justice, 58; and mobility, 58. *See also* justice

Chicago: early traffic engineering, 29; neighborhood block parties, 149; *Plan of Chicago,* 30

CicLAvia, 150, 179, 182; event impacts, 186; origins of, 178–79; reflections on, 187. *See also* Ciclovía

Ciclovía, 17, 147; in Bogotá, 150; in Denver, 176; guidance for, 150; in Los Angeles, 41, 178–79; as model of Open and Shared Streets, 147, 191; in New York, 150; in Oakland, 150; origins and evolution of, 41, 150–51, 178; in Philadelphia, 41, 150; in Pittsburgh, 134–35; in San Francisco, 150; variants of, 150, 176, 178–79

Cincinnati, *Official City Plan of Cincinnati,* 30

civil rights movement, 84; and disability rights, 9, 83–84, 86; and transportation justice, 63; and transportation planning, 38. *See also* Americans with Disabilities Act; disability: and justice

closure, street, 147, 155, 169; and Ciclovía events, 150–51, 154, 162, 186; as Covid-19 response, 124, 152, 208; historical precedents for, 148–50; legal issues surrounding, 109, 182; and Open Streets, 5, 158–59, 161–62;

Index   281

and pedestrian street plazas, 221–22; politics surrounding, 67, 125–26, 131, 146, 164, 167, 171–72, 223; process for long-term, 174–76; and traffic calming, 109. *See also* Open Streets

communities of color: equity planning and, 90, 144, 222, 226; impacts of transportation planning on, 35; response to Slow Streets, 118, 125–27, 130. *See also* racial justice

community building: Green Alleys and, 188–89; New Urbanism as, 39; Open Streets and, 157, 164; public street plazas and, 223; streets and, 22, 85–87, 180

Complete Streets, 2, 91; advocacy, 40, 42–43, 45; in Boston, 113–14; in Denver, 167–68; design guidelines, 41, 94, 97, 100; and green gentrification, 67; in Los Angeles, 180; mobility justice and, 60, 76; movement, 39–42, 82, 87, 109; in Oakland, 123; in Pittsburgh, 135, 140, 143; policies, 87, 89–90; in San Francisco, 205, 210; theory behind, 88

comprehensive planning: in Denver, 168; in New York, 154; in Oakland, 131; in Portland, 223

Connecticut, 107

Covid-19 pandemic, 3; in Boston, 119; in Denver, 168–69; as impetus for rethinking streets, 3, 44, 213, 220; in Los Angeles, 181–182; in New York, 155–56; in Oakland, 123–24; in Pittsburgh, 139–40; in Portland,

220–21; in San Francisco, 203; in Washington, D.C., 211–12

Crenshaw, Kimberlé, 11–12, 50, 69–71, 78, 90, 234. *See also* intersectionality

decision making, 55, 64, 74, 104, 209; and mobility injustice, 46, 63; procedural equity/justice and, 49, 58, 67–69, 75, 77, 90, 234; and roadway design, 25, 88, 92, 103

Denver Department of Transportation and Infrastructure, 166–77

design, roadway, xi, 2, 9–10, 16, 92–104; history of, 28–29, 33–37

disability: activism, 38, 83–84; and the ADA, 83–87; and justice, 63, 72, 74

distributive justice, 57–59; critiques of, 61–62. *See also* mobility justice

District Department of Transportation, 210–11, 213–14, 217

diversity, equity, and inclusion, 3, 18, 55, 229–30; and mobility justice, 61–65, 76–77

duty of care, 58, 60

emergency access: and Open Streets, 157–59; and parklets, 169, 202, 205–6; and public street plazas, 222–24; and Slow Streets, 110

engineering, traffic: autocentric, 34, 37, 46; critiques of, 39; evolution of traffic, 25, 30–33, 35–37; for highway capacity, 33; multimodal, 2, 41; relationship to urban planning, 34

environmental gentrification, 66

282   Index

environmental justice, transportation and, 39, 45, 62–63

equity: difficulty defining, 9, 48; disability and, 86; intergenerational, 66–67, 77; multimodal, 59–61, 76; procedural, 67–69, 76; social, 61–64, 76; spatial, 56–59, 76; transportation, 7, 63. *See also* intersectionality; mobility justice

equity indexes and planning, 141, 143, 173, 190, 204, 236

farmers markets, 148, 221

Federal Highway Administration, 95

feminism and antiracism. *See* intersectionality

feminist geography, 61–62. *See also* intersectionality

Floyd, George, 3, 44–45, 126, 149. *See also* racial justice

furniture, street, 5, 10, 238; and sidewalk life, 210, 214, 215; historical role on streets, 194, 210; on Open Streets and Shared Streets, 3, 159; on the roadway, 4, 18, 211–12

gender: and geography, 61–62; and mobility justice, 64; and transportation, 62, 72. *See also* intersectionality

gentrification: and concerns about Complete Streets, xi, 65–66, 90; and mobility justice, 77; transportation improvements and environmental, 49, 134, 167, 209, 219

Georgetown, 216, 217, 218–19; business improvement district,

211–12, 216; sidewalk extensions, 212–13

Green Alleys, 150; in Los Angeles, 151, 179, 187–89, 190; NACTO design guidelines for, 151–52

Green Book. See AASHTO: *A Policy on Geometric Design of Highways and Streets*

green gentrification. *See* gentrification

Highway Capacity Manual, 33, 93

horizontal elements. *See* traffic calming

inclusion. *See* equity

incomplete streets, critique of, 65

influenza pandemic, 1–2; and public streets, 27

infrastructure, 7–8, 47, 52–53, 75–76; engineering roadways as, 31, 35–37; green, 151, 167–69, 188; and highway capacity, 33, 93; engineering roadways as, 31, 35–37; streets as, 25, 29, 30–35

infrastructure, social, 7–8, 53–54

Institute of Traffic Engineers, 109. See also *Highway Capacity Manual*

intergenerational equity, 66–67, 77. *See also* mobility justice

interim design: and parklets, 193, 198; of public street plazas, 101, 171, 174, 198–99, 200, 225–26; and sidewalk widening, 206, 210, 212–13; of Slow/Shared Streets, 173

intersectionality, 11–12, 15, 50, 71; in geography, 71–72; and just streets, 75–79; Kimberlé Crenshaw's theory of, 11, 69–71;

and mobility justice, 72–76, 78, 234

intersectional mobility justice. *See* mobility justice

ITE. *See* Institute of Traffic Engineers

Jacobs, Jane, 38, 10

justice: and Complete Streets, 90; procedural, 49, 67–69; tension with spatial justice, 143, 177. *See also* mobility justice

just places, 65–67. *See also* mobility justice

just streets, definition of, 15–16, 76; diverse approaches to, 55–69; intersectional approach to, 69, 72–73, 75–76. *See also* mobility justice

just sustainabilities, 66, 68

LADOT. *See* Los Angeles Department of Transportation

law, traffic: autocentrism and, 75, 78; connection to engineering and design, 10, 28–29, 31; and justice, 58; and structural racism, 11, 70, 72, 75; *Uniform Vehicle Code*, 31

Lefebvre, Henri, 48, 52, 55

level of service, 33, 93, 94

livability. *See* livable streets

livable streets, 66, 77, 195; and traffic calming/Slow Streets, 105, 108–9, 110–11, 112, 131–32, 144, 172; as transportation planning goal, 141, 167

Logan Circle, 213–14

LOS. *See* level of service

Los Angeles, 10, 29, 38; bicycle planning, 185; CicLAvia, 41, 150, 178, 187; Complete Streets policy and design, 178, 180; Green Alleys, 151, 179, 187–89; Livable Streets programs, 180–81; mobility planning, 180; Slow Streets, 182–86; Vision Zero, 180

Los Angeles Department of Transportation, 178, 180–88, 190–91

Los Angeles Sanitation and Environment, 178–79, 187. *See also* Green Alleys

low-speed, low-volume streets: and bikeways/bike boulevards, 101, 102, 128–29, 135–39; in history, 106–8; and shared-use arrows, 98; and Slow/Shared streets, 97, 102, 106, 110–12, 114, 139–40; and traffic calming, 108–9, 112–13, 135, 180. *See also* bicycle boulevards; traffic calming

Manual of Uniform Traffic Control Devices, 35, 95–96

merchants. *See* street vendors

mobility: evolving approaches to, 7, 48–49, 51–54; infrastructure and, 7–8; planning, 118, 144, 180, 185; politics of, 7, 9, 51–52. *See also* mobility justice

mobility justice: Americans with Disabilities Act and, 86–87, 99–100; Complete Streets and, 90; distributive approaches to, 56–59; intersectional approaches to, 11–12, 69–79; intersectional definition of, 73–75; Mimi Sheller's writings on, 7, 63–64; multimodal approaches to, 59–61; multimodal design and, 103–4; need for clearer definition of, 8–9,

284 Index

11, 49, 55–56; Open Streets and, 191–92; parklets and public street plazas and, 228–30; place-based approaches to, 65–67; procedural approaches to, 67–69; Slow Streets and, 145–46; social justice approaches to, 61–64; Vision Zero and, 92
multimodalism, xi, 2, 81–83; in design, 93–103; and mobility justice, 59–61, 103–4; in policy, 83–92
Mumford, Lewis, 22
MUTCD. See *Manual of Uniform Traffic Control Devices*

NACTO, 9, 40–41, 82, 100; *Designing for All Ages and Abilities,* 102; and mobility justice, 103; *Streets for Pandemic Response and Recovery,* 44, 102–3, 111–13, 152–53, 200; *Urban Bikeway Design Guide,* 101–2, 111, 151–52; *Urban Streets Design Guide,* 101, 111, 199–200
National Advisory Board on Transportation Research, 33
National Association of City Transportation Officials. *See* NACTO
National Committee on Uniform Traffic Laws and Ordinances, 31. *See also* Uniform Vehicle Code
National Complete Streets Coalition, 40, 42, 45, 87–88, 89
National Council on Disability, 84
neighborhood bike routes. *See* bicycle boulevards
neighborhood slow streets. *See* Slow Streets

neighborhood traffic calming. *See* traffic calming
neighborways. *See* bicycle boulevards
Netherlands, 110
New Mobilities scholarship, 7, 51–52
New Urbanism, 39
New York City: block parties and, 149; comprehensive planning, 154; Covid-19 pandemic in, 44; history of traffic control in, 25, 28; influenza epidemic, 2; Open Streets, 5, 6, 10, 153–66; Play Streets, 140–50; street design guidelines, 154; Summer Streets events, 41, 150–51; transportation planning in, 154; Vision Zero planning in, 91
New York Department of Transportation, 154–56, 157–60, 161–63, 166–67
NIMBY, 132
Norton, Peter, 15, 21, 27, 28, 29
not in my backyard. *See* NIMBY
NYDOT. *See* New York Department of Transportation

OAKDOT. *See* Oakland Department of Transportation
Oakland, California: bikeway planning in, 123, 131; Covid-19 response, 123–24; pandemic Slow Streets, 124–29; permanent Slow Streets program, 130–33; racial diversity and response to Slow Streets in, 126–27
Oakland Department of Transportation, 123–33
Open Streets, 2, 5, 147–48; community involvement in, 156–57, 161,

Index   285

165–66; controversies surrounding, 162–63, 171–72, 182; in Denver, 167–77; design guidelines for, 150–51, 152–53, 184; full closure, 157–58; as interim design for permanent closure, 162, 174–76; in Los Angeles, 177–91; mobility justice and, 166–67, 177, 189–92; in New York City, 153–67; origins of, 150–51; partial closure, 158–58; signage, 157, 169, 182
Open Streets Project, 150–51
operations and maintenance: of Open Streets, 161, 165–66, 172; of public street plazas, 185–86
Owens, Major, 84

Pacoima, Los Angeles, 187–89
parades, 30; as precedent for temporary street closures, 41, 148–49
parking: as privatized use of the street, 194, 207, 214–15; history of on-street, 29; rethinking as potential public space, 41, 163, 195–96, 198, 199, 205, 206, 201, 221. *See also* parklets
Park(ing) Day: manifesto, 196; origins, 41, 195–96; as precedent for parklets, 195–96, 198, 200–201, 210
parklets, 3; as Covid-19 response, 201–4, 211, 220; design standards for, 101; leasing rates for, 206–7, 217; mobility justice and, 208–10, 218–19; origins in Park(ing) Day, 41, 198; in Portland, 219–28; and public access, 201, 202, 207, 217–18, 222; in San Francisco, 5,

41, 200–210; San Francisco's Pavement to Parks program and, 41, 198, 201; in Washington D.C., 210–19, 193–94, 199–200, 201, 204–5, 206, 213, 217, 223–25
paving: history of, 22–23, 25–26; programs and multimodal improvements, 123, 130, 131, 145
pedestrians: ADA accessibility and, 99; design standards for, 96–97; fatalities in U.S., 28, 43; malls, 194; pedestrianization, 148, 194, 235
permanent street closure: and public street plazas, 155, 174–76, 181, 187–88, 199; legal issues surrounding, 185; Open and Shared Streets and, 162, 168
Philadelphia, 2, 24, 150
Philly Free Streets, 41, 150
Pittsburgh, Pennsylvania, 134–44; Complete Streets policy, 134–35; Department of Mobility and Infrastructure, 135–44; mobility planning in, 140–41; Neighborhood Slow Streets program, 10, 139–41; Neighborhood Traffic Calming program, 135, 142–43; Neighborway program, 135–39, 143; Vision Zero, 134
Pittsburgh Department of Mobility and Infrastructure. *See also* Pittsburgh, Pennsylvania
planning, 30; bicycle, 123, 128–29; climate action, 135; Complete Streets, 88; equity and, 8; street layout, 24, 33–34; transportation, 39, 57, 63, 68, 141, 161, 168,

173, 185; Vision Zero, 92, 115, 123

Plan of Chicago, 30

Play Streets, 97, 149–50, 152, 153, 155, 181, 185

plazas, public street: in Denver, 174–76; in Los Angeles, 180, 185–86, 187–89; NACTO guidance for, 101, 199–200; in New York, 153–54, 198–99; in Portland, 219, 221–23, 224–28; in San Francisco, 196, 198, 201

A Policy on the Geometric Design of Highways and Streets. See also AASHTO

politics of mobility, 7, 9, 51–52

Portland, Complete Streets, 219; Covid-19 response, 220–22; equity planning, 221–22; parklets, 219–28; public street plazas, 219, 221–23, 224–28

Portland Bureau of Transportation, 219–28

Pride, parades, 149; plaza, 225

privatization debates: and parklets, 201, 207, 214–15, 217, 223, 226; and Slow Streets, 129

procedural equity/justice, 67–69; and multimodal policy and design, 92, 103, 104; and Open/ Shared Streets, 177, 191, 192; and parklets, 218; and Slow Streets, 122, 129, 143, 145. *See also* mobility justice

Project for Public Spaces, 196–98

PROWAAC. *See* Public Rights-of-Way Access Advisory Committee

PROWAG. See *Public Rights-of-Way Accessibility Guidelines*

public realm, 1, 54–55, 67, 133, 154, 175, 198, 206, 231

Public Rights-of-Way Access Advisory Committee, 85

Public Rights-of-Way Accessibility Guidelines, 99

public seating, 175, 196, 199, 200, 204, 207, 210, 225

public space: geographical approaches to, 54–55; inter-sectional mobility justice and, 76–77, 233; potential of roadways to be retrofitted as, 196–98, 200, 236–37, 238; pre-automobile streets as, 23–24; social infrastructure and, 53–54

public street plazas. *See* plazas, public street

Queens, New York, 6, 56, 156–57, 164

race, 3; critical race theory, 71–72; and intersectionality, 11, 70–71, 73; and mobility justice, 62–63; and pedestrian fatalities, 28, 43; social justice and, 62

racial justice, 12, 126. *See also* mobility justice

racism, 3, 11, 70; and highway planning, 34; and transportation, 39, 45, 63

Rawls, John, 56. *See also* justice

rights, 55; disability, 63, 83–87; mobility, 48, 52, 56, 64, 69, 83; traffic law and, 28, 31

right to the city, Henri Lefebvre and the, 48, 52, 55, 58

routine accommodation, 40, 87. *See also* Complete Streets

Index   287

San Francisco, 38, 200–10; business improvement districts, 205–6; Covid-19 response, 201–4; equity planning, 203–4; livable streets design in, 108; and Park(ing) Day, 195–96; parklets, 200–10; Pavement to Parks program, 201; Shared Spaces program, 202–10; Sunday Streets, 150; Valencia Street project, 208

school streets, 147, 152. *See also* Open Streets

Seattle Bicycle Sundays, 150

Shared Spaces, San Francisco, 202–10; design guidelines for, 204–5, 206; and equity, 203–4; and public seating access, 204

Shared Streets: in Denver, 168–74; design guidance for, 97, 101–2, 111, 114, 155; in Los Angeles, 180

shared-use bicycle marking, 98, 123, 137; and Slow Streets, 123, 137

sharrow. *See* shared-use bicycle marking

Sheller, Mimi, 7, 51, 63–64, 68, 72

sidewalks: extensions, 212–13; history in Roman roadway design, 23; Jane Jacobs on, 37; in nineteenth-century cities, 25; outdoor dining and, 5, 169, 174, 202, 211; public passage and public life, 54; as social infra-structure, 53

Slow Streets, 3, 5, 10, 105–46; in Boston, 113–22; design guide-lines, 111–13, 114, 132–33, 140; historical precedents for, 108–11; and mobility justice, 122, 142–44, 144–46, 235–37; in Oakland,

123–34; in Pittsburgh, 134–44; planning of, 115–18, 130–31; streets as, 48, 53–54; and traffic calming, 108–9, 114, 120–22, 135–39

Smart Growth America, 45, 75

social infrastructure, 7–8, 52–53; and Open Streets, 157, 164–67, 188–89; and public street plazas, 189; and Slow Streets, 117–18

social justice, xi, 44–45; distributive approaches to, 57–58; diversity and, 61–63; gender and, 62; and public space, 55; race and, 62–63. *See also* mobility justice

spatial justice, 8, 56, 58; and the ADA, 86; Edward Soja's approach to, 57

speed: asymmetries between vehicles and pedestrians, 27, 105; early limits to, 28–29, 107; limiting on Open Streets, 157–59, 169; limiting on Slow/Shared Streets, 97, 101, 102, 110–12, 131, 137, 169, 180, 184; and livability, 37, 67, 108, 130; and roadway hierarchy, 34, 94, 108; and traffic calming, 109–10, 135; and Vision Zero, 92, 114. *See also* Slow Streets; traffic calming

speed humps: in Boston, 115, 119–22; as mobility justice, 144–45; in Pittsburgh, 135, 142–43. *See also* traffic calming

streets: in the early American city, 1, 23–24; engineering of, 35–36, 93–103; in European cities, 22–23; geography of, x; in the industrial city, 24–26; legal definition of, 31–32; multimodal design of, 39–42, 81–104; as pipes for cars, 33–35; as question of mobility justice, 7, 12–13, 43–46, 47–50, 76–79; reclaiming of, 3, 231–39; as social infrastructure, 54–54; takeover by motorists, 2, 26–29; in the twentieth century, 26–30. *See also* Open Streets; parklets; plazas, public street; Slow Streets

street vendors: historical place of, 148, 163; return of, 164, 194

streateries, in Washington D.C., 201–19; permitting and design, 217–18. *See also* parklets

Summer Streets, New York, 41, 150, 154, 155, 159, 162

sustainability, and street design, 9, 41, 66–67, 77, 101, 112, 114, 122, 134, 231

tactical urbanism, 2, 113, 197; Covid-19 as opportunity for, 160, 169; Park(ing) Day, 195–98; San Francisco Shared Spaces, 201, 209–10; Slow/Shared Streets as, 169

Thirty-Fourth Avenue Open Street, 6, 156–58, 159, 163–64

traffic calming: in Boston, 114–22; design standards for, 108–9, 112–13; history of, 108–9, 110–11; horizontal elements in, 109, 120; as mobility justice, 145–46; in Oakland, 130, 131; in Pittsburgh, 135–44; in San Francisco, 108; vertical elements in, 109, 112

traffic engineering, 33–37, 88–89; Association of State Highway and Transportation Officials, 35–37, 82, 93–96, 96–98, 100; history of, 25, 33–37, 40; Institute of Traffic Engineers and, 35, 109; Transportation Research Board, 33, 82, 93

traffic laws: definition of street, 31; origins and evolution of, 32–33, 107–8. *See also* Uniform Vehicle Code

Transit Street Design Guide, NACTO, 41

transportation equity, 40, 45, 60–61, 63, 87, 235; multimodal design and, 103; parklets and, 218; placemaking and, 209; public street plazas and, 189, 208–9. *See also* mobility justice

transportation geography, 51; of the street, 47; and New Mobilities, 51–52

transportation justice. *See* mobility justice; transportation equity

transportation planning: in Boston, 113–14, 121–22; in Denver, 167–68, 172–77; and equity/ justice, 4, 77, 235–37; and inequities, 63, 68; in Los Angeles, 178–80; in New York, 154, 161, 182–86, 190–91; in Oakland, 123, 128–29; in Pittsburgh, 135, 140–41, 143–44; and *Plan of Chicago,* 30; in San Francisco, 201, 204–8; in Washington D.C., 210–11

transportation racism, 39, 45, 63; and highway planning, 34

Transportation Research Board, 33, 110; *Highway Capacity Manual,* 33, 93

TRB. *See* Transportation Research Board

Trust for Public Land, 151, 179

underserved neighborhoods, 88, 118, 151, 166, 191, 208, 218, 229

Uniform Vehicle Code, 31–33

United States Department of Transportation, 45, 82, 96–97

universal design. *See also* disability justice

Urban Bikeway Guide, NACTO, 41, 101–3, 111–12

Urban Streets Design Guide, NACTO, 40, 101–3, 111–12

UVC. *See* Uniform Vehicle Code

vehicles: and the evolution of paving, 24, 25, 29; and the industrial city, 24–26; and Roman roadway design, 22

vendors. *See* street vendors

Vision Zero, 2, 9, 82, 90–92; action planning, 114–15, 118, 123, 167–68, 177, 180, 208; origins of, 91; principles, 91–92

Washington, D.C.: Covid-19 response, 211; early parklet adoption, 210; historical design, 24; Streateries Program, 210–19

Weicker, Lowell, 84

Whyte, William, 196

woonerf streets, 122, 145, 235; as inspiration for shared street design, 97, 105, 111; origins of, 110–11

David L. Prytherch is professor of geography at Miami University in Oxford, Ohio. He is author of *Law, Engineering, and the American Right-of-Way: Imagining a More Just Street* and coeditor of *Transport, Mobility, and the Production of Urban Space*.